"Readers are in excellent hands with *Helping Your Anxious Child*. It is written by leading international experts in child anxiety who together have worked with thousands of families where children have struggled with anxiety. The strategies they describe have been tried and tested in their many rigorous studies. But critically for busy families, the style of the book is extremely practical and, most importantly, written with empathy, compassion, and hope."

—**Cathy Creswell**, professor of developmental clinical
psychology at the University of Oxford, and coauthor of
Helping Your Child with Fears and Worries

"I highly recommend *Helping Your Anxious Child* to parents who are serious about empowering themselves and their children to understand anxiety. The authors clearly lay out structured steps you can use to guide and support your child. The readings and activities in the book are based on decades of research about anxiety and anxiety conditions. The activities for parents and children are relevant and can be used in everyday life."

—**Judith Law**, CEO of Anxiety Canada Association—a national
mental health charity based in Vancouver, ON, Canada

"Anyone looking for effective strategies to help an anxious child will find that this book is an absolutely incredible resource—it is packed with user-friendly tools to help families understand anxiety, and it will equip children with the essential skills they need to approach new situations with confidence and joy. I *highly* recommend this book for all parents looking to support children by putting anxiety-reducing strategies into action!"

—**Donna B. Pincus, PhD**, CAS Feld Family Professor of
Teaching Excellence, and professor of psy
brain sciences at Boston University

"In a world awash with information for parents, it is a great pleasure to recommend a book soundly based on the best available scientific evidence. The authors are leading researchers who also bring the practical know-how that comes with extensive clinical experience to produce an immensely readable book packed with practical ideas and advice for parents of children struggling with anxiety."

—**Warren Cann**, CEO of the Parenting Research Centre, and founding director of www.raisinghildren.net.au

"The authors have produced a timely and informative book for parents of children with anxiety disorders. The book is based on many years of the authors' invaluable research, and is perfectly linked to their extensive and rich clinical experience. The many illustrative examples and helpful worksheets make the book a must-read for all parents who struggle to help their children overcome fears and become confident."

—**Silvia Schneider, PhD**, professor of clinical child and adolescent psychology at Ruhr University Bochum in Germany, and director of the Center of Research and Treatment of Mental Health

Praise for the 2nd Edition:

"In *Helping Your Anxious Child*, parents are provided a step-by-step guide for assisting their children in overcoming a panoply of worries, fears, and anxieties. The strategies described are well-established ones, backed by considerable scientific support. Parents will find this book engaging, easy to read, and full of important ideas about how best to help their children."

—**Thomas H. Ollendick, PhD**, University Distinguished Professor in the department of psychology at Virginia Tech

Helping Your Anxious Child

THIRD EDITION

A Step-by-Step Guide for Parents

RONALD RAPEE, PhD

ANN WIGNALL, DPsych | SUSAN SPENCE, PhD

VANESSA COBHAM, PhD | HEIDI LYNEHAM, PhD

New Harbinger Publications, Inc.

Publisher's Note

This publication is designed to provide accurate and authoritative information in regard to the subject matter covered. It is sold with the understanding that the publisher is not engaged in rendering psychological, financial, legal, or other professional services. If expert assistance or counseling is needed, the services of a competent professional should be sought.

NEW HARBINGER PUBLICATIONS is a registered trademark of New Harbinger Publications, Inc.

New Harbinger Publications is an employee-owned company.

Cover design by Amy Danie

Acquired by Elizabeth Hollis Hansen

Edited by Jean Blomquist

Library of Congress Cataloging-in-Publication Data

Names: Rapee, Ronald M., author. | Wignall, Ann, author. | Spence, Susan, author. | Cobham, Vanessa, author. | Lyneham, Heidi J., author.
Title: Helping your anxious child : a step-by-step guide for parents / Ronald Rapee, Ann Wignall, Susan Spence, Vanessa Cobham, Heidi Lyneham.
Description: 3rd edition. | Oakland, CA : New Harbinger Publications, [2022] | Includes bibliographical references.
Identifiers: LCCN 2022016710 | ISBN 9781684039913 (trade paperback)
Subjects: LCSH: Anxiety in children--Popular works. | Anxiety in children--Treatment--Popular works. | BISAC: FAMILY & RELATIONSHIPS / Children with Special Needs | PSYCHOLOGY / Psychotherapy / Child & Adolescent
Classification: LCC RJ506.A58 R37 2022 | DDC 618.92/8522--dc23/eng/20220625
LC record available at https://lccn.loc.gov/2022016710

Printed in the United States of America

25   24   23

10   9   8   7   6   5   4   3

To my "girls"—Wendy, Alice, and Lucy

—Ron Rapee

To Mike, Nick, and Tom

—Ann Wignall

To my family and friends

—Sue Spence

To Tom, Will, Alex, and Gabby

—Vanessa Cobham

To Emily and Zoe

—Heidi Lyneham

Contents

Acknowledgments

The anxiety management principles and program described in this book are based on the clinical treatment program *Cool Kids*, developed at Macquarie University, Sydney, Australia. *Cool Kids* is an evolving program that is based on many years of scientific research, theory, and clinical feedback. These developments could not have come without the invaluable input from a countless number of researchers and practitioners. It is simply not possible to mention or thank all the many people who have influenced this program. However, special thanks go to Maree Abbott, Sally Fitzpatrick, Jennie Hudson, Susan Kennedy, Maria Kangas, Lauren McLellan, Carolyn Schniering, and Viviana Wuthrich. We would also like to acknowledge the pioneering work of Paula Barrett, Mark Dadds, and Phil Kendall.

Introduction

Welcome to *Helping Your Anxious Child*. Being the parent of an anxious child can be a roller coaster. While anxious children are often thoughtful and caring, they can also be exasperating and place extra demands on parents in terms of time and emotion. Often extended family and friends do not see the distress being experienced by both the child and their immediate family. When a child is continually scared or worrying and begins to miss out on so many of life's rewards, most parents are desperate to help. So, it is understandably frustrating when nothing you do seems to work. Sometimes the things you try seem to make children worse in the long term, and because most people think that children will "just grow out of it" at some point, many families suffer for a long time before they find out that something can be done.

Anxiety is a common problem among children and adults alike, and there are many successful treatment programs run by professionals that have been developed to provide much-needed help. The program you are about to embark on is different. It is an adaptation of the proven professional programs designed to allow parents to teach anxiety management skills to their own child.

This book is designed to guide parents through a structured course of readings and activities that will help you to teach your child to manage their anxiety and will help you to learn new ways of responding to anxious behavior. The techniques and methods that are covered come from many years of careful, scientific evaluation, including testing the use of this particular book (see, for example, Cobham et al. 2010; Lyneham and Rapee 2006; Rapee et al. 2006; Rapee et al. 2021). Each chapter includes children's activities, to encourage children to be actively involved in taking control of their anxiety, and practice tasks that will help you and your child practice new skills in everyday life. The book is primarily aimed at children aged around seven to twelve years. However, very similar principles apply to younger children, so throughout the book we provide some examples and instruction on how you can help a younger child. We have also included a chapter at the end of the book (chapter 11) where we describe how the skills in this program can be adapted for teenagers.

We hope that you enjoy the program and that your child conquers their fears and worries by successfully learning anxiety management skills.

How to Use This Program

We know that every child is different and so is every family. So, there are no hard-and-fast rules in running this program, and if you think of a better way to do something, then we encourage you to try it. But, we have had many years of experience in running programs like this one and in working with children and their parents. Based on this experience, we can share with you some of the principles that work best for the majority of families.

First, the activities and readings in this book are best completed in the order they appear. Each set of readings and activities is designed to build on the last set. If you jump ahead, you may find that you haven't yet learned the previous skill and that will make progress much more difficult. Some children, however, will move more quickly or more slowly than others. So, how fast you work through the chapters is up to you and should be based on your child's own personal circumstances. In the activities, you will be encouraged to include several examples of the same task. If your child catches the idea of a particular activity after one or two examples, it is not necessary to complete the rest of the examples. If your child needs extra practice to grasp the ideas, then complete all of the examples. For some children, you may need to spend two or three weeks on the same chapter and exercises and repeat them all. Don't be afraid to try again—it is much better for your child to be a little bit bored than to not understand.

You will need to set aside time in your schedule to work on the program if you want to see your child managing anxiety. We recommend that you make a particular set time each week to be your "anxiety management session." This does not mean that you only work on your child's anxiety at that time—far from it—but this will be the main time that you read over the next chapter, talk with your child about the tasks and activities, and plan the next week's exercises and practice. For example, you may decide that Sunday mornings after breakfast will be your anxiety management session time. Think of it like another season of dancing or football or piano. Every Sunday morning for a few months, you will read the next chapter, do the parent activities, and sit with your child to work on their anxiety management skills. You need to make sure this is possible. For example, plan your weekend activities around this time and make sure that the rest of your family are either part of the program or occupied somewhere else.

You will see three types of activities described in this book.

Parent Activities: Reading the chapter and doing the parent activities are tasks that you need to do before you sit down with your child. Most of the time these will be issues you need to think about or skills that you need to learn in order to help your child. To make this easier, we have included the free, downloadable Parent Activity Worksheets at http://www.newharbinger.com/49913. (See the very back of this book for more details.)

Child Activities: These are the activities, exercises, and lessons that you need to do with your child so that they can learn to manage anxiety. Each child activity provides a short, simple description of what you need to explain to your child (based on what you have read in the chapter) and an example of a completed worksheet that uses the anxiety management skill. Your child will need blank copies of the worksheets so they can practice the skills during the week. You can make your own blank worksheets by using the completed examples in this book to guide you. Alternatively, you can download the Helping Your Anxious Child Activity Book, offered free to users of this book at http://www.newharbinger.com/49913. In the downloadable workbook, each activity is available and contains child-friendly explanations of the relevant skill for you to read with your child and blank worksheets (based on those used in the examples within the chapter) that your child can complete with your help.

Child Practice Tasks: These practice tasks are the most important component. They describe exercises that your child will have to practice throughout the week in order to learn to manage anxiety. These practice tasks will need to be done many times, sometimes for several weeks, until your child gets really good at the particular skill. Worksheets for these tasks are also included in the downloadable workbook.

A Few Things to Keep in Mind

The readings and activities should be completed over two to four months. Although it may be tempting to move through the entire program in the first week when you are feeling enthusiastic, it is better to work through it at a consistent pace. That way you won't burn out before the program finishes, and it will help create the habit of tackling anxious thoughts, feelings, and behaviors on an everyday basis.

The program will work better if all parents and significant caregivers work through the readings and activities. One of the most important features of a successful program is being able to put the skills into practice in all parts of the child's life, and this is much more likely if all parents know what to do. The same goes for any other adult— such as stepparents, grandparents, or nannies—who your child spends a significant amount of time with. If some of the anxiety occurs at school, then it might be helpful to meet with your child's teacher and talk about what you are trying to achieve. But if some of the people in your child's life are not interested in what you are doing, don't give up. We have seen some spectacular successes, even in cases where one parent had no interest whatsoever in helping with the program. The program is also very successful in single-parent families.

Finally, don't get discouraged by slow progress and setbacks. Keep in mind that your child has had many years to develop anxious ways of behaving and thinking; it will take more than a few weeks as well as a lot of persistence to change these patterns. Especially at times when you or your child are stressed—don't give up; find an enjoyable activity to do (such as play a short game together, read a story, or go for a short walk) and then, when things are a little calmer, come back and keep on working.

Seeing a Mental Health Professional

We mentioned earlier that this book is designed to provide parents with all the information they need to help their child overcome anxiety. That's true. But we all know that knowing something and doing it properly are two different things. That is why we strongly recommend that you see a qualified mental health professional about your child's anxiety if you possibly can. A mental health professional will be able to properly assess your child and let you know whether this program is appropriate. A professional can also help you apply the information in this book to the specific circumstances of your life as well as that of your child. And a professional can help to keep you motivated at times when nothing seems to be working, or can help you adapt the program to get over those tough hurdles.

But if a professional gave you this book or told you to get it, then we are confident it will help. Our scientific research with children who had been diagnosed with an anxiety disorder tells us that when parents were given a copy of this program and told to help their own child, with no extra professional help, around one in five children were completely free of an anxiety diagnosis after going through the program, and many more made strong gains. When several short sessions with a therapist were added to help parents stay on the right track, over 60 percent of children who completed the program were diagnosis free (Lyneham and Rapee 2006).

What to Expect During This Program

- *Don't* expect that you'll have things sorted out in just a few weeks.

- *Do* expect that there will be noticeable changes before completing the program.

- *Do* expect to make progress in a zigzag fashion rather than a straight line, that is, two steps forward and one step back.

- *Do* expect that any narrow, or highly defined, worries (e.g., where the only worry is being afraid of dogs or going to sleep in the dark) will be easier to make progress on than broad, or generalized, worries (e.g., getting worried about *any* new situation or social event that comes up).

- *Do* expect that children will need to keep practicing skills for some time after the program has finished, until their new skills in thinking and behaving are everyday habits.

Will Anxiety Go Away Completely?

Someone who has no anxiety at all would be in a lot of trouble! Anxiety is a normal emotion that helps us perform to the best of our abilities and protects us in dangerous situations. The aim of this program is to bring anxiety down to manageable levels. We want children to manage anxiety so that they get the helpful effects, like revving up before a big game, without the bad effects, like avoiding situations that might otherwise be fun. As you will learn later, anxiety is also part of a person's makeup or personality. This program will teach your child new ways of coping so that anxiety will no longer rule their life. But you will find that even after finishing the program, your child will probably always be a slightly more emotional or sensitive person than some other children you know, and that is not a bad thing.

PARENT ACTIVITY: Getting Ready for the Program

Here are a few points to think about to get you ready to run this program with your child. You will need to put time and effort into helping your child learn to manage anxiety, just like you would if you were helping your child learn the piano or to improve their reading. Your child will also need to have the time to put into this program.

1. As the parent, set a time each week to read over the chapter, do any parent activities, and prepare for the anxiety management session with your child.

   When can you do your preparation?

   _____

2. Plan a time that you and your child will set aside each week to complete an anxiety management session (around thirty to sixty minutes). Make sure that the time is "reserved" and doesn't get pushed aside. Also make sure that other members of your family have something to do and won't disturb you.

   When can you do the weekly anxiety management session?

   _____

3. It will also be much better (but not absolutely necessary) if other important people in your child's life are willing to help.

   Who in your child's life should be involved in helping your child learn to manage anxiety?

   _____

   _____

   _____

Be prepared to spend additional time outside of the anxiety management session to practice skills. Ideally, there should be some practice every day.

CHAPTER 1

Understanding Anxiety

Emily had a secret problem. She was twelve years old and still afraid of the dark. At night, when her family was asleep, she would often hear strange noises outside and she would panic, imagining that they were being robbed or that they'd all be murdered while they slept. Emily still kept a night-light on in her room and would often run to her parents' room on particularly bad nights and slip into their bed. She'd never take the garbage out at night or go upstairs alone after dark, and she usually insisted on her parents checking her room before she went to sleep. Because of her fear, which was a secret to everyone except her parents, Emily never accepted invitations to sleep over at friends' houses and found excuses to not go to summer camp. Emily's parents had tried to push her to face her fears and sleep in the dark, but she became so upset and they had so many fights that eventually they just gave in to her fears. Now her parents feel frustrated at the limitations that Emily's fear causes both in her own life and for everyone else in their family.

Ten-year-old Connor had a different problem. He was extremely shy. At home, he would talk freely with his family. At school or with strangers, Connor was different. He was terrified that he would do the wrong thing and make a fool of himself. He hated to speak in front of the class. Even though he could play the piano beautifully, he was too scared to perform at the school concert. In the school yard, he was usually alone, afraid to join in with the other children.

Problems like Emily's and Connor's are common, normal, and quite easily handled. But they can often cause unpleasant and potentially serious interference in children's lives and in the lives of their families. Their stories give you a quick look at some of the many different ways that anxiety can affect children's lives.

Managing anxiousness and helping your child develop confidence and control in life is much the same no matter what form the anxiety takes. In this book, we will describe some of the common types of children's anxieties, increase your understanding of children's anxiety, and teach you how you can help your child master their fears. We will discuss all sorts of anxieties—from the minor, temporary fears that many children experience, to the longer, more severe, and invasive problems that can so extensively restrict a child's life. Most importantly, we will describe, in detail, skills and strategies that you can use to help your child learn to control their fears.

We will begin our discussion of anxious children by describing several children who we've seen and who have benefited from these strategies. We'll come back to these children throughout the course of this book and use them to show how each of the techniques can be applied to the real world.

Some Real-Life Anxious Children

Talia's Story

Talia is a typical nine-year-old with a big group of friends and a cheeky streak. She loves music, is a member of the school basketball team, and rarely worries about a thing. But Talia is scared of water. She learned to swim when she was five years old, but she's never enjoyed it and has always avoided deep water as much as possible. When her father takes her out beyond where she can stand, she begins to panic, clings tightly to him, and begs him to take her back. No one can figure out why Talia is afraid of the water—she has never had a bad experience there and has never known anyone who has drowned. Both of her brothers love swimming. Yet something about the water has always been frightening to Talia, and, try as she might, she just can't talk herself out of it. Now that Talia is getting older and starting to go to pools with friends, she is running out of excuses and her swimming phobia is beginning to become a problem.

Kurt's Story

Ten-year-old Kurt is a worrier. He worries about his schoolwork, he worries about his parents' health, and he worries that he will forget to feed his dog and she will starve. Kurt's parents no longer let him watch the evening news because he spends the next two days worrying about all the tragic stories he has seen. They also don't tell him about new things that he is going to have to do until the very last moment, because when they do, he pesters them mercilessly with his constant questions about what is going to happen. This interrogation also happens whenever Kurt has to do something unpleasant, such as take a test at school or go to the dentist. Kurt will ask his parents for information and reassurance hundreds of times.

Kurt also worries about germs. He's scared when he touches certain things that germs have gotten onto his hands and that he will get sick and die. He worries about infections and all sorts of illnesses. As a result of his worries, Kurt washes his hands again and again all day long. For example, after going to the bathroom, Kurt will scrub his hands for several minutes. He will also rush off to wash whenever he has touched something he thinks may be contaminated, such as door handles and seats where other people have been sitting. Kurt refuses to go to certain places, such as hospitals or the cafeteria at his school, because of the germs he thinks are there. He will sometimes get particular ideas about things that are contaminated that will then become taboo. For example, he went through a phase of avoiding the backyard because the dog had once thrown up there. Last week, Kurt caught the train with his mother and they sat opposite a man who sneezed several times. When he got home, Kurt raced straight to the shower and washed for forty-five minutes.

Ethan's Story

Now that he's twelve years old, Ethan's parents believe that he should be doing a lot of things by himself. But Ethan has little self-confidence and worries a great deal about what other people think of him. He has always been a nervous, sensitive, and shy child and he grew up having very few friends. Since beginning middle school this year, Ethan has retreated even more into his shell. It took him most of the year to make his first friend, Tony, who is also a bit of an outsider. In class, Ethan's teachers report that he rarely says a word and that he becomes very upset if he is asked to answer a question or speak in front of the class. At home, Ethan is quite talkative with his family but becomes quiet if anyone he doesn't know well comes over. Ethan has very specific rules about what clothes he can and cannot wear, he will always get his parents to deal with salesclerks and cashiers, and he will never answer the telephone. Despite his parents' urging, Ethan has never joined a club or team and spends most of his time at home alone, building models. From time to time, Ethan talks about feeling lonely, and he has gone through a few periods of feeling quite down and miserable.

Lashi's Story

Lashi is a seven-year-old girl whose parents separated when she was five. Since the separation, Lashi has begun to worry a great deal about her mother. She is terrified that her mother will be killed in a car accident or by a burglar and that she will never see her again. Lashi cries whenever her mother leaves her, and she refuses to be left alone with a babysitter or even to sleep over at her grandmother's home. As a result, Lashi's mother has hardly been out since the separation. She is beginning to lose her friends and has no chance to meet a new partner. Sometimes Lashi is willing to stay overnight with her father, but she spends the whole time asking about her mother, and lately she hasn't been willing to stay with him at all. Lashi's parents still get on well despite the separation, and they agree that they need to work together to help Lashi overcome her worries. It is a real struggle every morning to get Lashi to go to school, and sometimes Lashi's mother gives in and takes a day off work to let her stay at home. Lashi also worries about burglars breaking into the house and is scared of the dark. Over the past few weeks, she has begun to sleep in her mother's bed, something her mother has allowed because it is just too much of a struggle to argue. Lashi's mother loves her daughter very much, but just lately she has really begun to get fed up with the limitations on her life and is starting to feel angry and resentful.

In addition to her main anxiety, Lashi also has a fear of injections, doctors, and hospitals. Most of the time, this is not a big problem, but occasionally, it makes it very difficult for Lashi to go to the doctor for treatment and even to visit a sick friend. Having shots is the biggest problem—Lashi missed her last vaccination because she would not allow the nurse to give her an injection.

Hayley's Story

Hayley is eleven. Her parents are worried about how Hayley will ever cope when she goes to high school given how much she worries about everything. Hayley worries when her parents go out, worries about keeping her friends, about doing well enough at school, about events from the past and in the future, and about possible dangers. She always expects things to go wrong and does not like to go outside her comfortable routine. Hayley even worries about how much she worries. She has a couple of close friends at school but fears that one day they will suddenly decide that they don't like her. She doesn't want to make new friends in case that ruins her current friendships. Hayley is a very bright girl, and she produces flawless work almost all of the time, spending hours making sure that everything is absolutely correct, but Hayley performs very badly during long tests mostly because she gets stuck on an early question trying to answer it perfectly and then doesn't complete the rest of the questions.

Recently Hayley has developed a very big fear of choking when she eats. This started after a bad case of tonsillitis. After that, she stopped eating certain foods such as hard fruits and many meats because she finds them difficult to swallow. All other foods have to be chewed for a long time before she can swallow them. She now has different dinners *than her parents and sisters and has lost some weight. Her parents have tried to force her to eat, but Hayley only panics and starts hitting people and throwing food across the room.*

Ang's Story

Ang is a five-year-old boy who is active, energetic, and curious. At home, he is just like any other little boy. He is constantly kicking a ball, fighting with his older sister, or running around the apartment. But whenever someone comes to the door, he runs to his room to hide, and he refuses to make eye contact or even to say a word to anyone other than his very closest relatives. When Ang goes out with his family, he is a different child. He is quiet and shy; he clings to his mother; and he refuses to play with other children or interact with anyone aside from the family. Ang cries every morning when his mother tries to leave him at preschool, and on the worst days, he throws huge tantrums and clings to his mother, not letting her go. Once she manages to leave, his teachers report that Ang usually settles in after a while, but they say that he rarely talks to any of the other children and often plays alone. Once he gets back home, Ang again transforms into a happy bubbly boy; however, he is scared most nights to sleep alone and he is very sensitive to loud noises or anything that is outside his usual routine.

These children show just some of the ways that anxiety can affect a child's life across the childhood years. There are many types of anxiety and many ways that children can show its effects. In fact, the forms that children's worries can take are as varied as the number of children themselves. As you can see, fears do not always have to be "weird" or "crazy." Many normal and common types of concerns can become a problem for children if they interfere with something children want or need to do. Fears and worries can also clearly vary in their intensity and effects.

The good news is that problems such as these can be managed very well. In the rest of this book, we will describe the skills needed, including detective thinking, facing up to fears, and learning better social interaction. Each skill will be described in detail, examples and activities will be provided, and we will apply the concepts to the cases of children we've introduced. Finally, we will discuss the future, what you can do to help your child maintain their gains, and what to do if problems reemerge. Throughout the program, your child will not only be building their confidence, but will also be earning rewards and time with you and the rest of the family. In our experience, most children going through the program enjoy learning the skills even if at times they get a bit scared of what they may have to do or embarrassed about what they think and feel.

Is Your Child's Anxiety a Problem?

Everyone feels anxious from time to time. For most people, anxiety doesn't really affect their day-to-day life. Understanding more about "normal" fears and worries, and the ways in which fears can affect a child, will help you to decide whether your child needs help.

Normal Fears

Fears are a normal and natural part of life. All children experience fears and phobias at particular stages of their lives, and this is a normal part of growing up. Infants will develop a fear of strangers and fear of separating from the main caregiver at around six to nine months of age. Naturally, the exact age and the amount of fear will vary slightly from child to child, but all children will go through this stage and most fears will show up at similar times. As a child gets older, they will begin to show other natural fears. Fears of animals (e.g., dogs) and insects (e.g., spiders), fear of the water, fear of the dark, and fears of the supernatural (e.g., ghosts and monsters) often occur in young children in the toddler years and beyond. Around middle to late childhood, children begin to be more aware of other children and will begin to become self-conscious and develop a strong desire to fit in. These worries usually increase over the following years and peak in mid-adolescence, when how a teen looks and what the other kids think become the most important things in the world.

When these fears develop, they're usually just part of the normal developmental process that we all go through. But sometimes, fears and worrying can reach a point where they start to cause a problem for the child. These excessive fears are often temporary and transient but may still cause such distress that, as a parent, you want to help your child hurry through this stage. On the other hand, some children will experience fears and worries to a much greater degree than their peers, and some continue to experience fears long after other children their age have outgrown them.

When Does Anxiety Become a Problem?

How do you decide if your child's fear is "abnormal"? Quite simply—you don't! There is no such thing as an "abnormal fear." All fears are normal—some are simply more intense or more extensive than others. Even fears that might at first appear strange, such as a fear of germs that causes a child to wash a lot, can simply be seen as normal fears that have become too extreme. After all, most people worry at least a little about germs—just ask yourself if you would eat dinner out of your dog's bowl! So, children with anxiety problems can simply be thought of as having normal worries that have become extreme and more intrusive than the worries of other children.

A better way to think about these things is to consider whether your child's anxiety is a problem in their day-to-day life. Does it interfere with activities or cause difficulties for your child? These difficulties may be many and varied. For example, it may simply be that your child's fears cause them to be upset and distressed. Or they may stop your child from doing things that they like or from making friends. Or it may be that worrying is affecting your child academically or on the playing field.

The bottom line is this: if your child's anxiety is adversely affecting their life, then they will benefit from learning about how to overcome it. In making the decision to work on these skills, you should remember that change will take dedication, hard work, and commitment. But it can also often be enjoyable. The activities are not in any way harmful or dangerous, and they usually reap many additional benefits such as improved self-esteem, confidence, and general happiness.

How Common Are Anxiety Problems?

Many adults believe that childhood is a time of carefree days and no responsibility. It may surprise you to know that, in fact, anxiety is the most common problem reported by children of all ages. Diagnosable anxiety disorders are found in around one in ten children, and less extreme but still distressing fears are even more common. The particular disorders vary somewhat with age. Fear of separating from caregivers is more common at the younger ages, while social fears are more common at older ages. Anxiety and worry affect children of all ages, from infants to adolescents. Girls or boys, rich or poor, brilliant or average—it makes no difference—anxiety can affect anyone.

Interestingly, even though anxiety disorders are so common in the real world, they are not the most common problem in child mental health clinics. Mental health centers for children are much more likely to see children with aggressive behaviors, attentional difficulties, eating disorders, or suicidal tendencies. What seems to be happening is that even though anxiety is common in children, most parents do not think of taking their anxious child to a professional for help. This may be because parents believe that anxiety is simply a part of their child's personality and that there is nothing they can do about it. Or it may be that, because anxiety doesn't affect the parent or teacher as much as these other problems, they don't realize how much the anxiety is affecting the child. In addition, in many areas mental health services for children are more prepared for, and used to dealing with, aggression problems than anxiety. As a result, parents often feel that they are making "mountains out of molehills" in worrying about their anxious child and may be discouraged from seeking help.

How Does Anxiety Affect Children?

Some parents may think, "So what? Everyone gets nervous sometimes. It doesn't hurt anyone, so why all the fuss?" To some extent, these parents may be right. Anxiety is not as dramatic a problem as a child contemplating suicide or engaged in drug abuse. But anxiety is a sign of real personal suffering—it's not an act or a way of getting sympathy.

Anxious children tend to have fewer friends than other children their age. Because many are shy, they have difficulties meeting new children and joining clubs and groups. For this reason, they often have a limited number of friends, and they may not interact with their friends as much as others do. In turn, lack of friendships can have an important impact later in life, increasing loneliness and reducing the opportunity for peer support.

Anxiety can also affect a child's academic achievements. Many anxious children do very well at school because their conscientiousness and perfectionism make them try harder. But they may not be doing as well as they could. This is especially the case for those children who worry a great deal. We often find that these children delay homework and struggle with their lessons, not because they are incapable, but because their worry stops them from approaching the tasks confidently. Anxious children may also get less out of the class and the teacher because their anxiety stops them from making full use of the resources (e.g., they may not ask questions in class). In addition, many anxious children may do well in the classroom situation but fail when it comes to exams because their worry about failing stops them from being able to concentrate. We also know that anxious children are more likely to miss days of school than other kids (Lawrence et al. 2015), and they are more likely to leave the school system earlier (Lee et al. 2009). In the longer run, research has shown that anxious children have more restricted career choices and opportunities (Caspi et al. 1988). Many careers such as sales, media, or legal work may be out of the question for shy adolescents because of their worry about performing in front of others.

While many anxious children will change as they grow and mature and may well become confident, outgoing adults, some will develop into anxious adults. Anxiety disorders in adulthood can be a serious hindrance in life. Anxious adults are more likely to abuse drugs and alcohol, miss work or be unemployed, have illnesses and visit a variety of medical specialists, and be depressed and even suicidal. Depression is likely to start even earlier, usually during adolescence. We aren't trying to suggest that this will happen to your child. But even if the effects of anxiety for your child are at the mild end— perhaps a few missed opportunities—it would be better to do something now than to wait until more severe problems develop.

If you're a parent with an anxious child, you need not fret or worry excessively—anxiety can be managed—but it's good to be motivated to do something to help your child.

Types of Anxiety

Everyone is individual, and no two anxious children will behave in exactly the same way. The amount of anxiety will also vary from child to child. Some children are afraid of one or two specific things. For example, a child may be generally confident and outgoing but simply be scared of going to sleep with the light out. At the other end of the spectrum, some children may be worried about many areas of life and may seem generally nervous or sensitive. For example, a child may worry about any new situation; be scared to meet new children; be afraid of dogs, spiders, and the dark; and worry about their parents going out at night.

There are also certain common anxiety patterns that we see time and again, and we will describe these in the following sections.

Specific Phobias

A child with a specific phobia is afraid of a particular situation or object and usually tries very hard to avoid contact with the thing that frightens them. Some common specific phobias include the dark, dogs, heights, spiders, storms, and injections. Talia, whom we introduced earlier, has a specific water phobia.

Separation Anxiety

Separation anxiety is the fear of being away from a main caregiver, most commonly, a child's mother. Children with separation anxiety become very upset when they have to separate from their main caregiver for any reason. In severe cases, they may follow the parent from room to room so as not even to be out of their parent's sight. More commonly, these children will avoid going to school, get upset when their parents try to go out, refuse to sleep over at other people's houses, and try to keep their parents with them at all times. Some children will report stomachaches or other physical problems when they separate, and many will throw tantrums when separation is threatened. The reason for this behavior is a fear that something terrible will happen to the parent or the child while they are apart and that, consequently, they will never see each other again. Lashi, whom we introduced earlier, developed separation anxiety after her parents separated, but many children don't have such an obvious trigger.

Generalized Anxiety

Generalized anxiety is a general tendency to be worried or anxious about many areas of life. These children are often described by their parents as "worrywarts." They worry about many general problems such as health, schoolwork, sport performance, bills, burglaries, and even their parents' jobs. They are particularly concerned about any new or novel situation they have to face and will often go to their parents repeatedly to ask questions and to seek reassurance. Many parents report that television shows such as the evening news or TV dramas will send their child into a fit of worrying for days. Kurt and Hayley, whom we introduced earlier, have generalized anxiety.

Social Anxiety or Social Phobia

Social anxiety or social phobia refers to fear and worry in situations where the child has to interact with other people or be the focus of attention. These children are more commonly described as shy, and the central problem is a fear that other people will think badly of them in some way. As a result, they may avoid many situations that involve interaction with other people, including meeting new people, talking on the telephone, joining teams or clubs, answering questions in class, or wearing the "wrong" clothes. Ethan, whom we introduced earlier, has social anxiety, and young Ang has a very early form of social anxiety that is sometimes referred to as behavioral inhibition.

Obsessive-Compulsive Disorder

In obsessive-compulsive disorder, the child will usually repeat certain actions or thoughts over and over again, often for long periods. Children with obsessive-compulsive problems may have particular thoughts or themes that play on their mind again and again. For example, they may worry about dirt or germs continuously, or they may continually be worried about keeping things orderly and neat. In addition, these children will usually perform some actions repeatedly, often in a superstitious or ritualistic way. For example, they may wash repeatedly in a particular pattern for long periods of time, or they may organize and reorganize their belongings in a very specific pattern. Kurt's main problem is one of obsessive-compulsive disorder.

Panic Disorder and Agoraphobia

Panic disorder is a fear or worry about having panic attacks. Panic attacks involve a sudden rush of fear that comes with a number of physical symptoms (including racing heart, sweating, dizziness, tingling, and breathlessness). During a panic attack, children may believe that they are dying or that something terrible is happening to them. Panic disorder is not common in young children and is more likely to be found in older adolescents and young adults. Sometimes these adolescents will begin to avoid many situations because they worry that another panic attack might happen. If they start to avoid several different situations due to a fear of panic attacks, then this is called agoraphobia.

A Note on Traumatic Events

In the context of exposure to a highly stressful or even potentially traumatic event, it is normal for most children to experience distress in the initial days and weeks. For the vast majority of children, this distress reduces naturally with the passage of time and the support of family and community. For some children whose distress does not reduce naturally, you may see the development of a new or significantly worsened anxiety or fear. For example, a child whose community experienced a natural disaster may develop a new fear about being separated from their parents or a specific phobia about something they associate with the disaster (e.g., wind, if it was a cyclone or hurricane disaster). In this kind of case—where the child's issues focus on anxiety and fear—this book has the potential to be an excellent resource for you as parents. However, after exposure to a potentially traumatic event, the most common psychological response is not anxiety, but rather a different type of presentation—referred to as post-traumatic stress disorder or PTSD. Children experiencing PTSD present differently compared to children experiencing anxiety. For instance, children with PTSD may keep remembering the event or have bad dreams about it, perhaps even including the trauma in their play. They may suddenly act or feel as if the event is happening again and become very upset. They'll often try hard to avoid situations that remind them of the trauma and may become distant in their feelings. They may show jumpiness, sleep difficulties, and irritability. Children experiencing PTSD require a different type of treatment compared to children experiencing anxiety. If you are concerned that your child may be experiencing PTSD, we would strongly encourage you to seek professional psychological treatment and support for the family.

PARENT ACTIVITY: My Child's Anxiety

When reading through the descriptions of other children's anxiety, you probably thought to yourself, "That's my child." Thinking about these similarities and differences will help you to identify which major areas are difficult for your child. This will help you to think about possible goals and areas to focus on.

Highlight each issue that you think describes a "problem" for your child—in other words, something that interferes with your child's life in some way, more than it does for most children their age.

SOCIAL FEARS	SEPARATION FEARS
☐ Shy	☐ Worries about getting lost
☐ Has difficulty meeting people	☐ Worries about someone close to them getting hurt or sick
☐ Has difficulty joining in groups	☐ Gets upset when they have to be away from Mom or Dad
☐ Has few friends	
☐ Avoids interacting with peers	☐ Gets upset when parents go out
☐ Doesn't like to be the center of attention	☐ Avoids going to playdates alone
☐ Believes others will think badly of them	☐ Refuses to sleep at other people's homes unless parents are there
☐ Avoids wearing different clothes	☐ Complains of feeling sick when they must separate
☐ Doesn't speak to people	☐ Afraid of something terrible happening to Mom or Dad (e.g., they may be in a car accident)
☐ Scared of asking or answering questions in class	
☐ Worries that someone will laugh at them or that they will be embarrassed	

OBSESSIVE-COMPULSIVE FEARS

☐ Does the same thing over and over again

☐ Complains of thoughts that get "stuck" in their mind

☐ Worries continuously about germs or being dirty

☐ Has to do or keep things in a certain order and very precisely

☐ Does a certain action in a ritualistic way

☐ Gets very upset if they can't perform ritual

GENERALIZED WORRIES

☐ Is extremely conscientious

☐ Worries about making mistakes

☐ Has difficulty performing in exams

☐ Worries about schoolwork or performing well enough

☐ Worries about money, bills, family, health, or safety

☐ Is afraid of new situations

☐ Asks lots of questions or often seeks reassurance

☐ Worries a lot after seeing news programs or scary movies

SPECIFIC FEARS

☐ Avoids very specific things that they are afraid of

☐ Is afraid of the dark, heights, insects, animals, doctors, dentists, storms, or water

☐ If confronted with feared object, becomes panicky

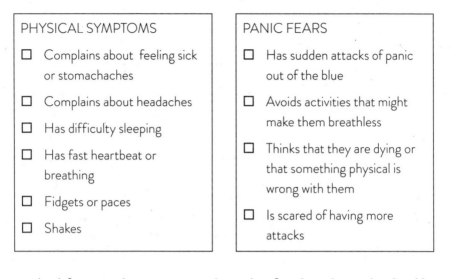

PHYSICAL SYMPTOMS	PANIC FEARS
☐ Complains about feeling sick or stomachaches	☐ Has sudden attacks of panic out of the blue
☐ Complains about headaches	☐ Avoids activities that might make them breathless
☐ Has difficulty sleeping	☐ Thinks that they are dying or that something physical is wrong with them
☐ Has fast heartbeat or breathing	
☐ Fidgets or paces	☐ Is scared of having more attacks
☐ Shakes	

Look for areas where you seem to have a lot of marks under one heading. You may find that there are several marks under the physical symptoms list as these are very common across all of the anxiety areas. Then you will find one, two, or three other areas that seem to have more marks than not. With children, it is very common for there to be more than one area that causes problems. Or there might be a few marks in other areas, but there will be one area that is definitely the main problem.

Which areas appear to be problems for your child?

_____

_____

_____

Why Is Your Child Anxious?

Some fears can be very understandable and based on obvious causes. For example, children may be scared to go to school because they are being bullied, or they may be scared of the dark following a burglary at home. In other cases, the fears and worries that children experience are much harder for parents to understand. For example, the child who worries that they are stupid may be doing perfectly well at school and elsewhere in life. Or a child may be scared that Mom will be killed in a car accident even though Mom always makes sure she picks them up on time. Or a child may worry about and imagine every possible disaster even though nothing really bad has ever happened to them. In these cases, the anxiety may be an entrenched part of the child's personality, and you may feel as though your child has been sensitive and "high-strung" for all of their life.

No one knows the complete answer to the question "Why is your child anxious?" But research has identified a number of factors that are likely to play a role in some way. The following sections discuss some of the things that might cause or at least keep anxiety going in children. In the illustration, you can also see that each of the factors interact with each other, which also helps to keep anxiety going.

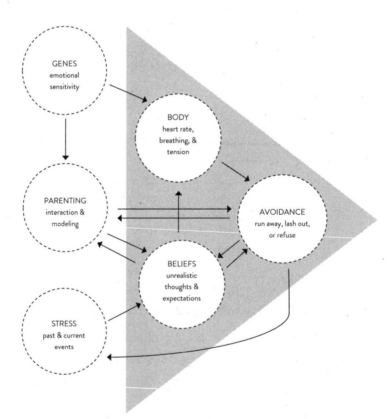

Genes

There is little doubt that anxiety runs in families. People who are anxious can often identify some close relative who always seems to be anxious, and it's common for at least one parent of anxious children also to be somewhat anxious. In some cases, this might involve a serious level of anxiety, while in others it might simply be that a parent tends to worry a little more than average. Children with only a single, specific phobia are much less likely to have anxious parents.

Research has shown that what is passed on from parent to child is not a specific tendency to be shy or to worry about the dark, but a general personality that is more emotionally sensitive than other people's (Eley 1997). Just as people vary in how tall they are or the color of their hair, people vary in how generally emotional they are. Anxious children tend to have a personality that is more emotional than the average. A large part of this is due to their genes. On the positive side, this means that they are likely to be more caring, kind, honest, and loving. But on the negative side, this emotionality means that they are more likely to worry, brood, feel down, and be fearful. There are both positives and negatives to any child's personality, and we can't and don't want to change these. But the techniques in this book will show you how your child can learn to control some of the things that really interfere with their life.

Parent Modeling and Interactions

All children are influenced by and copy their parents. Just think of the young child who walks out of Mommy's room covered in makeup, wearing high heels and jewelry. It is reasonable, then, to expect that children may also copy their parents' ways of coping with the world. If a parent is anxious and copes by avoiding situations, then the child may learn that this is the way to handle fears. We are not saying that you are entirely responsible for your child's anxiety; there is no way that modeling could explain even the majority of anxious behavior. But if your child already has some anxious tendencies and either you or your partner is anxious, your child may pick up a few of these behaviors, and this may strengthen their already anxious nature.

Similarly, the way you react to or handle your child's fears might also play some part in maintaining the anxiety. While all parents differ, some parents react to their anxious child in an overly protective way. This is very understandable. Parents love their children and so when faced with a child who is scared, vulnerable, and worried, parents only too naturally rush to their aid. But, in some cases, this helping behavior allows the child to avoid the things they fear. Some parents begin to anticipate their child's anxiety and will start to help their child even when it isn't necessary. This is especially the case if the parent is also anxious. If this pattern becomes established, the child is not urged to face their fears and as a result may begin to learn that "the world really is dangerous" and "I cannot handle it myself."

Stressors

When a child is bitten by a dog, the child will become wary of dogs for a period of time. When a child's parents separate and divorce, the child will often lose some confidence and become more sensitive for a time. These are natural responses that happen to most children after a stressful event. If a child experiences stressors like these and is already sensitive and anxious, then these stressors may have an even bigger impact than usual and may add to their anxiety. Common stressors include parental separation, family violence, death of a loved one, being bullied at school, doing badly in school, getting sick, and specific incidents (e.g., being in a car accident, being robbed, being bitten or stung, and being in a fire). Experiences like these cannot be identified in all or even the majority of cases of anxiety, but they may be important in triggering anxiety in some children.

In addition, we are starting to learn that people often create their own stressors. It appears that the very fears and worries that anxious children have can often lead to more stress in their lives, and this can increase their anxiety. For example, an anxious child may have some unusual behaviors that, in turn, lead other children to tease them. Or an anxious child may stop their parents from going out at night, which may increase pressure on the parents and then lead to more tension in the family.

Reactive and Sensitive Bodies

When you are anxious, your body becomes more "pumped up" or aroused. Researchers often refer to this as the *fight-flight-freeze response* because its purpose is to help protect people by preparing them to combat or escape potential danger. The fight-flight-freeze response includes changes such as rapid heart rate, increased breathing, sweating, and nausea. Many anxious children have bodies that react intensely when a threat is perceived. How reactive their body is, is in part determined by their genes. Anxious children also notice what is happening in their body quickly, which tends to intensify the reaction. Worried, anxious children often complain of stomachaches, headaches, vomiting, diarrhea, or tiredness as a result of this chronic arousal, and they struggle to think logically and creatively when anxious because their body is using all of its energy to prepare them to escape the danger. Feeling sick and having aches and pains will also increase the desire for an anxious child to avoid activities. For example, they might often use feeling sick as the "reason" why they don't want to go to a party or can't go to school.

Inaccurate and Negative Thoughts and Beliefs

Anxious children mentally focus on any possible danger in the world. This includes physical danger (e.g., my parents will die; we will go broke) and social danger (e.g., other kids will laugh at me; I will make a mistake). Anxious children focus on these types of beliefs, often misinterpret unclear events as dangerous, focus their attention on any possible danger, and remember all the bad things, forgetting the good. Importantly, these ways of thinking keep their anxiety going because the world always seems like a dangerous place. Take the case of ten-year-old Kurt, whom we described earlier. Kurt was constantly thinking about his parents getting sick or hurt, about making mistakes in his homework, and about his dog starving to death. In addition, he was always asking his parents about things that could go wrong, and if you asked Kurt about his last school test, he would always remember it as a negative experience. If Kurt heard a noise outside the house, he would assume it was something terrible. Because of all these thoughts and interpretations, the world really did seem like a very terrible place to poor Kurt, and it is no wonder that he was always scared.

Avoidance

Anxious children avoid things. This is a basic and automatic part of their personality—to run away. This might include obvious avoidance like not wanting to go to school or refusing to take the garbage out in the dark, or it might include less obvious, subtle avoidance, such as working really hard on their homework so they never make a mistake, helping all night with the music at a party so they don't have to talk to anyone, or taking ages to decide what to wear so that they don't look bad. *But avoidance—whether it is obvious or subtle—is the key to keeping anxiety alive.* Avoiding keeps the thoughts that we described above real because children never learn that those thoughts are not true. By avoiding anything that is a little frightening, children are not able to learn positive lessons such as "I can cope," "It's not that bad," or "It won't hurt me." Take the case of Ethan whose main problem involves believing that other people will think he is stupid or incompetent. Ethan would avoid talking to kids, would stay quiet and "hidden" in groups, and would make excuses not to talk on the phone or ask people for advice. But by avoiding all these things in both obvious and subtle ways, Ethan was never able to learn that people would not think he is incompetent.

PARENT ACTIVITY: Anxious Factors For My Child

We have described several factors that probably help to keep your child feeling anxious and worried. Not all of these factors will be important for every child.

However, avoidance is the key and is a part of any anxiety problem. Think about your child and family and reflect on which factors are important to your child.

We cannot emphasize enough that this activity is not an exercise in self-blame. It has been an observation of many therapists that parents want to know at least a bit about the causes of anxiety, but when it comes down to the crunch, it doesn't matter where it came from; what matters is that we can do something about it!

GENES Family members who you would describe as "emotional" or "nervous"	
PARENTING Situations where you help your child, or allow them to not participate to reduce their fears	
STRESS Events in your child's life that have or could increase fear	
BODY The way that your child's body responds when they are anxious	
BELIEFS Key topics that your child worries about or "dangers" that they focus on	
AVOIDANCE Ways that your child avoids anxious situations by running away, lashing out, or refusing activities	

How to Help Your Anxious Child

The skills you will learn in this program are aimed at the factors that we have just been talking about. To get a better idea of how it all fits together, the illustration below shows you how each of the skills fits with each of the factors that maintain anxiety.

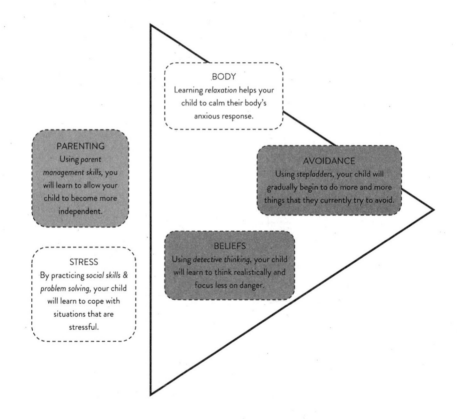

Although the importance of each factor for an individual child varies, there are skills that are essential for anxiety management, so-called core skills. The core skills work on the highlighted parts of the model: avoidance, anxious beliefs, and parenting. These skills are all learned in the first few weeks of the program and should be practiced until your child's anxiety is not causing significant problems. The more variable factors in the model, such as body reactivity and stress, are targeted with the optional additional skills: relaxation and social skills. It is essential that every family learn the core anxiety management skills of stepladders, detective thinking, and parent management. You can then select the additional skills that are relevant for your child, if needed.

Putting Together a Program for Your Child

If you work with a professional therapist, it is their job to help tailor and fit the best program for your child's unique situation. If you are going to work through this program mostly by yourself, then you will need to do this. You may want to read ahead to see how the different skills and techniques that we cover in this program work together. In chapter 10, we describe the specific programs that were used by each of the children whose stories appeared earlier. You may like to skip ahead to that chapter and have a quick look at how these different programs are put together. To give you another view of the program, we describe below the structure that we use in our standard clinical program that we run at Macquarie University in Sydney, Australia. The Cool Kids program is run in ten sessions that are spread over twelve weeks. A description of what we cover each week is shown in the table below. This might give you an idea of an approximate timetable for running the program with your child.

Macquarie University Cool Kids Program

Week	What we cover	Practice Tasks	Chapter in this book
1	Understanding anxiety	Linking thoughts and feelings	1 and 2
2	Detective thinking	Detective thinking	3
3	Detective thinking and parent management	Detective thinking Parent monitoring	3 and 4
4	Stepladders	Stepladders, detective thinking	5
5	Shortcutting detective thinking and advanced stepladders	Stepladders, detective thinking	6
6	Troubleshooting stepladders	Stepladders, detective thinking	7
7–9	Troubleshooting all skills & learning additional skill if needed Relaxation and/or social skills	Stepladders, detective thinking, and additional skills	8 and 9
10	Future goals and coping with setbacks	Plans for the future	10

PARENT ACTIVITY: What Are Our Goals?

It's time to think about what you might like to get out of the program. How far you get will depend on how much time you are prepared to put into it and how hard you and your child work at the new skills. Having goals in mind will help boost motivation and can also be used later to see how far you have progressed.

As we said earlier, parent activities are designed for you, the parent, to do in order to help you to help your child during your anxiety management session together. You will find several worksheets to help you, including this one, in the free Parent Activity Worksheets section of http://www.newharbinger.com/49913.

In your first anxiety management session, there will be a children's activity where your child will get a chance to talk about their own goals. But first, we would like you to identify what you would like to see at the end of the program.

What would you like your child to be able to do, which they currently don't do because of anxiety? Examples: spend time with a friend after school, catch the bus every day, greet people when they say hello, fall asleep within a half-hour of going to bed, go to summer camp, visit friends who have dogs	
What would you like your child *not to do* and how often do they do these things now? Examples: avoid going to school, sleep in your bed, ask questions, get stomachaches—every day, once a week	

List broader goals that you would like to achieve. Example: confidence in reacting to new situations.	

We will look back at these goals at the end of the program to see how far your child has come and what you still want to achieve.

BARRIERS

Are there any practical barriers that might get in the way of running this program? Example: Your child might be doing too many after-school activities to fit in something else, or you may have a partner who doesn't support this program.	

Spend a few minutes thinking about these barriers and then about ways you might try and overcome them. For example, if your child does too many activities after school, is there an activity that could be paused for a few months?

In Summary

Anxious children believe that the world is a dangerous place. Because of this belief, they will often interpret very innocent events as examples of danger. For example, a normal noise outside at night might be interpreted as a burglar. Most importantly, anxious children avoid things they fear. Because of this avoidance, they never have an opportunity to find out that what they are scared of probably won't happen and that they can cope if it does. This maintains anxiety by not allowing children to learn that what they fear is usually not true. Where parents allow their children to avoid their anxieties—perhaps by doing things for them and protecting them from possible worry—parents are also allowing these beliefs to stay.

In this program, we will help you to teach your child how to think more accurately and constructively about the world and to expect less danger in situations; we will teach you different ways of handling and interacting with your child; and we will show you how you can encourage your child to approach the situations they fear in a gradual and consistent manner. Together with these strategies, we will also cover some additional techniques that may be of help in some circumstances. These include coping strategies such as improved social skills and relaxation.

Above all, this is a book for parents and other caregivers. We are teaching you, the caregiver, to help your own child overcome anxiety. This means that your child will need to work closely with you through the program. Although high anxiety can occur at any age in a child—from preschool age to early adulthood—this book will be most valuable for children who are not yet teenagers. As we all know, once we reach adolescence, listening to our parents is not our highest priority! Toward the end of the book, we have included a chapter about how you can use the skills as your child enters their teenage years. But for the most part, this book will be of greatest benefit for children.

Motivating Your Child to Begin This Program

It can be difficult to get anxious children to try anything new. Usually they tend to expect the worst and feel nervous at the thought of having to do something that they haven't tried before. They may worry that the program will be too difficult or that they will be forced to do frightening things that they feel they can't do. Many anxious children also like to try to appear perfect in front of their parents (and peers) and so may have difficulty admitting their limitations. At the same time, your child is probably aware of how uncomfortable it feels to be anxious and would most likely prefer to be free of anxiety.

Likewise, starting a program like this can be a little scary for a parent. Working through the anxiety management exercises in this book will not be easy. You will be asked to look at some of your own feelings and behaviors at some points. And you may have to be prepared to make some of your own changes if your child is really going to improve. Above all, working on this program will take time and energy—the program won't work if you or your child is not fully committed.

Therefore, it is important to have your child's full cooperation, and you will also need to make this program your number one priority for the next few months. The program will work best if you and your child see this as a combined adventure. The two of you will need to form a team, working toward some common goals. A good way to encourage your child's cooperation and motivation is to discuss the negative aspects of being anxious and the benefits that might come from learning to control anxiety. Remember—most children love doing things with their parents. If you treat this as a game or adventure that you are going to do together, your child will be much more likely to go along with you.

Before you start, it is a good idea to sit down with your child and talk about the program you are going to do together. Here are a few points to cover:

- Feeling anxious is normal, and there are many children who feel just the same way.

- You and your child will work on this program together—they are included every step of the way. You might describe it as an adventure in which the two (or three) of you will be a team.

- Your child will not be forced to do anything they do not want to do.

- New skills will be learned one small step at a time.

- The program will be fun and will also include rewards that can be earned.

- At the end of the program, your child should feel braver and more confident.

Remember that this program will not take away all the normal protective anxieties that a child may have in certain situations (e.g., being scared of walking down a dark alley). Instead, it aims to teach skills to manage the bits of anxiety that are "over the top" and that get in the way of your child doing what they want in life.

ACTIVITIES TO DO WITH YOUR CHILD...

As we mentioned earlier, at the end of each chapter you will find activities to do with your child that will help you teach the anxiety management skills. It is very important that you and your child regularly work on the activities and practice tasks. You can download the Helping Your Anxious Child Activity Book from the New Harbinger website: http://www.newharbinger.com/49913. This workbook contains all of the activities to print out and use with your child. It also provides child-friendly explanations of each skill and blank worksheets for your child to complete.

In general, once children are about seven years old, they will benefit from actively learning the skills by completing the activities in the workbook. For younger children, three to six years, the program will be predominantly for parents to learn and then use the skills in everyday interactions with their child. If a children's activity has a task that is particularly suitable for even the youngest children, this will be highlighted in the children's activity instructions.

Reward your child for their efforts in completing the work by consistently showing encouragement and interest in what they have done. If you stop paying attention to the tasks, your child will very quickly follow. Most children appreciate stamps, small stickers, or tokens that they can cash in later for bigger rewards. Giving your child a star or sticker each time they complete an exercise is a good way to help make the program fun and to motivate your child to continue. However, attention and interest from you as well as your praise will be the most powerful rewards and the best ways to motivate your child. We will say more about using rewards later. One really simple principle is the "minute-for-minute exchange"—that is, for every minute your child spends working on the program, they get a minute of an enjoyable activity such as screen time or story time with a parent.

CHILDREN'S ACTIVITY 1: Meet Some Other Children with Anxiety

Read stories with your child about different children who have anxiety, either the ones from earlier in the chapter or from their Activity Book. Hopefully, this can get you started talking about their own fears and worries, and how they are not alone and are not "crazy." For younger children, there are a number of picture books that tell stories about children who are scared or worried that you could borrow from a library to read.

CHILDREN'S ACTIVITY 2: Me and My Anxiety

Talk with your child about their own fears and worries. First list or draw all the things that people could be afraid of or worried about. Then circle each one that you were afraid of when young (or even what worries you now) and then have your child circle each one that they find difficult. Be very careful not to turn this into an "interview," and do not start telling your child to stop worrying about these things. Just accept your child's view and ask questions so that you and your child can understand more about the fear.

CHILDREN'S ACTIVITY 3: My Goals

Begin by talking with your child about what they might get out of doing the program. A good way to phrase it might be to ask questions like "Are there things that are hard for you to do now because they make you nervous?" or "Are there things that you would like to do without being scared?" Or you may focus on more concrete positives (especially if you have a younger child), for example, "Would you like to be able to make friends more easily?" While there may be lots of things that you personally want out of the program (like being able to leave your child with a sitter while you go out at night), you need to focus here on what positives your child might get out of the program (like becoming a "big" boy or girl, being able to go places independently, feeling brave, and having more friends). Write down the main goals that your child comes up with. It is a good idea to put this somewhere that you and your child will see regularly to remind yourselves of why you are doing the program, especially when things get a little tougher. Encourage your child to decorate these goals and be proud of where they are heading.

As part of setting goals, plan a special activity that you will do together at the end of the program as a reward for working hard. This activity should be just for the parents/caregivers and the child doing the program. The point is to make your child feel special and that their (and your) hard work is going to be rewarded. We suggest allowing three months to complete the program. The removal or loss of this activity should never be used as a threat during the program, but it can be used as a means of motivating everyone to remember that working on the anxiety is a commitment that will have benefits in the long run.

CHAPTER HIGHLIGHTS

In this chapter, you and your child learned...

→ that you can identify problematic fears by examining the impact that anxiety has on everyday life;

→ how anxiety affects three aspects of a person: their thoughts, their body, and their behavior;

→ that anxiety can be divided into several different types and that it is common for children to experience difficulties in more than one area;

→ that there are different factors that can cause or maintain anxiety, including genes, negative thinking, avoiding, parent reactions, parent modeling, and stressors; and

→ how each anxiety management skill is targeted at a particular factor that keeps anxiety going.

Your child will need to do the following:

* Complete the children's activities with the help of a parent or other adult.

* Set goals and make a commitment to learning to manage anxiety.

CHAPTER 2

Feelings, Thoughts, and Actions

There are some simple pieces of information that can really help children learn to manage their anxiety better. Younger children might need to spend a little more time in this section, whereas older children might cover it fairly quickly.

Learning About Feelings

Many children have difficulty in naming feelings and in being able to describe the differences between emotions. It's important to make sure that your child understands and can recognize different emotions before moving on to teach ways of controlling anxiety. If your child struggles to name and recognize feelings, you can help them by labeling and discussing feelings in everyday situations and by playing games based on feelings. For example, play a game where your child acts out a feeling, first just being given the name of the feeling (e.g., sad, angry) and then being given a situation (e.g., winning a prize, losing a wallet). Your child then acts out the feeling they would probably have in that situation. Try to make it fun and silly. If the rest of the family is willing to get involved, you can make a set of cards or pieces of paper with different feelings written on them and have each person take turns in picking one of the cards and acting out that feeling without using words. Other members of the family can then try to guess what the feeling is. Another helpful activity is to name the feeling that a person in a video or picture might be having.

Your child should understand that there are several different forms of anxiety. For example, fear, worry, tension, shyness, embarrassment, and terror all have a focus on possible danger at their core. While there may be slight differences among them, as far as this program is concerned, they are all basically the same.

The Worry Scale

An important step is to teach your child how to measure their fears. This will help your child understand that strong emotions do not come from nowhere or "out of the blue." In addition, your child needs to learn that we are not trying to "get rid of" anxiety, but are simply teaching them to control it better. Being able to distinguish between different levels of fear will become important later in the program.

We use the worry scale to show different degrees or levels of anxiety. The thermometer uses a scale from 0 to 10 on which different levels of anxiety are marked from 0 (very relaxed) to 10 (extremely worried). This is a personal judgment, and everyone will have different perceptions for different situations. For very young children, you might create a smaller picture scale that uses just three or four faces from very scared to happy. What is important is that your child learns to recognize that anxiety is not an all-or-nothing feeling but can vary in degree.

After teaching your child about the worry scale, it is important to have your child practice giving worry-scale ratings. Ask your child how anxious they are in different situations through the day. This will help your child to become more aware of their anxiety levels and will also give the two of you a common language to use to describe anxiety (e.g., "I feel at 4 now" or "I'm at 7 at the moment").

The Worry Scale

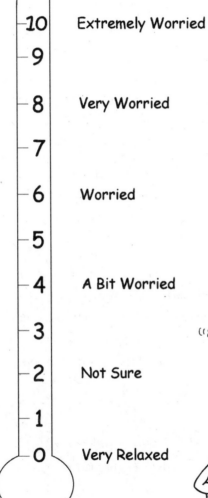

10 — Extremely Worried

9 —

8 — Very Worried

7 —

6 — Worried

5 —

4 — A Bit Worried

3 —

2 — Not Sure

1 —

0 — Very Relaxed

The Three Parts of Anxiety

You will remember that when children experience anxiety, you are likely to notice it affecting them in three ways.

- First, in the *expectations, beliefs, and thoughts* that they have. Anxious children will have thoughts that center around some type of danger or threat. For example, they may worry that they'll be hurt, that someone close to them may be hurt, or that they'll be laughed at.

- Second, anxiety is experienced *physically* in the body. When a child becomes anxious, their body prepares for danger by increasing heart rate and breathing and tensing muscles, but this can also lead to sweating, nausea, stomachaches, headaches, or agitation.

- Third, and probably most importantly, anxiety affects children's *behavior*. When children are anxious, they may freeze, fidget, pace, cry, cling, and shake. In addition, anxiety almost always involves some type of avoidance.

It is important for your child to develop an understanding of these parts and how they influence each other by becoming aware of how their own anxiety works. At your anxiety management session for this week, your child will identify how anxiety might affect them across the three systems—physical symptoms, thoughts, and behaviors. Some of the information you might cover follows.

How Anxiety Affects the Body

When we become frightened, our body goes through many changes. These may include any of the following:

- breathing fast
- butterflies in tummy
- needing to go to the toilet

- wobbly knees
- tense muscles
- dizziness

- crying
- sweating
- stomachache
- shakiness
- blushing

- headache
- feeling too hot
- fidgetiness
- increasing heart rate

You can begin to get younger children to think about these changes by asking them to think of a frightened animal such as a cat. Ask what physical changes would happen if a cat was asleep and woke up suddenly to see a dog standing next to it (e.g., fur standing up, big eyes, tensed-up body, and scared expression). After this, you can ask your child to think about how their own body feels during anxious times. It is often useful if you or other family members are willing to discuss what happens to your and their bodies when anxious, to show both the similarities and the differences in how people react to anxiety.

How Anxiety Affects Thoughts

It is also going to be important for your child to become more aware of their worried thoughts and beliefs. In fact, this is one of the more important parts of this section since you will be moving on in later weeks to help your child change their anxious thoughts. Your child will learn that certain feelings go along with certain thoughts, and that anxious feelings tend to go along with thoughts of danger. In addition, your child needs to begin to become more aware of the particular bad things that they tend to expect.

When teaching your child about thoughts, try to get them to suggest thoughts that indicate some sort of event rather than simply describing the feeling. For example, a thought such as "This is going to hurt" is good because it describes a bad outcome that a person might be expecting. However, a thought such as "I am scared," which simply describes the feeling, doesn't tell you anything about what your child is scared about. One of the hardest things for children in this part of the program is to learn the difference between thoughts and feelings, so it is best to try not to confuse these things.

It is a good idea to introduce the term "worried thoughts" here. Your child should begin to understand that when we feel scared, nervous, or shy, it is because we have some sort of worried thought or belief. Of course, sometimes these worried thoughts might be quite hard to identify, and some children will say, "I just feel that way." If your child does this, don't push it yet. It is enough in this case to get your child to "guess" what they might be thinking.

How Anxiety Affects Behavior

It is a good idea to get your child to think about how they behave or act when anxious. This is likely to include different ways of avoiding or escaping from the frightening situation but may also include other behaviors such as pacing, hitting, throwing tantrums, asking for help, or biting nails. To try to raise your child's awareness of what they typically do when anxious, first tell your child what you do, then ask what they have seen other people do (family members, friends, or TV characters), before finally asking what it is that they typically do. As with worried thoughts, some children may not recognize or admit to all their behaviors. Again, don't push too hard at this stage.

PARENT ACTIVITY: Learning About My Child's Anxiety

Since you are going to be helping your child through this program, it is a good idea for you to learn a little more about these patterns as well. Over the next few days, watch your child carefully—notice their anxious behaviors, thoughts, and feelings. (Visit http://www.newharbinger.com/49913 to download this worksheet.)

Situation		
BODY I notice...in their body	THOUGHTS My child says or asks...	ACTIONS My child does...

Situation		
BODY I notice...in their body	THOUGHTS My child says or asks...	ACTIONS My child does...

Based on the gathered information, what is it about your child that alerts you to the fact that they are worried or scared? (Think about typical things they say, physical symptoms, mood swings, etc.) This information will also be helpful during later activities, so keep it handy.

Linking Situations, Thoughts, Feelings, and Actions

Once your child has learned the different ways that anxiety works, the next step in the program is to help children understand that there is a link between a situation, their thoughts, how they are feeling, and what they do. To do this successfully, your child will need to be able to identify situations that they have been in, what they thought during that time, how they were feeling in that situation, and what they did next. This is the first skill that will require a short period of daily practice before your child will be able to confidently identify thoughts separate from their feelings.

We use a form to help children record the link between situations, thoughts, feelings, and actions. The following is a completed example. The form asks children to describe the situation that made them anxious, their thoughts at the time, how they actually felt (e.g., frightened, worried, shy, nervous, etc.), the degree of fear or worry on the worry scale and what they did.

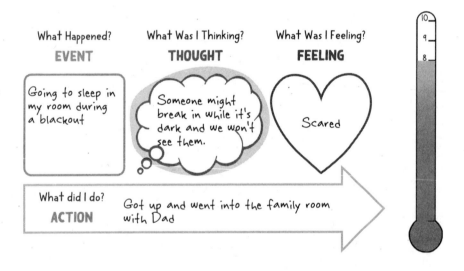

ACTIVITIES TO DO WITH YOUR CHILD...

Complete the following activities with your child. Remember that you can either create these yourself or use the downloadable Activity Book available at http://www.newharbinger.com/49913.

CHILDREN'S ACTIVITY 4: What Is Anxiety?

Talking with your child about worries and fears and how being anxious can sometimes be helpful (e.g., by getting you scared if you smell smoke in the house or by revving you up for a big test or game). You need to make sure that you use the right level of language for your child's ability. Obviously, you will need to use very different words for a preschool child or an older child.

Explain that sometimes we get anxious when there really isn't anything to be afraid of, such as getting scared by a noise outside at night that is being made by the next-door neighbor's cat. Some kids, in fact, get a lot more anxious a lot more often than other kids and consequently they miss out on fun activities or spend a lot of time feeling bad.

Tell them about the three parts of anxiety: how the body reacts (e.g., fast heartbeat), what the person thinks (e.g., that the dog in the park is dangerous), and what the person does (e.g., leaves the park so that the dog can't get them). Try to use examples to help them to understand that when they feel anxious, they can tell that's how they're feeling by what happens to their body, what they think, and what they do.

CHILDREN'S ACTIVITY 5: The Worry Scale

Show your child the worry-scale thermometer. Explain that sometimes we only feel a little bit worried, but at other times we feel really, really scared. So that we can tell other people how scared we are very quickly, we can rate the feeling of worry on a worry scale, just like you can read the temperature on a thermometer. Have your child use the worry scale to describe their degree of worry in a list of different situations, including silly ones (like waking up and finding that a lion is in the bed), ones that are likely to get a very low rating (such as visiting Grandma for her birthday), and situations that you know your child finds very frightening. Encourage your child to give ratings across the range on the worry scale.

CHILDREN'S ACTIVITY 6: Anxiety and My Body

Create an outline of a body that your child can use to show where anxiety affects them. You may choose to draw one freehand, but a fun alternative is to get a huge sheet of paper, have your child lie on it, and then draw an outline of your child with a pen on the paper. Your child can then use this personal "portrait" to color and show where and how anxiety affects them. If needed, use the list from the section "How Anxiety Affects the Body" above to remind your child of possible body symptoms. Help your child feel okay about these symptoms by comparing them to the ones that you get when worried or scared.

CHILDREN'S ACTIVITY 7: Thoughts, Feelings, and Actions

Talk with your child about how feelings depend on what you are thinking. Look at magazine pictures and ask your child how the person is feeling and then have them guess what that person might be thinking. Use pictures of situations that could be either positive or negative, such as a child ice skating. Ask your child to identify a thought that would make the person feel happy and then a thought that might make the person feel worried or scared. Once the thoughts are identified, ask your child what the child in the picture may do next (which should differ depending on the different thoughts).

You may need to do this activity with several different situations until your child identifies a range of thoughts and actions. At the end of the activity, point out how different people can have different thoughts and that even the same person can have different thoughts about one situation.

Note: Young children (under seven years) might find it very hard to identify their thoughts or to link their thoughts with their feelings (below). If your child is finding this too hard, encourage them to guess what they might be thinking or to guess a typical "worried thought" that another child might have.

CHILDREN'S ACTIVITY 8: Linking Thoughts, Feelings, and Actions

Draw a picture similar to the example earlier where the main thought, feeling, and action for a situation can be recorded. Ask your child to think of a time when they felt really happy and to think about where they were, who else was there, and what they were doing. Write a short description of the event or situation in the first box. Now ask your child to try to remember what they were thinking or saying to themself in their head. This might be a bit hard to remember if the situation happened a long time ago. If your child can't remember exactly what they were thinking, try to guess what it might have been in that situation. Write this in the thought box. Then ask your child to describe how they were feeling. Write this in the feeling box and have your child rate how worried they were in this situation using the worry scale (probably 0). Finally, write in what action the child did next in that situation.

Next, repeat this exercise, this time having your child think of a time when they felt terribly worried or afraid. Finally have your child practice completing the linking thought, feeling, and action record using situations that have happened in the past day or two.

CHILDREN'S PRACTICE TASK 1: Learning About My Thoughts, Feelings, and Actions

As we said before, it's important for your child to learn to become more aware of their own patterns of anxiety. You can do this by having your child keep a record of their anxiety for a week or two, recording a number of examples of situations, thoughts, feelings, and actions where they felt anxious. Use a linking thought, feeling, and action form and have your child make an entry on the sheet whenever they feel anxious, worried, shy, or scared, even if only a little. This may be many times a day or only once a day. But you should try to encourage your child to make at least one entry each day. Remember to praise and reward your child for these efforts during the week. This exercise is generally suitable for children ages seven and up.

CHAPTER HIGHLIGHTS

In this chapter, you and your child learned...

→ how to recognize and distinguish between different types of feelings;

→ how to use the worry scale to rate the intensity of anxious feelings;

→ what happens to your body when you are anxious; and

→ that in each situation there are thoughts, feelings, and actions.

Your child will need to do the following:

* Complete the children's activities with the help of a parent or other adult.

* Complete Practice Task 1. Over approximately one week, fill in a linking thought, feeling, and action picture whenever they feel even a little anxious.

CHAPTER 3

Detective Thinking

Learning to think in a calm, constructive, and accurate way is a very useful strategy to help any person, adult or child, to overcome anxiety. In this program, we use the term "detective thinking" to describe a process of learning to challenge faulty and unrealistic thoughts and beliefs. This is a simple "game" where your child will learn to identify their worries and then act like a detective and find clues to tell them whether that worry is realistic or not. It will be particularly helpful as a part of your child's anxiety coping skills, especially for children who have reached a certain level of maturity (usually after about seven years—for younger children, we provide a simplified version later in the chapter).

However, it is not an easy technique to use properly, even for adults. Therefore, in order to be able to really help your child use this skill, it is best if you can learn to use it yourself. For this reason, we have written this chapter in two parts. In the first part, we teach the ideas and methods of detective thinking to you so that you can fully understand how it works. Because it is a complex technique, we recommend that you also use detective thinking in your own life for a while to help you with any situations of worry, stress, or anger. Putting it into practice in this way will help you to better understand how to do it. In the second part of the chapter, we show you how you can teach detective thinking to your child, and make it a little simpler to learn than the full technique that you will be using.

If you have identified some fears and worries in your own life, then learning to use the detective thinking strategy and allowing your child to see and hear you using it is a great way to model that anxiety can be reduced using skills that can be learned.

The Basics of Detective Thinking

Before you can learn to change your thoughts, and in that way manage your feelings as well as help your child, there are some basic principles that you need to understand.

The Relationship Among Events, Thoughts, and Feelings

Most people think that events happening outside of themselves cause feelings. In other words, if you experience a certain event, then certain feelings will be the inevitable result. For example, how many times have you said, "*You* made me so angry" or "That noise scared me"? However, outside events such as the actions of another person or traffic jams cannot be fully responsible for your feelings. One way to understand this is to realize that two people can experience exactly the same event and feel differently about it. The same person can also experience the same event at different times and feel quite differently about it at each time. Why is this?

The answer lies in the content of your beliefs, thoughts, or self-talk—in other words, your feelings depend on what you are telling yourself about an event. As you will see in the following examples, your beliefs about a situation or event determine how you will feel about that situation or event.

Imagine that both Tony's wife and Jim's wife are an hour late in coming home from the movies. Tony tells himself that his wife probably decided to have a coffee with her friend (this is his belief about the situation). As a result of holding this belief, he is not concerned about her, although he is somewhat annoyed that she didn't think to call and let him know. Jim, on the other hand, tells himself that his wife must have been involved in a car accident (this is his belief about the situation). As a direct result of holding this belief, he is worried sick.

This example clearly demonstrates that it is not the situation per se (wife being late) that results in the emotions experienced by each man. Instead, it's the beliefs or thoughts held by each that are responsible for the different reactions. The event might act as a trigger, but the emotion that the trigger prompts depends on how the event is *interpreted* by the person. Let's look at another example in which we can see different emotions experienced by the same individual, apparently in response to the same situation.

Celine has just finished a hard day's work and she is feeling tired and irritable. She gets home just as her husband, Aaron, is feeding their young son, Charles. When Aaron leaves for a few minutes, Charles begins playing with his food and, laughing, suddenly picks up the bowl and puts the whole meal on top of his head. He thinks this is hilarious, but Celine is furious about the mess. On another night, exactly the same thing happens. But this time, Celine has just been given a promotion at work and is feeling pretty good. This time, when Charles tips the bowl over his head, Celine thinks it is the cutest thing and laughs along. Here again, we can see an example of two different emotions being triggered by the same event. But this time it is happening in the same person. The difference lies entirely in what is going on inside Celine's head. In one case, Celine thinks about the mess and the inconvenience and becomes angry. In the other case, Celine thinks how cute her son is and how much fun he is having and she feels good.

Although it is tempting to believe that an event itself determines the way in which we react to it, in actual fact, our beliefs and thoughts based on our interpretations of that event directly determine how we react. As you and your child work through this program, try to remind yourself that our emotions are not directly caused by the things that go on around us. Instead, our feelings and emotions are the direct result of the way that we *think about*, or *interpret*, events and situations. Here is an example:

EVENT	BELIEF/THOUGHT	FEELING
You hear the screeching of car brakes	The dog's been run over	Panic
	Those kids are at it again	Anger
	Lucky they missed	Relief

Two Common Errors in Thinking

Most people who worry a lot or feel stressed tend to make two errors in their thinking. First, they commonly overestimate how likely it is that bad events will occur. Second, they usually assume that the outcomes or consequences of those events will be catastrophic and unbearable.

OVERESTIMATING THE PROBABILITY THAT SOMETHING BAD WILL HAPPEN

Someone who is an anxious person often believes that bad things are very likely to happen to them, even though this may not be true. Think, for example, of someone who is very shy, having to get up and give a speech at a wedding. They might well think, "I just know that I am going to say the wrong thing." Now it is possible that this person will end up saying something a little inappropriate. But it's quite hard to say the wrong thing at a wedding, and the chance that that person will say the wrong thing is probably not very high. Thinking "I am going to say the wrong thing" implies 100 percent probability—that is, that the person will definitely say the wrong thing. Clearly, this is an overestimate.

Similarly, if you're late coming home, your child would feel anxious if they think "Mom and Dad have had an accident." But this thought again implies 100 percent probability—"Mom and Dad have *definitely* had an accident." While there may be some chance that you have had an accident, the reality is that it is probably pretty unlikely. So, if your child is thinking that it is definite, that is an overestimate that only serves to intensify anxiety.

OVERESTIMATING THE BAD CONSEQUENCES

To highly stressed people, life often seems very threatening. Not only do they believe that unpleasant things are highly likely to happen to them, but they also believe that if those things do happen, the consequences will be absolutely catastrophic and unbearable.

Interestingly, most people who assume the worst are unaware they are doing it. In other words, they typically have never asked themselves the question "What's the worst thing that could happen, and could I cope if it did happen?" For instance, imagine that you are on your way to an appointment. As you sit in your car, stuck in traffic, you think to yourself, "Oh no, I'm going to be really late." As part of this thought, you are assuming that being late will be really terrible. In other words, you are saying to yourself, "I am going to be late, and that is the end of the world." But if you could ask yourself the question "If I am late, what will really happen and will I be able to cope with that?" you will probably find that being late is not really as tragic as you are assuming.

As another example, imagine that your child is very anxious about making a mistake on their homework. As part of this fear, they are probably assuming that making a mistake will be the "end of the world." In fact, while the teacher may make a comment about it, making a mistake in homework will probably have no serious effects at all. This shows you the second type of common problem in thinking—overestimating the negative consequences of things.

Changing Your Beliefs

So, if our feelings come directly from our beliefs about a situation, and anxious people tend to believe that bad things are more likely to happen to them than they really are, it seems reasonable that if we could change those beliefs, we could control our anxiety to some extent.

Before we go any further, we need to point out an important limitation. No one can ever control their thoughts and beliefs 100 percent, so no one is going to be able to control their feelings 100 percent. That is not what we want to do. What we are aiming for is to teach you how you can help your child to adjust their *extreme* beliefs so that they are more accurate most of the time. By doing this, your child will also be able to reduce their extreme emotions of fear so that they are more manageable. This is one small step in learning to overcome anxiety. .

The answer to reducing extreme anxiety is to learn how you might change your beliefs from extreme ones to less extreme ones. For example, instead of thinking, "My partner has been in a car accident and they have been killed," it would be more accurate to think, "There is a chance that my partner has been in a car accident, but it is more likely that there is another reason for their lateness, and even if they have had an accident, it's probably not a huge one." If you believed the second thought, your anxiety would be much less than with the catastrophic thinking.

The key to changing your emotions is belief. In other words, there is no point in simply saying to yourself, "My partner hasn't been killed in a car accident" if you don't believe it. You have to convince yourself that the less extreme thought is true. Luckily, in most cases it is, and so it is usually not too hard to think of the less extreme thought. In most cases in life, the extreme, catastrophic belief is just not very accurate or realistic. Usually, if you look at the actual evidence, the less extreme belief is the more accurate or likely one. That is why we call this technique *detective thinking.* Most people who are anxious tend to think in unrealistic or faulty ways. By learning to think more constructively, they can learn to control their anxiety.

Of course, this raises an important point in that, at times in life, things will happen that are bad. At these times, it is quite understandable and appropriate to be anxious. The goal then is not to try to teach your child never to be anxious. Rather, you can teach your child ways of managing anxiety when that anxiety is excessive and out of proportion to the situation.

Looking at Evidence

The key to changing your thoughts is to really believe the new thoughts—that is, to convince yourself that your original belief is simply not true. We do this by learning to look at the actual evidence. In other words, you need to become a sort of detective or scientist with respect to your life and to look at the evidence for every negative thing that you believe. That is why we talk about *detective thinking,* and in a moment we will be showing you how you can teach your child to think about their thoughts like a detective.

To do detective thinking for yourself, this is what you need to do: Every time you find that you are stressed, anxious, or worried, you need to ask yourself, "What is the negative thing that I am expecting?" or "What do I think is going to go wrong here?" The answer to this question will give you your negative thought or belief. For example, imagine that you have been called into your boss's office and you have no idea why. You find yourself feeling worried. So, you could ask yourself, "Why am I worried—what is the negative thing that I am expecting?" Your answer might be, "She is going to criticize me for something I have done wrong." This is your negative belief. Notice that a question such as "I wonder why she wants to see me?" is not a negative belief and is not what is making you worried. You need to ask yourself "What *bad thing* am I expecting?"

Once you have identified your negative belief, you need to look at the evidence that either supports or doesn't support it. There will be many types of evidence you can look at, and each thought will require slightly different evidence. However, there are four common types of evidence that we use most often:

- **Past experience.** One of the easiest sources of evidence is to ask yourself how often you have been in a similar situation and how many of those times it worked out badly. Remember to be very honest with yourself—don't just look at the bad times, but take into account *every* time you have been in a similar situation. For example, you might ask yourself, "How many times in the past has my boss called me in, and in how many of those times has it turned out that I did something wrong?"

- **General information.** You can also often get good evidence by looking at general information relating to a situation or event. This information may take the form of commonsense, logic, general knowledge, or even official statistics or research. For example, you might ask yourself, "Do I usually make mistakes that I am unaware of?" or "Is my boss someone who normally criticizes?"

- **Alternative explanations.** A very useful strategy is to try to think about other possible reasons for the event. The negative interpretation that you had might be one explanation, but are there others? For example, you might consider that your boss has called you in to clarify something she didn't understand, to give you a new task, to ask your opinion on something, or even to offer you a promotion. None of these is necessarily correct, but it shows you that your negative expectation is only one possibility out of several. Therefore, the negative expectation is not definite and the feared outcome is less likely than you originally thought.

- **Role reversal.** Finally, a very good source of evidence for some situations, especially interpersonal ones, is to mentally turn the situation around. Pretend that you are the other person and that other person is you or that it is happening to someone else. Then ask yourself how you would feel or what you would think if the situation was reversed. For example, you might ask yourself, "If my colleague had been called in by the boss, would I assume that they would be criticized?" In most cases, we are far less negative about other people's lives, and this is a powerful way to realize that you seem to have different expectations for yourself and others.

Looking at all of the evidence in this way can help to convince you that your negative belief ("She is going to criticize me") is just not very likely or at least is not as likely as you originally assumed. But there is one further step to changing your beliefs.

As we said earlier, anxious people tend to overestimate both the likelihood of something bad happening and also how bad it will be. The evidence we have looked at so far should help to reduce the likelihood estimate. But what about the consequences? To examine this, you need to ask yourself one last question—"So what?" In other words, you need to ask yourself: What would really happen if the bad thing that I am expecting actually did occur?" "Would it be the worst thing that could happen?" "Could I cope with it?" This will help you to identify two possible types of answers. One possibility is that you will realize very quickly that the bad thing you were worrying about isn't so bad. The other possibility is that you will come up with another negative belief, and you will then need to look at the evidence for that.

For example, you might ask yourself, "So what if my boss does criticize me about something I did wrong?" One possible answer might be, "I guess it doesn't really matter—I can deal with it." If you *really believe* this, then you should find your worry immediately dropping off. On the other hand, you might come up with a negative consequence such as "If my boss criticizes my work, she will fire me." In this case, you have now identified another extreme thought and you should go ahead and look at the evidence for this. For example, you might look at the logic of the statement (just because my boss has identified one mistake, does that mean I would get fired?) or at past experience (have you ever been criticized by the boss before and did you lose your job that time?).

Learning to apply detective thinking to your life is not easy and takes a lot of practice. In reading this section, you may be thinking, "Why are these guys telling me all this—I'm not the one with the problem." This may be true, but the reality is that we can all use detective thinking at times. We all have times that we get angry, anxious, upset, or stressed when it really isn't necessary. At these times, learning to think more constructively and accurately can help to make a difference. But it will only work if you learn it well and really practice at times when you are not too emotional. More importantly, as we said before, you need to learn to do detective thinking so that you can teach it to your child. The best chance your child has for learning to think more realistically is if you and your child's other caregivers can use detective thinking. This will help your child learn by copying you, and you will also be better able to help your child if you know what you are doing and what to look for. For these reasons, we strongly urge you to practice detective thinking right along with your child.

Hopefully, by finding evidence for your own past worry, you can see how analyzing the evidence can help to provide a belief that is more accurate and less likely to cause extreme worry. You may also see how difficult it is to learn this skill at first. The parent activity below will help you to think about evidence for one of your recent worries and will provide you with some questions you can use in the future to help you think of evidence. You can then use the Detective Thinking Worksheet to do some more practice using detective thinking on any other worries or other distressing thoughts.

PARENT ACTIVITY: Finding Evidence for My Own Worry

This is by no means an easy skill to learn, for adults or for children. Before you move on to teaching your child about the skill, try it for yourself. (If you prefer, visit https://www.newharbinger.com/49913 to download this worksheet.)

Detective Thinking Evidence Sheet	
EVENT	
THOUGHTS	Worry Rating:
EVIDENCE What has happened in the past? What do I know about this situation? Possible alternative explanations? What is most likely to happen? What would other people expect? How bad would it really be? Could I cope?	
MORE ACCURATE THOUGHT?	Worry Rating:

Teaching Your Child About Detective Thinking

The points we have been discussing are not easy ones to understand, and it is often hard to apply these principles to your own thoughts and beliefs. It is reasonable to wonder then how you are going to teach these ideas to your child. In short, the answer is that you will teach your child a simplified version of these principles. Your child will need to practice by regularly using their Detective Thinking Worksheet that we will show you in the section "An Example of Detective Thinking" below. This worksheet is very similar to the Detective Thinking Worksheet that we described for parents above and that hopefully you have tried using. The Detective Thinking Worksheet for children has slightly easier wording and questions for your child to follow.

By the time you have worked through this chapter, your child should have a good understanding of several important points. These points are made in the exercises and readings that you will be working on with your child. However, it is also important that you emphasize and reemphasize these points whenever you can. The key points are these:

- Thoughts are the things that we say to ourselves in our heads.

- Thoughts are important because they cause feelings and behaviors.

- Thoughts can be either calm or worried.

- Worried thoughts can often be changed to calm thoughts by being a good detective and looking at the evidence.

The material that you will be working through with your child in this chapter consists of three distinct but related stages, each of which builds upon the stage before. The first stage involves helping your child to understand what thoughts are and to become skilled at identifying their own thoughts—you started this in the last chapter. The second stage involves helping your child to understand why thoughts are important, and the third stage involves helping your child to challenge worried thoughts by acting as a detective and examining the evidence. In the following sections, we will include some instructions that you can use to explain these ideas to your child, and at the end of the chapter, we'll offer activities to help your child better understand the ideas.

Why Are Thoughts Important?

At this point, you will need to briefly explain the underlying idea of detective thinking to your child just as we described it at the beginning of this chapter; the children's activities at the end of the chapter will help you with this. Of course, depending on your child's age, this will most likely need to be a more simplified version than was described earlier. It is important to discuss with your child why thoughts are important, making sure that they understand that more than one thought is possible in a situation and that what thought they have will determine how they feel. The consequence of this is that if children change their thoughts, they can also change how they feel.

The Detective Approach

As we discussed earlier, one of the most common mistakes that anxious children make in their thinking is to overestimate the probability that bad or dangerous things will happen to them.*

For this reason, anxious children need to learn to evaluate how likely it is that their negative, anxious interpretations of situations are true or accurate. In turn, they can learn to think calm thoughts that more accurately reflect the actual evidence. This will help them to really believe their calm thoughts. In children's terms, we talk about becoming a detective to find clues about whether an anxious thought is true.

---

* As you read this section, it is possible that you might think that your child's worries are "real and justified." In other words, perhaps your child is not overestimating. For example, your child's anxieties may be completely focused around real, physical bullying at school, or your child may have a learning disability and be justifiably worried about failing school. If this is true for your child, then this approach is not suitable for those specific worries. This program, and detective thinking in particular, is aimed at managing *excessive* or *unrealistic* anxieties, not fears based on real dangers or difficulties.

In the same way that you have been examining your own negative thoughts and beliefs, your child will need to learn to find evidence about their negative expectations. Just as for you, it is important that your child really believes their calm thought. For this reason, it is important that you do not simply tell your child that a worried thought is silly or unlikely, as they probably won't believe you and it will often upset them further. Instead, your child needs to come to work it out for themselves, through the process of gathering evidence, that their negative interpretation is unlikely.

In this approach, what children are being asked to do is very similar to the work done by detectives. Both are searching for evidence and clues in order to reach the "truth." To make it more fun, it is a good idea (particularly with younger children) to get them to choose a favorite detective or super-hero character (such as Harry Potter, Hermione Granger, Scooby Doo, Captain Marvel, Spider-Man, Captain America, Jessica Jones, or Sherlock Holmes). Once children get used to thinking about their favorite detective in this way, you can use this character as a prompt. In other words, when your child begins to worry, you simply need to remind them to try to think like their detective.

The overall approach involves three steps. The **first step** is for children to work out what they are worried about. They need to identify their worried thought. Remind your child of the difference between thoughts and feelings. It's best if the worried thought is a clear statement of what your child expects to happen. For example, a thought such as "I am scared that Dad has been killed in a car accident" is a good, clear description that your child can use with their detective thinking. In contrast, a thought such as "I am scared because Dad isn't here" doesn't say what your child is really afraid of and so cannot be worked on easily. You will need to drill down a bit further by asking about exactly what your child is worried is going to happen.

The **second step** is for your child to gather as many clues as possible about their worried thought. This is where your child gets to play detective and try to work out how they might really "know" whether the thing they are afraid of will really happen. The easiest types of evidence to find include the following:

- What has happened before in this situation?

- Did the really scary, terrible, awful thing actually happen?

- What general things do I know about this situation?

- What else could happen in this situation?

- What is more likely to happen?

- What has happened to other people in that situation?

Notice that we don't automatically ask children to think about consequences ("What if it did happen?"). Children, especially younger ones, tend to have a lot of trouble with this as they are very concrete and do not have a lot of life experience of different consequences. With older children and teenagers, there will be many times when you can ask them about possible consequences yourself, such as "How bad will it actually be?" as well as "Could you cope with the bad outcome if it did occur?" Whether you ask consequence questions may also depend on the situation. If the worry relates to something social, like getting in trouble at school or being laughed at, then consequences are easy (and important) to discuss. However, if, for example, the worry is about a parent dying or something similar, it will be best to stick with evidence that shows that what they are scared of probably won't happen.

Finally, based on the evidence children have discovered, they will be in a position to take the **third step**—to reevaluate their worried thought. Hopefully, they will be able to realize that the worried thought is not actually very likely and that a calm thought is more likely. Remember, this exercise is about *detective* thinking, not positive thinking. This means that there will be some occasions when the worried thought is actually the more likely one. As an example, think of the child who goes out after dark and finds themself in a dark lane and sees someone breaking into a house. It is important to remind children that in such situations, feeling frightened is very natural and useful. The detective thinking that you are teaching your child is designed to help replace worried thoughts with calm, accurate thoughts at those times when your child's fears are excessive and not in situations where it makes good sense to be afraid.

To help you explain the instructions for detective thinking, we have written a possible explanation you could use with your child. It is the exceptional child (and parent) who understands the ideas and can use detective thinking right away. You will need to be patient and keep reminding your child of the concepts, making sure they do lots and lots of practice. Practice can also be useful for you; we find that many parents have quite a bit of difficulty with this skill. It's not shameful to admit you are having difficulty—don't be afraid to reread the earlier sections and keep practicing. And remember the detective thinking technique is not useful for preschool-aged children or for children who think in a very concrete way—for these children, see the options later in the chapter.

How to Explain Detective Thinking to Your Child

The children's activities will help you to teach your child about detective thinking. The following dialogues and examples will help guide you in how to teach your child this important skill. You can either read the examples to your child or put the information into your own words.

You know now that some thoughts are unhelpful. They make you feel worried and scared; and they can make you do things that lead to bad results for you. Luckily, there are things you can do to beat the worried thoughts.

The first step is to catch them. You've already had some practice at this. Whenever you notice that you are feeling worried or scared or nervous, what you need to do is to catch the worried thought that is causing you to feel this way. Then, write it down on the Detective Thinking Worksheet, next to the "What am I worried about?" heading. You can also use the worry scale to write down how bad your worry is.

The next step is to become a detective and hunt down all the clues about your worried thought. A detective's job is to look for evidence and clues so that they can find out the truth. This is exactly what you need to do too. You need to look at your worried thought and ask yourself, "How do I know if it is really true?" Then you need to look for clues to decide whether or not this worried thought is true. Here are some questions you can ask yourself to make sure that you consider all the evidence. (You can point these out to your child on the Detective Thinking Worksheet, or it may be helpful to write these out on cards to help prompt your child while they are learning the skill.)

- **What has happened before in this situation?** Have you been in a situation like this before? Did anything bad happen? Did something bad happen every time you were in the situation?

- **What information do you know about this situation?** Is this really a bad situation? Have any of your friends or people you know had anything like this happen to them?

- **What else could happen in this situation?** Could there be another reason for this happening? Might something else happen?

Once you have collected your evidence, the last thing you need to do is to think it all through and work out how much you believe in your worried thought (based on the evidence). The questions to ask yourself here are "Based on my clues, what do I really think will happen? Can I think of a different, calm thought?" Write your calm thought on the last line of the Detective Thinking Worksheet. Finally, you should ask yourself, "If I really believe my new calm thought, how worried would I be?" Use the worry scale to write down a number.

An Example of Detective Thinking

The case of the big dog is an example of how Kurt talked with his mother about one of his smaller fears, dogs. You will need to go through lots of practices like this with your child over several weeks to help your child really learn how to use the detective approach. An example of Kurt's Detective Thinking Worksheet appears below. Read through the example below with your child. While you are going through it, look at the Detective Thinking Worksheet to show your child how the various parts were recorded by Kurt and his mother.

KURT'S EXAMPLE: THE CASE OF THE BIG DOG

Mother: I want you to imagine that you are walking down the street one day when a big dog comes running up to you. (Kurt's mother writes, "There's a big dog coming toward me" on the "Event" line of the Detective Thinking Worksheet.) If you were scared of the dog, what might you think to yourself, Kurt?

Kurt: If it was a really big dog, I would be scared that he was going to bite me.

Mother: Well done, Kurt! You've just worked out your worried thought. Let's write that down here on the "Thoughts" line. (She writes, "The dog's going to bite me and I won't be able to stop him.") Let's look at the worry scale, and you tell me, how worried do you think you would be?

Kurt: I think maybe a 7, no, a 9.

Mother: Okay—we'll write that in here. Now let's pretend that we are detectives and look at the evidence for whether this will or will not happen. What sort of evidence can you think of?

Kurt: The dog has big teeth.

Mother: Sure, it does have big teeth. Can you think of any evidence for how you know whether the dog will bite you? For example, what has happened before when a dog came running up to you?

Kurt: I was at my auntie's house once, and her big black dog, Jack, came running up to me.

Mother: What happened when it ran up to you?

Kurt: Nothing; it was friendly.

Mother: Good work. So a dog has run up to you before at your auntie's house, and nothing bad happened. That sounds like an excellent bit of evidence to me. Let's write that down on the "What is the evidence?" line. (Mother writes, "A dog has come up to me before, and it didn't bite me.") What did you do when it came over?

Kurt: Well, I patted it. Its fur was really dirty.

Mother: Wow, you were so brave that you even patted it. That's fantastic. So, rather than the dog biting you, what could the other possibility be?

Kurt: It could be friendly, and I could pat it.

Mother: That's right. Rather than the dog wanting to bite you, the alternative possibility is that it's friendly and wants you to pat it. Do you think this could be a good piece of evidence?

Kurt: Yes.

Mother: Yes, I think so too. Good detective work. Let's put the alternative possibility in the evidence section. (On the "What is the evidence?" line, she writes, "The dog is being friendly and wants me to pat him.") I have one more question for you: are all dogs mean, or are lots quite friendly?

Kurt: Lots are quite friendly.

Mother: Okay, that's another useful piece of evidence. (She writes, "Lots of dogs are friendly" on the "What is the evidence?" line.) Now that we have looked at some evidence, do you really think that the dog is going to bite you?

Kurt: I guess not.

Mother: Good work. From the evidence we came up with, it is probably more likely that it's friendly and that nothing bad will happen. That sounds like a calm thought to me—let's write it here. (She writes, "The dog is probably friendly, and nothing bad will happen" on the last line.)

Mother: I'm wondering, how would you be feeling if you were thinking that the dog was going to bite you?

Kurt: Scared.

Mother: And how would you be feeling if you were thinking that the dog was friendly?

Kurt: Good.

Mother: Can you tell me a number for how worried you would be—from your worry scale?

Kurt: Only a tiny bit—I think a 3.

Mother: Great work. We can see that the worried thought about the dog would make you feel scared, and this other calm thought would make you feel happier and more relaxed around the dog.

Detective Thinking Evidence Sheet

EVENT What is happening?	There's a big dog coming toward me.
WORRIED THOUGHTS What am I thinking?	The dog's going to bite me. I won't be able to stop him. Worry Rating: _9
WHAT IS THE EVIDENCE? What are the facts? What else could happen? Did it happen last time I worried? What is likely to happen? What has happened to other people?	A dog has come up to me before, and it didn't bite me. The dog is being friendly and wants me to pat him. Lots of dogs are friendly.
WHAT IS MY CALM THOUGHT?	The dog is probably friendly, and nothing bad will happen. Worry Rating: 3

Consolidating Detective Thinking

As we have said, detective thinking is going to take a lot of practice before your child (or you) can use it in situations where they feel anxious. To help you find evidence for different types of thoughts, we have written a list of questions you can use to gather evidence as well as a series of examples of completed Detective Thinking Worksheets. The questions give you some ideas of different ways you can help your child try to come up with evidence. The examples are for you to read and get a better idea of detective thinking. You might also go through a few of these with your child.

Once you start to practice detective thinking, you should start with some smaller practice worries, and later you can use the skills on your child's own big worries. Practice task 2 requires your child to practice detective thinking on a day-to-day basis. You should keep practicing detective thinking until your child is able to confidently use this skill without needing your help.

Detective Thinking Questions

Here is a list of many possible questions that you could use to help your child discover evidence. Remember that the questions in the left-most column of the Detective Thinking Worksheet are only prompts. There are many other questions that can be used to find evidence, and for some situations, particular questions would be inappropriate (such as the question, "So what if it did happen?" to a fear about parents dying).

We should also point out here that your child doesn't necessarily have to find lots and lots of evidence or fill the whole page for every worry. Sometimes finding just a single bit of evidence that is really believable is enough to change a worry. The key is to get your child to realize that what they are scared will happen, probably won't. Whether this takes lots of little bits of evidence or just a single, key discovery is not important.

SOME USEFUL QUESTIONS

Here is a more detailed list of possible questions that your child might use for various worries, depending on the type of event (situation) and the type of thought that they are having. You don't need to use every question for every worried thought, just pick the questions that are likely to find useful evidence.

- What is the evidence that this will not happen?

- What else could happen?

- Are you jumping to a conclusion that this will happen?

- Does the evidence suggest that your thought is correct?

- What is the best outcome that could happen?

- What would be the worst outcome that could happen?

- Could you cope if it did happen?

- What is the most likely outcome?

- How will this look in two weeks, a month, or a year's time?

- Are there other explanations for how that other person reacted?

- What are the real chances of this happening? (Try a calculation.)

- What has happened in the past?

- What happens to other people in this situation?

- Are you trying to be perfect?

- Can you really control what will happen?

- Are you underestimating what you can do to deal with this situation?

- Are you being too hard on yourself?

- Are you trying to read someone else's mind?

- If you had a friend in this situation, what would you say to them?

- What would your superhero/detective character think, based on the evidence?

SOME SAMPLE DETECTIVE THINKING WORKSHEETS

Here are some Detective Thinking Worksheets filled out by the children we introduced in chapter 1. Children often find it much easier to come up with and accept evidence for other people's worries. You can read over these samples with your child to let them see how other children do detective thinking. You could even ask your child to try and think of other evidence that these children might have used.

Lashi's Examples

Detective Thinking Evidence Sheet

EVENT What is happening?	I am waiting to be picked up from school and Mom is ten minutes late.
WORRIED THOUGHTS What am I thinking?	Mom's been in a car accident. Worry Rating: _8
WHAT IS THE EVIDENCE? What are the facts? What else could happen? Did it happen last time I worried? What is likely to happen? What has happened to other people?	Mom is only ten minutes late. She could be stuck in traffic or have lost track of time or be stuck on the phone to Nan. Mom has been late to get me twice before; both times she did arrive. There are lots of kids still here; not all their parents could be dead. I won't call her yet because she will be driving and I would distract her.
WHAT IS MY CALM THOUGHT?	Mom is running late; she will be here soon. Worry Rating: _3

Detective Thinking Evidence Sheet

EVENT What is happening?	I am spending the day at Grandma's.
WORRIED THOUGHTS What am I thinking?	What if Mom gets sick? Worry Rating: 6
WHAT IS THE EVIDENCE? What are the facts? What else could happen? Did it happen last time I worried? What is likely to happen? What has happened to other people?	Mom was not looking sick when I left. If she did get sick, she is with friends and they will help her. She could be having a great time. Most times when she gets sick, it is only a cold or tummy bug, not something serious. Mom can take care of herself when I'm at school, so why not now?
WHAT IS MY CALM THOUGHT?	Mom is not sick; if she did get sick, she could take care of herself. Worry Rating: 2

Kurt's Examples

Detective Thinking Evidence Sheet

EVENT What is happening?	I just closed the front door.
WORRIED THOUGHTS What am I thinking?	My hands are dirty; if I don't wash them, I will get sick. Worry Rating: _9_
WHAT IS THE EVIDENCE? What are the facts? What else could happen? Did it happen last time I worried? What is likely to happen? What has happened to other people?	There is nothing visible on my hands. I have closed a lot of doors in my life and I haven't gotten seriously sick. My body has the antibodies to cope with germs. A lot of very rare things would all have to happen in a row for me to actually get sick. A lot of people don't even bother to wash at all, and they don't get sick.
WHAT IS MY CALM THOUGHT?	My body can cope with a few germs if there were any there to catch. Worry Rating: _5_

Detective Thinking Evidence Sheet

EVENT What is happening?	We are going away for the weekend.
WORRIED THOUGHTS What am I thinking?	Something might go wrong. **Worry Rating:** 7
WHAT IS THE EVIDENCE? What are the facts? What else could happen? Did it happen last time I worried? What is likely to happen? What has happened to other people?	The weekend is planned out. If something unexpected comes along, it might be a good thing, like a fair. If the car broke down, we could get it fixed and then go home; the worst that could happen would be being bored for a while.
WHAT IS MY CALM THOUGHT?	It is unlikely that something will go wrong, but if it does, I can cope. **Worry Rating:** 4

Ethan's Examples

Detective Thinking Evidence Sheet

EVENT What is happening?	I'm in a class discussion, and everyone has to contribute.
WORRIED THOUGHTS What am I thinking?	I'll say something stupid and get laughed at. Worry Rating: 7
WHAT IS THE EVIDENCE? What are the facts? What else could happen? Did it happen last time I worried? What is likely to happen? What has happened to other people?	I did the homework. I know what the story is about. I know what to say. Most people look very bored already; they probably won't even listen. If they laugh, it could be that I was actually funny. Even if they laugh, in three days they won't remember and it won't really matter.
WHAT IS MY CALM THOUGHT?	I know what I am talking about, but most people won't even notice. Worry Rating: 4

Detective Thinking Evidence Sheet

EVENT What is happening?	I'm being taught a new skill during PE.
WORRIED THOUGHTS What am I thinking?	I look like an idiot; I can't do it. Worry Rating: __10__
WHAT IS THE EVIDENCE? What are the facts? What else could happen? Did it happen last time I worried? What is likely to happen? What has happened to other people?	Everyone is learning, and only some seem to be able to do it. The idea is to practice till you get it right. I can usually do new skills okay; I don't need to be perfect at it.
WHAT IS MY CALM THOUGHT?	Just give it a try; that's the only way to learn. Worry Rating: __5__

Hayley's Examples

Detective Thinking Evidence Sheet

EVENT What is happening?	I'm doing math homework and am *stuck* on question 2.
WORRIED THOUGHTS What am I thinking?	I have to answer this question or I'll get in trouble. Worry Rating: _9
WHAT IS THE EVIDENCE? What are the facts? What else could happen? Did it happen last time I worried? What is likely to happen? What has happened to other people?	I only have to give it a try; I don't have to get it right. I worked out question 1, and this is the same kind of thing. Not all the kids will be able to do it. If I really can't do it, I won't get in trouble; I just might have to stay in to get some help at recess.
WHAT IS MY CALM THOUGHT?	If I do my best, that's all that will be asked. I just have to be patient and stay calm. Worry Rating: 4

Detective Thinking Evidence Sheet

EVENT What is happening?	I spoke to a new girl in my class.
WORRIED THOUGHTS What am I thinking?	My friends won't want to play with me. Worry Rating: _6_
WHAT IS THE EVIDENCE? What are the facts? What else could happen? Did it happen last time I worried? What is likely to happen? What has happened to other people?	I was being polite. She was nice; they might like her too. They may not even know I spoke to her. Sometimes I speak to people that I know they don't like, but they still play with me. I remember they spoke to someone new last term, and I still played with them afterward.
WHAT IS MY CALM THOUGHT?	They aren't going to care; they might even be interested in meeting her. Worry Rating _1_

Talia's Example

	Detective Thinking Evidence Sheet
EVENT What is happening?	I was invited by a friend to go with her and her family to a local swimming pool.
WORRIED THOUGHTS What am I thinking?	I can't go. Someone will push me in and I might sink and drown. Worry Rating: _6
WHAT IS THE EVIDENCE? What are the facts? What else could happen? Did it happen last time I worried? What is likely to happen? What has happened to other people?	There is a shallow end of that pool so I could hang around there. I don't have to jump in the deep end. Plenty of people go to the local pool and they don't drown. I do know how to swim. Other kids will be there and they won't be scared. There is a lifeguard on duty. My friend will have a parent there too, and they will be watching out for us. Last time I went to the pool I didn't drown. We won't be spending all the time in the pool. We will be chatting at the edge.
WHAT IS MY CALM THOUGHT?	I know how to swim and there will be adults watching to keep us safe. Worry Rating: 4

A Simple Version of Detective Thinking for Younger Children

As we have noted earlier, some children might find it too hard to learn the full detective thinking process, perhaps because they are too young, they have learning difficulties, or they are very "concrete" in their thinking style. Although these children might have trouble engaging in the logical evidence process of detective thinking, they can often benefit from a more simple strategy of "thought replacement."

Thought replacement is a simpler process where the child identifies, or even guesses, worried thoughts and calm thoughts. The steps involve first asking your child what "worried thought" they might be having (or some other child might have in the same situation) when they are feeling frightened, and then asking your child to identify a different "calm thought" that they might have instead. For many children, simply reminding themselves of a calm thought when they start to feel frightened can help to start to bring their anxiety down.

You might find it helpful to use thought bubbles similar to the self-talk activity later in this chapter, where a person or two people had different thoughts about the same thing. When your child is anxious, have them write or draw the situation, then add two thought bubbles, In one, write their worried thought. Then get them to identify or guess a calm thought for the situation. Using a superhero as a prompt can often be useful—for example, "What would Captain Marvel (or other superhero) think if her mommy was late picking her up from school?" Obviously using the full detective thinking process is usually better. But for some children, simply learning to come up with a calm thought when they feel frightened can help to reduce their fear. If you decide to use this technique, you should still practice the exercise: have them identify the worried thoughts and alternate calm thoughts they might have in various situations when you are calmly sitting at home. Then when you are out and about and your child starts to show some increasing anxiousness, you should take the opportunity to remind your child to think of their relevant calm thought. Later, when you start to practice stepladders (see chapter 5), reminding your child about their relevant calm thought should form part of the stepladder planning and its practice.

A Final Important Comment

You shouldn't be too perfectionistic or allow your child to be perfectionistic while learning these skills. The goal is for your child to learn to replace worried thoughts with more accurate, calm ones—and to *believe* them. Exactly how they get to this point is not so important and may vary slightly from child to child. Some children, especially very young ones, may not be able to do the exact sort of evidence collecting that we have suggested here. But they may still begin to think more calmly if they practice coming up with calm, realistic thoughts. For some children who are really having difficulty learning to gather evidence (e.g., for more concrete thinkers), simply learning to identify their own worried thought and then repeating a calm thought can still help reduce their anxiety.

Finally, remember that this is not the only technique for overcoming anxiety. If your child really cannot master the detective thinking (after a good and serious try), you might want to move on and rely on some of the other skills that we will cover in the next chapters. They will naturally start to discover evidence when they start to face their fears with stepladders, and there is a chapter on relaxation that can be helpful as an alternative anxiety-reducing strategy.

ACTIVITIES TO DO WITH YOUR CHILD...

CHILDREN'S ACTIVITY 9: Why Are Thoughts Important?

Explain to your child that every event leads to thoughts, feelings, and actions. Emphasize that the same situation can lead to two different thoughts and that the thoughts cause different feelings and actions. Use the example below or something similar to make this point. Or, if you prefer, download "Why Are Thoughts Important?" from the Activity Book at http://www.newharbinger.com/49913.)

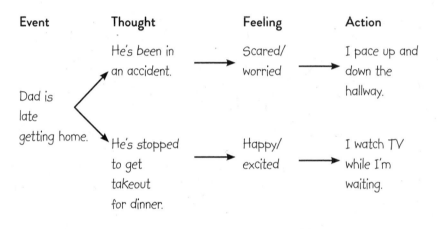

Point out that the feeling can be changed by first changing the thought, as the thought comes first. Emphasize that sometimes we have calm thoughts that make us feel good and do helpful things. At other times, we have worried thoughts that make us feel bad and do unhelpful things.

Read Sam's and Tim's stories and ask your child to identify whose thoughts were helpful and why.

Sam's Story

Sam is at the movie theater with his family. Just before the movie starts, he sees a friend from his class on the other side of the room. Sam waves and calls out to the friend. The friend does not respond. Sam thinks to himself, "He must not have heard me. I'll go over to where he's sitting after the movie has finished and say hello."

Sam feels fine. He sits excitedly in his seat and enjoys the movie. When it has finished, he goes over to the other side of the theater where his friend is sitting and says hello. His friend is pleased to see Sam, and they make plans to meet up the next day to play.

Were Sam's thoughts helpful? _____

Why? _____

_____

How did Sam feel after this event? _____

_____

What does Sam do? (What is his behavior?) _____

_____

Is it a good outcome? _____

Tim's Story

Tim is at the movie theater with his family. Just before the movie starts, he sees a friend from his class on the other side of the room. Tim waves and calls out to the friend. The friend does not respond. Tim thinks to himself, "Oh, he ignored me. He must hate me. Everyone saw that he ignored me. I can't believe what a loser I am."

Tim feels embarrassed and miserable. He doesn't enjoy the movie at all because he's too busy worrying about what happened with his friend. When he sees his friend at school on Monday, Tim avoids him.

Were Tim's thoughts helpful? _____

Why? _____

_____

How did Tim feel after this event? _____

_____

What does Tim do? (What is his behavior?) _____

_____

Is it a good outcome? _____

CHILDREN'S ACTIVITY 10: Self-Talk

This activity is designed to help your child better understand the idea that a person can think in different ways in the same situation and that these different thoughts will lead to different feelings and behaviors. Find photos or cartoons of a child in situations such as approaching a big dog, meeting a new child, giving a speech, and waiting for someone to come home. (Suitable cartoons are included in the Activity Book at http://www.newharbinger.com/49913.) Using the pictures, have your child write two different thoughts that the child in the picture could be having. Encourage your child to identify a calm thought and a worried one.

Then, using a table with the column headings "Situation," "Thoughts," "Feelings," and "Actions," have your child fill in the spaces for a calm response and a worried response for situations such as these: "I haven't done my homework," "I want to invite a new friend to my house," "My team has a semifinal tomorrow," and "Summer camp starts on Monday." With each one, point out the way in which it is the thought that changes how you feel and what you decide to do.

CHILDREN'S ACTIVITY 11: Detective Thinking

For this activity, you will need to create your own blank Detective Thinking Worksheets based on the earlier examples. You can copy the sample forms that we showed earlier in this chapter, or you can use the version provided in the Activity Book, which is available at http://www.newharbinger.com/49913. You will need a lot of blank worksheets for this task and for the coming weeks of practice.

Keeping in mind the information you read earlier about teaching detective thinking to your child, explain first that children who worry a lot tend to think that bad things happen a lot or that if a bad thing does happen, it will be a catastrophe, and second, that one way to feel less worried is to work out if the worried thought is realistic. Explain that you can do this by looking for "clues" about whether a worried thought is true or not.

Go through the steps to detective thinking:

- Write down the event, thought, and how strong the feeling is on the worry scale.

- Ask yourself questions (such as "What are the facts?" and "What is likely to happen or has happened before or to other people?") to help find the evidence.

- List all the things that could happen in the situation.

- Use the clues to come up with a calm thought, and rate how worried you would be if you had this thought instead.

Read through one or two of the examples given earlier in the chapter to show your child how detective thinking works.

Teaching your child to use detective thinking is best demonstrated by completing examples. Help them to find evidence and calm thoughts for two simple examples, such as a situation like "There's a big dog coming toward me" and the subsequent thought, "The dog's going to bite me, and I won't be able to stop him" or the situation "There's a strange noise outside" and the thought "A robber is trying to break in."

CHILDREN'S ACTIVITY 12: Applying Detective Thinking to Big Worries

This activity should be done *after* your child has had at least one week of consistent practice of doing detective thinking on their smaller worries. Once your child starts to understand the process, have them complete Detective Thinking Worksheets for bigger worries, trying to cover at least two situations. Remember to use the questions listed earlier to help your child gather the best evidence for each situation. If your child is having trouble, let them "coach" you on one of your own worries. Get your child to ask you the questions and help you come up with evidence for the worry, and then help you come up with a calm thought. It is often easier to practice when the situation is not personal.

In particular, encourage your child to come up with a lot of evidence for these big worries. The more evidence your child finds, the more likely it is that they will find a calm thought to believe. (This activity is also available in the Activity Book at http://www.newharbinger.com/49913.)

CHILDREN'S PRACTICE TASK 2: Detective Thinking

Detective thinking is not an easy skill to learn. The key is practice. Detective thinking will continue for the rest of the program. Children should fill in a Detective Thinking Worksheet every time they feel at all nervous, shy, worried, or frightened. The more that children practice, the better they will get at it, and the more likely they will be to use detective thinking when they're actually feeling anxious. To begin, you'll probably need to be quite involved and help your child considerably. As they get better, you should help less and less. Older children might pick up the skills in a few days while younger children may need help for many weeks. But remember, this isn't a race—each child needs to take whatever time is needed to master the skill. (Visit http://www.newharbinger.com/49913 to download this practice task.)

Each afternoon or evening you should sit down with your child and think through the day and go over detective thinking for any bad experiences or remembered worries. Even doing them after the fact is good practice. Obviously, the key is for your child to be able to use detective thinking when in a frightening situation. Therefore, whenever you notice your child getting nervous, try to prompt them to use this skill. Early on in the process, you will need to prompt in detail, helping your child with the exact steps and questions; obviously this means that you will need to commit this process and the evidence-gathering questions to memory. As your child gets better at the skill, prompts may simply take the form of reminders, such as "What would a detective think in this situation?"

CHAPTER HIGHLIGHTS

In this chapter, you and your child learned that...

→ in any situation, it is possible to have more than one thought about what is happening.

→ thoughts can lead to different feelings, such as feeling calm or worried in response to the same event.

→ worried thoughts are often faulty, but by being a detective, a person can find evidence to help discover a more accurate thought.

→ the process of detective thinking, involves the following actions:

   → identifying the worried thoughts in your head

   → using questions to help find evidence that suggests that the worried thought is not true

   → using the evidence to create a calm thought

→ a calm thought can help you to feel less worried.

Your child will need to do the following:

* Complete the children's activities with the help of a parent or other adult.

* Practice detective thinking as often as possible. The more your child can do it, the better they will get at it—but it needs to be done at least once per day. Detective thinking and filling out Detective Thinking Worksheets will need to continue for at least the next two to three weeks, but probably quite a bit longer.

CHAPTER 4

Parenting an Anxious Child

There are many different ways of handling a child's anxiety. Some of the more common strategies include reassuring a child (e.g., repeatedly telling the child that "everything will be all right"), telling a child exactly how to handle the situation, empathizing with a child's anxiety by discussing in detail what makes you anxious and afraid, being tough with a child and not letting them avoid the situation, removing a child from the feared situation, allowing a child to avoid the situation, prompting a child to independently decide how to cope constructively with their anxiety, ignoring a child's anxiety, and becoming impatient with a child. You probably find that you use several of these strategies at different times with differing rates of success. As a general rule, some of these strategies are effective in managing child anxiety and some of them are not. Each strategy will be reviewed in more detail.

PARENT ACTIVITY: What Are My Current Strategies?

Listed below are some of the common ways that parents react to their child's anxiety. Thinking about your own parenting strategies, comment on how useful or successful each is with your child. You can add your own strategies to this list as well. (Visit http://www.newharbinger.com/49913 to download this worksheet.)

Strategy	Successful or useful?
Providing reassurance	
Telling child what to do	
Empathizing	
Being tough	
Allowing avoidance	
Prompting independence	
Ignoring	
Becoming impatient	

In case you're beginning to wonder whether the way in which you parent your child is going to be called into question, rest assured—it's not! The above list has been generated with the help of other parents who have been involved with this program in the past. It's not meant to gauge how "good" a parent you are. Rather, it is intended to show that lots of other parents face similar difficulties and often respond to them in similar ways.

Being the parent of an anxious child can be really tough, and no doubt there are times when you feel that you just don't know what to do or say in response to your child's anxiety. There are probably many times when you feel that nothing that you do or say seems to work. When a person is really caught up in a situation or problem, it's very difficult for that person to view the situation objectively.

There is no right or wrong way of handling a child's anxiety, and each child and each family is different. However, there are some things that parents can do to reduce the anxiety that their child will experience in the long run. On the other hand, sometimes parents and children slip into a pattern that isn't very helpful for addressing a child's anxiety. Hopefully, this chapter will help you gain some objectivity in thinking about the strategies that you currently use to handle your child's anxiety. By carefully considering the advantages and disadvantages associated with each strategy, you will be able to make informed decisions regarding whether or not a certain strategy is likely to be effective in the long term with your child.

Unhelpful Ways of Dealing with Anxiety in Children

While it is true that there are no wrong ways to handle a child, sometimes parents might react to their child's anxiety in ways that help to keep the anxiety going or even to increase it in the longer term.

Excessively Reassuring Your Child

Based on parents' reports, this strategy appears to be very commonly used with anxious children. Examples of ways in which parents attempt to reassure their children include physical affection or closeness or telling the child that "everything will be all right" and that "there is nothing to be afraid of." Within reason, these are all great strategies, and if they feel right for you, you should continue to use them to some degree. It is only when you find yourself constantly having to reassure your child that alarm bells might start ringing. Loving your children and giving them comfort, security, and reassurance when they are hurt is an important part of parenting. We would never say that you should not reassure your child. In fact, too little reassurance can be as bad as too much. Children who never get reassurance or comfort from their parents are likely to feel insecure and alone. But because of their personalities, anxious children often feel they are not able to rely on themselves and will ask for reassurance far more than other children. That's when you can start to get into a vicious circle.

Reassurance is a natural parental response to a child's distress. Unfortunately, to an anxious child, reassurance is like water off a duck's back: it has very little effect. More importantly, even if reassurance might help to relieve your child's anxiety a little in the short run, in the long run, the more reassurance you give as a parent, the more reassurance your child will demand.

What is really important is to think about *when* you give your child lots of attention and praise. Obviously, when a child is really hurt or has gotten a fright from a potentially serious situation, then you cannot give too much love and attention. Let's say your child was crossing the road and a car screeched to a stop only inches from your child's terrified face. There is no way that you could give too many hugs and kisses in a situation like this. But when your child's fear is excessive, then your hugs and kisses simply give your child the message that there really is something awful to worry about. Let's say your child starts to cry when you want to go out for the evening and a sitter arrives. Leaping in and showering your child with hugs and kisses only gives the message that "this really is an awful situation."

Reassurance is a form of positive attention for your child. This means that every time your child gets anxious and you reassure them, you are actually rewarding your child's anxiety. In some cases, this might make the anxiety seem almost worthwhile for the child. At the very least, it can help to teach children that they cannot cope by themselves and that they need you to handle difficult situations. For this reason, you may find that for your anxious child, you will actually need to hold off your reassurance even more than you would for a nonanxious child simply so that your anxious child is encouraged to learn that they can do things for themself.

WHAT CAN YOU DO INSTEAD?

So what do you do when your child does seek help or reassurance? The best strategy is to help teach children how they can come up with answers themselves rather than always expecting you to do it for them. There are two common ways of doing this. One way—prompting your child to cope constructively—is described in detail later in this chapter (see "Helpful Ways of Dealing with Anxiety in Children"). Another alternative is to prompt your child to use detective thinking. In other words, rather than simply giving your child reassurance (e.g., "Don't worry; it will be all right"), it would be much better to get your child to apply their own detective thinking to the worry.

When you are dealing with a child who has become used to asking for reassurance a great deal, you may need to gradually give less and less help over time. For example, if you decide to encourage your child to use their own detective thinking rather than coming to you for reassurance, you may need to spend a little time with your child going through detective thinking the first few times. After a short while, you can expect your child to do more and more of the detective thinking independently. Eventually, if your child comes to you seeking reassurance, you should be able to ask your child what their detective would say, ask them one of the evidence-finding questions to help them to consider other possibilities, or simply to tell them to do their own detective thinking about the problem.

If you are going to make a change from always helping your child as much as they want, to withdrawing a little, it is very important that you let your child know. Actually, this applies to any of the unhelpful ways of dealing with children's anxiety discussed here. A sudden change without explanation might leave your child feeling hurt, unloved, and afraid. No matter how young your child is, you should explain clearly what the changes are going to be and why you are making them. It's also a very good idea to introduce rewards (and of course lots of praise) when your child successfully solves a problem by themself. Finally, it is absolutely essential that you and other adults in your child's life are consistent. No matter how hard it is, it is important not to give in to your child's requests for reassurance (within reason). Don't enter into extended arguments with children. Rather, inform them clearly and calmly that you are confident that they know the answer and you are not going to discuss it anymore. Then ignore any further requests for reassurance. Don't forget to reward and praise your child for successful self-reliance (i.e., for not seeking reassurance). This relates to another strategy you can try as an alternative to excessive reassurance: being actively on the lookout for and rewarding brave, nonanxious behaviors.

As you will see in the following example, for Kurt and his mother, this process does require that parents keep to their decision despite their child asking the questions. Children learn that persistence often pays off, so as a parent, you will need to outlast their persistence and stick to your plans.

Kurt's Example

Whenever they're going on a family outing, Kurt bugs his parents with repeated questions about what will happen, who will be there, what they should take, what he should wear, and so on. In the past, Kurt's parents have tried everything to get him to relax and ask fewer questions. Usually, however, they end up answering his questions for a while, eventually losing patience and yelling at him. Finally, Kurt's parents decided that it was time to tackle this problem in a different way.

To begin, Kurt's mother sat down with him at a calm time to discuss the issue. She told him that she loved his usual questions and his curiosity but that when he was worried about things, he would often begin to ask too many nagging questions. She explained that she knew he was very smart and that he was now old enough to answer many of his own questions. She said that the next time he began to worry and ask too many questions, she would help him to do his detective thinking to try to come up with his own answers. After that, Kurt's mother explained that she and his father would ignore any further "worry questions." They would be very pleased with him if he could do his own detective thinking and not ask them any worry questions.

A week later, Kurt's family was invited to a friend's house for lunch. As the time approached, Kurt began with some questions. He was particularly worried about whether he would know anyone and about the possibility that the other kids might not like him. As soon as he began to ask questions, his mother sat down with him and went through his detective thinking with him. She encouraged him to think about how many times he had previously been to visit family friends and had known people, whether other kids usually found him likeable, what he was likely to think (based on previous experience) of the other children there, and so on. After Kurt had been through the evidence, his mother praised him and went about her work. The next time that Kurt asked a question about the visit, she said to him, "You know that we have already talked about this and done the detective thinking. You know that you have the answers and that you don't need me to tell you. If you ask again, I am not going to answer you, but I am very happy to talk about anything else you would like to discuss." When Kurt asked again, his mother simply ignored the question. When he did not ask any questions for ten minutes, she said, "Kurt, do you realize that you haven't asked me anything about our outing today for the last ten minutes? I'm really

*proud of how brave you are being. Keep up the good work." Kurt asked
no more questions about the visit that day. After the visit, Kurt's parents
let him stay up a little later to watch a movie he had been excited about.*

Being Too Involved and Directive

When a child is extremely anxious, some parents will try to take over
and direct their child. In other words, they will tell the child exactly what to
do, how to behave, and what to say in the anxiety-provoking situation, or
they will do things on behalf of their child.

Ethan's Example

*Take Ethan's parents, for instance. Ethan becomes very anxious when in
social situations with other children. On one particular occasion, Ethan
and his father went to the birthday party of a younger cousin. Ethan
spent most of the time sitting beside his father and not mixing with the
other children. At one point, a clown arrived and began handing out
candy. Ethan's father could see that Ethan would have loved to have
some candy but that he was not going to step forward and ask for any
because he was too shy. So his father leaped up and went to the clown to
get some candy for Ethan. Ethan blushed from ear to ear but was very
pleased with the candy.*

The manner in which parents sometimes take over for their anxious
children is an excellent example of what we call a *vicious circle*. Usually,
parents only adopt this strategy after the repeated experience of watching
their child feel helpless with anxiety. Most parents don't tell their kids what
to do in anxiety-provoking situations out of natural bossiness. Rather,
parents behave in this way because they feel so much for their child when
they see the child become gripped by fear. In the short term, this strategy of
stepping in helps to reduce the children's fear and gets them what they want.
However, if you think about it, this reliance on parental direction is actually

a form of avoidance. In the above example, Ethan has learned that he is unable to handle the feared situation himself and that he can only do it with his father's help. In the long term, this helps to further reduce his self-confidence and to keep his anxiety going.

Even though it can be very painful, it is vitally important that you do not do too much for your child. The bottom line is that children often learn best by being allowed to make their own mistakes. Also, children can only learn that situations are not dangerous, and that they can cope, if they are encouraged to experience the situation. We will discuss this principle in much more detail in the coming chapters. For now, it's important for you simply to think about whether you sometimes become too involved with your child's activities or take things over for them.

So, how much involvement is "too much"? Unfortunately, there's no simple answer to this question. There is no way to quantify how involved to be, and, of course, every parent and child and situation will be different. What you need to ask yourself is whether you think that you help your child more than other parents do and whether your child relies on themself less than other children their age. You may need to think about concrete examples of times when your child has appeared helpless and you felt you had to step in. Talk to other parents and ask what they or their child would do in such situations. And above all, ask yourself, "Did I *really need* to step in? What would have been the worst thing to happen, if I hadn't?" As we said earlier, with an anxious child, it's possible that you might need to help even less often than you would with a less-anxious child.

WHAT CAN YOU DO INSTEAD?

So, when you feel tempted to become involved and tell your child exactly what to do in a situation where they are anxious, what else could you do? To start with, remember that if you plan on changing the way in which you respond to your child's anxiety, it is important to have a conversation with them about this during a time when things are calm (i.e., not when they are extremely anxious). Explain what is going to change and why. Make sure you communicate your confidence in your child's ability to learn how to solve their own problems. Just as with excessive reassurance, the best strategy is to help children learn how to solve their own problems rather than doing this for them. This brings us to one of the helpful strategies for responding to a child's anxiety: prompting your child to cope constructively. This involves making use of a step-by-step problem-solving approach that is introduced at the end of this chapter. Helping your child to follow this approach—thus increasing their capacity to cope with anxiety-provoking situations—is an excellent alternative to being too involved and directive. Of course, you can also prompt your child to use strategies such as detective thinking and facing up to feared situations (discussed in the next chapter) as well. While at first you will most likely be quite involved in helping your child to work through the problem-solving steps, it is important to gradually reduce your role in supporting your child to engage in constructive coping. Eventually, you want to get to a point where you just need to remind them of the problem-solving approach and they are able to work through this process themselves.

Permitting Avoidance

Anxious children try to avoid lots of activities. As a parent, it is hard to continually push your child to face fears, so sometimes you might give in and let your child avoid them. If this happens occasionally, it's understandable. Obviously, in the short run, your child's anxiety and distress will drop, and you will also make yourself very popular by allowing your child to get out of doing things that they do not want to do. However, if it becomes a common habit, the long-term consequences of permitting avoidance in your child are very serious. As long as children continue to avoid, they will not overcome their anxiety.

Hayley's Example

Hayley's worries get much worse whenever there is a new or rare activity that she is meant to participate in. Hayley's parents know that events like the school athletics day or family outings with friends will cause several sleepless nights and a lot of tears. It has been this way for a very long time. When there is no other choice, Hayley is made to go to these events, but her parents often let her stay home or they decline the invitations themselves whenever possible as it is all too hard. Hayley has not gone to athletics days for the last two years, and last Christmas, Hayley, her siblings, and parents did not attend the family Christmas party because it was being held at her aunt's place rather than her grandparents' house where it had been in previous years. Sometimes Hayley's parents try to get around this problem by not telling her about events until they are in the car and on their way; for example, they might use this strategy when visiting the dentist. This often backfires; Hayley becomes panicky, and they have to turn back anyway.

Hayley knows she does not have to do activities that worry her a lot and will now just say to her parents, "I just don't think I can do that." Consequently, she is missing out on many enjoyable activities, as well as ones that are necessary for her education and health.

WHAT CAN YOU DO INSTEAD?

So, when your child is highly anxious and distressed, desperate to avoid a certain situation, and your instinctive response is to allow them to do this, what can you do instead? We will be focusing on the alternative to permitting avoidance in the next chapter. For now, it is enough to know that it involves gradually facing up to feared situations. At this stage, it's important that you don't push your anxious child too hard to face up to all of their feared and avoided situations, but you will need to gradually encourage them to face their fears. We know that this is often not easy and anxious children are masters of controlling a situation so that they can avoid their fears. If you are feeling guilty or distressed, reminding yourself that you are doing this for the benefit of your child in the long run (like urging them to take a bitter medicine or have a painful vaccine), can sometimes help. In the next chapter, you will find very specific advice about how to help your child face their fears in ways that are most likely to lead to successful outcomes.

Becoming Impatient with Your Child

Unfortunately, as many parents tell us, it's all too easy to become impatient and frustrated with an anxious child. Nothing you do or say seems to help. At times, it can feel as though children are deliberately clinging to their anxiety. Often it feels like "they could do it if only they would try harder." While it's understandable that you might sometimes lose your patience, obviously becoming angry with your child will only serve to make them more frightened and dependent.

Lashi's Example

Lashi's dad came to pick her up on Friday afternoon for an overnight visit. Lashi's mom had plans to go out with her best friend to a movie while Lashi was away; she hadn't been to a movie in eighteen months and was really looking forward to it. Lashi had been worried about visiting her dad all week. She thought that her mom would have a terrible accident while she was not there and that her mom would die because no one would be able to call for help. She had discussed this with her mom at length, and they had made an agreement that after the movie, Lashi's mom would call her to say good-night.

Before school on Friday, Lashi dragged her feet a lot and would not help to get her bag ready to take for the night. Her mom didn't want to rock the boat, so, although she yelled several times in frustration, she sent Lashi to school and got the bag ready herself. When the afternoon came and Lashi's dad arrived, Lashi became distraught. She clung to her mother and was shouting and screaming in the front yard. Lashi's mom lost her temper, smacked Lashi twice, and put her into the car so her dad could quickly drive off.

Lashi's mom felt awful. She knew Lashi was scared, but she had just had enough. She didn't end up enjoying the movie, and when she called Lashi afterward, even though she had settled pretty well, Lashi's mom offered to pick her up and bring her home. Lashi jumped at the chance and came home, and her mom then spent extra time with her to make up for losing her temper.

WHAT CAN YOU DO INSTEAD?

So, when your child's anxiety makes no sense to you and/or you feel like you've had enough of trying to deal with it, what are your alternatives? As we can see from Lashi's example, although entirely understandable, when parents become impatient and angry with their child's anxiety, the consequences tend to be unhelpful all around. In that example, Lashi's mom felt terrible about the way she had reacted and those feelings spoiled her enjoyment of the outing that had caused Lashi's anxiety in the first place.

If you feel yourself losing patience with your child, it is helpful to ask another person (such as your partner) to help, or to leave the situation for a short while to gather your thoughts. It can sometimes be useful to try to remind yourself what you are asking your child to do. Imagine having to confront something really terrifying (like walking into a biker's party and asking them to turn the music down) and you might be able to understand the difficulty that your child has to face.

Returning to the example, instead of expressing her impatience in the ways that she did (becoming angry and smacking Lashi), the mom could have tried asking Lashi's dad if he could help Lashi to move to the car. She could then have said good-bye to Lashi in her usual way and walked away from a situation in which her own emotions were beginning to feel out of control. She may have then been able to remind herself of how scared Lashi was that something terrible would happen to her mom.

PARENT ACTIVITY: Analyzing Unhelpful Strategies

To help become aware of the "traps" that you are currently falling into, complete the following table. (Visit http://www.newharbinger.com/49913 to download this worksheet.) Think about the times that you use some or perhaps all of these strategies. Record which of your child's worries typically prompts you to use the strategy and what the problem is with that—that is, what is your child learning when you use that strategy?

Strategy	What worry prompts this strategy?	What is your child learning?
Excessive reassurance		
Being too directive		
Permitting or encouraging avoidance		
Becoming impatient		

Helpful Ways of Dealing with Anxiety in Children

While there is no single way to handle a child's fears, and everyone will have their own ways of doing things, there are ways that parents can act that will help their child to learn that "nothing bad will happen" and "I can handle it."

Rewarding Brave, Nonanxious Behavior

All children, no matter how anxious, will at certain times do things that are frightening for them. As a parent, you should look out for any examples of this type of bravery, no matter how small, and reward your child for them. This will make it more likely that the bravery will happen again. Think of it as fanning the small embers of a fire to get it to grow. At first, you need to look for any example of bravery and make a big fuss over it. Later, as your child becomes less anxious, you can reward only the more obvious examples. Make sure you don't set your expectations too high. Remember, what may seem like a small thing to you may be extremely difficult for a nervous child. You will need to make sure you look for behaviors that are brave based on your child's personality, not on anyone else's standards. By pointing to and focusing on successes, you will help your child to build self-confidence as well as help your child realize what they are capable of.

In addition to looking for naturally occurring bravery, at times you may want to encourage your child to do things that are a little challenging. Again, this needs to be rewarded. We will discuss this strategy in more detail in the next chapter.

Rewards can fall into two broad types—material and nonmaterial. Material rewards are the ones most of us think of immediately. These might include money, food, stickers, or toys. The child is given the reward, say, a small toy, after the brave action is noticed. Nonmaterial rewards include praise, attention, and interest from the parent. Parental attention is an extremely powerful reward. Most children, especially younger ones, will do almost anything for the approval and praise of their parents. Spending extra time with children (e.g., playing a game or going for a bike ride) is a great way to reward them for brave, nonanxious behavior. Whenever possible, we suggest you use nonmaterial rewards because they have the added benefit of giving your child a sense of security and self-esteem.

It is also important to keep your rewards varied. If your child keeps getting the same reward over and over, that reward will very quickly lose its impact. There are several points to remember when using rewards:

- To be effective, rewards must be meaningful to the child. There is no point in rewarding a child with something they don't like. The easiest way to make sure that the child will work for a reward is to discuss it. Find out what they want most at this moment.

- Discuss clearly with your child exactly what they need to do to get rewards. There is no point showering rewards on children if they think the rewards came for no reason. It is important that the child knows exactly why they are getting the reward and how it could be gotten again. Praise should be clear and specific. You want your child to know exactly what they have just done that you liked and want them to repeat in the future. For example, saying, "David, you were able to go by yourself with Mrs. Jones into class this morning instead of needing me to come in with you. I was really proud of you" is much more useful than saying, "You were a good boy today, David."

- The rewards must be in keeping with the activity, and you need to make sure that you give the child a reward that is the right size for the difficulty of the activity. For example, if your child is terrified of dogs and has just spent the last half hour with the neighbor's dog, which they have never approached before, it is not fair to give only a small token or two minutes of your time. On the other hand, if your child has done something that was only slightly difficult, you are leaving yourself with nowhere to go if you reward them with a new television.

- Most importantly, rewards must be given as soon as possible after the brave action has occurred and they must be delivered if promised. Consistency is essential for effective parenting. Children will learn very quickly to stop trusting a parent's word if they find that promises are not delivered. *If you promise your child a reward, it must be delivered.* Similarly, rewards lose their effectiveness the greater the time between the event and the reward. If your child does something brave on Monday and you give a small reward the following Saturday, the whole impact will have been lost. For maximum impact, the reward should be delivered immediately. That is why your own time and attention can be so much better than buying a gift. Of course, there will be times when delivering an immediate reward is just not practical. For example, you may decide to reward your child by going skiing together. Obviously, this can't be done immediately and may need to wait until the weekend. In this case, it is useful to give some sort of interim reward. For example, you may make up a small voucher that clearly says the reason for earning the voucher on it, and your child can exchange it during the weekend for the ski trip. At the very least, if the reward is delayed, you need to make an immediate fuss and give attention to the brave act and make it very clear that the later reward and the brave act are connected.

- If you have other children, you may find that they become resentful of the extra attention and rewards that your anxious child is getting. One way around this might be to introduce a reward system for all children in the family. You can introduce a chart where each child can earn rewards, although the rewards might be earned by different behaviors for each child. In this way, you can build bravery in all your children if needed, or you could use the rewards for your other children to increase helpful habits such as obedience, brushing teeth, tidying their rooms, and so on. If they are older (mature) siblings, explain to them that their little brother or sister is doing some extra hard work to overcome their fears and that this is something that they would not normally be expected to do, so it deserves extra rewards. If they want to earn rewards too, they have to work on something equally as difficult or unusual (like doing an extra half-hour of music practice each day or learning how to touch-type).

TEACHING YOUR CHILD ABOUT REWARDS

In the same way that we emphasize rewards as an important part of parenting management, we believe it is also important for children to learn what rewards are. Although most children have no trouble telling you what things they would like to receive as rewards, they generally only think of rewards as big and small material items, not as the wide range of items that are actually possible. There are two purposes here: first, to get an idea of what rewards your child would like to earn throughout the program (remember rewards must be meaningful to your child, not you) and second, to get your child to begin to reward themself for the efforts made. In this chapter's activities, your child will be learning to identify rewards.

Ignoring Behaviors That You Don't Want

This is really the flip side of the previous strategy. It involves removing your attention from your child's anxious behavior and attending again (and praising) when the anxious behavior has stopped. The idea is that when you notice a behavior that you are not happy with (e.g., your child repeatedly complaining about feeling sick before school), you need to stop any interaction with your child as long as they are doing that behavior (complaining). Of course, it is essential that your child understand exactly why you are ignoring them and exactly what they need to do in order to regain your attention. Using this strategy should be immediately followed by specific praise for something good that the child is doing (e.g., complaining stops for one minute). Ignoring is a particularly useful strategy for dealing with reassurance seeking (as we discussed above in the section "Excessively Reassuring Your Child"). This strategy must always be used carefully and only in relation to a specific behavior. It's important that your child understands that it is the particular behavior in which they are engaging that is unacceptable to you and not their general character. In addition, as we discussed earlier, it is important to remove your attention from your child's reassurance seeking in a gradual and systematic way and to encourage children to use a strategy where they can do it themselves (such as their detective thinking).

Kurt's Example

All the way to school each day, Kurt used to ask his dad whether he had fed the dog, put her outside, and filled up her water bowl, even though he had never forgotten to do these things before. His dad made an agreement with Kurt that he would no longer answer these questions but would instead start singing along with the radio. He reminded Kurt that he himself was perfectly capable of remembering whether those things had been done and also reminded Kurt of the evidence that he had never forgotten these things before. The next day when Kurt asked the questions, his dad said, "I don't answer those questions anymore—try and think of the evidence yourself"; he then turned on the radio and started singing. Kurt looked annoyed, even got mad one morning, but after a week, he no longer asked the questions and soon stopped worrying about these things.

Prompting Your Child to Cope Constructively

When you talk with your child about the things that make them anxious, it's important that you express your empathy and understanding in a calm and relaxed manner. Children need to feel listened to, understood, and supported, but it is equally important that they are encouraged to constructively solve the problem of their anxiety rather than focusing on how bad they feel. A stepped problem-solving approach will be introduced later in the chapter as a way of handling anxious moments.

Parents who use this strategy typically prompt their children to think for themselves about how to constructively handle an anxiety-provoking situation. This is quite different from parents who tell their children exactly what to do in the anxiety-provoking situation.

Ethan's Example

Ethan is highly anxious about a debate that he has to take part in at school. He is very upset and imagines the worst possible outcome. Ethan is sure that he will make a mess of his speech and look like a complete idiot. He complains that he has a headache and that his stomach hurts.

Ethan's mom comes and sits down with him. She says to him, "Ethan, I can understand that you feel worried about the debate. But the fact is that you have to do it for class, and at the moment, you're just not helping yourself. You're saying a lot of negative things about how things are going to go, and that must be making you feel worse. Plus, you're talking yourself into feeling sick. What you're doing right now isn't making you feel any better, is it?" Ethan agrees with his mother. She then goes on, "Okay, so what can you do that might help? What can you do that would make you feel better?" Ethan answers this by saying that staying away from school on the day of his team's debate would help him feel better. His mom points out that Ethan's teacher would probably just postpone his team's debate until he came back to school, and she also says that Ethan will have to do more public speaking tasks now that he is in high school; if he puts it off now, the next time will be even harder. Ethan can see the logic of this, especially the first point. He suggests that maybe if he practiced the speech with his mom, he might feel better about it. She praises him for coming up with a constructive way of dealing with his anxiety and agrees to practice with him.

In this example, Ethan's mom is prompting Ethan to come up with his own solutions. She is not encouraging him to rely on her because she is not directly intervening. Instead, she is encouraging him to take responsibility for managing his own anxiety in a constructive manner. At the same time, she is firmly not allowing him to avoid the debate.

Encouraging your child to use the detective approach to evaluate the probability of their negative, worrying thoughts being true is an important component of this strategy. Prompting your child to independently decide how to cope constructively with anxiety is a good long-term strategy, because it involves showing faith in your child's abilities. You would be surprised at how often children are able to rise to meet their parents' expectations. If you believe that your child possesses the ability to overcome challenges and to solve problems, they are more likely to believe this too.

Modeling Brave, Nonanxious Behavior

Children learn how to behave by observing others, and most significantly, their parents, especially when children are younger. Thus, as a parent, everything that you do or say has added significance because you are serving as a model for your child. And who do you think your child is likely to most closely relate to with respect to their anxiety—the calm, relaxed one in the family or the slightly nervous, worried one? Naturally, when it comes to their fears and worries, anxious children will most strongly relate to a parent who, like them, might also seem to have a few fears of their own. So, if one or both parents can think of a few of their own fears and worries, then parents have the power to really help their child cope with anxiety.

The very best type of model is a *coping model*—that is, a model that can show that they experience fears and worries and then shows how to cope constructively with these difficulties. This type of model is much more effective than one who never seems to have any difficulties. So, if you fit the bill, it is really important that you don't try and hide your fears from your child or pretend that you never get scared. All this does is show your child that it is embarrassing or "weird" to be scared. Instead, you need to see managing your fears and worries as a shared activity—something you and your child can work on together.

Once you start talking openly with your child about your own fears, you can begin to use yourself as a model or practice example for your child. For example, you can ask your child to help you with your detective thinking. Children will love this, and it will help them to really understand how they can think more accurately. Later, when we start to work on building stepladders (see chapter 5), you and your child can each have your own stepladders and can use this to make anxiety management more fun. For example, your child can help you work on your stepladder and approach your fears, which will help them understand more about overcoming fears. Or you could set up a challenge where you see who can work their way up a stepladder first.

Of course, for some parents of anxious children, the parent's own anxiety can actually be a serious problem. If you believe that you have a problem with anxiety and are having trouble handling it yourself, it is important for you to see a mental health professional so that you can begin to model more effective coping for your child.

Talia's Example

Talia was beginning to prepare to face her fear of water. One day when her grandma was over, Talia found out that her grandma was also scared of water and that she had never learned to swim. They talked for a while about the things that her grandma had missed out on because she didn't know how to swim. Together they decided they could both face their fear of water and learn how to swim. They booked swimming lessons for each other and made a pact to have learned to swim one swimming pool length by the summer holidays when they would go swimming together. Even though Talia didn't live near her grandma, they kept each other up to date on their progress by phone. Talia felt confident that if her grandma could do it, so could she.

PARENT ACTIVITY: Analyzing Helpful Strategies

In this activity, you need to think through how you might apply the helpful strategies. Keep in mind both your child's most common worries and how you might overcome the unhelpful strategies that you analyzed in the last activity. (Visit http://www.newharbinger.com/49913 to download this worksheet.)

Strategy	What worries or anxious behaviors could I use this strategy on?	How might I do this? What would I say or do differently?
Rewarding brave, nonanxious behavior		
Ignoring behavior I don't want		
Prompting constructive coping		
Modeling brave, nonanxious behavior		

Important Principles to Remember When Dealing with Children

There are a number of common difficulties for parents in successfully managing their child's behavior. Although some of these principles may seem obvious, they are easy to forget.

Being Consistent

It is important that you try to reward (or punish) your child consistently. Children need to learn that certain behaviors lead to desirable consequences and that others lead to undesirable consequences. In this way, you can encourage your child to behave appropriately. You need to discuss this with your partner and decide on a joint strategy. Similarly, your parenting will work best if everyone who is involved with raising that child is also on board, including stepparents, grandparents, and so on. Naturally, this will not always be possible, and this is when things might start to get difficult. But the more you can have consistent rules and consequences for your child, the better your child will be at learning to manage their behavior.

Keeping Your Emotions in Check

At times, all children can be very frustrating and worrying! This is especially true for anxious children. What could be more frustrating than running late to get out the door when your child is refusing to get dressed because they are scared to go into the other room alone? As understandable as it is to get mad, you need to remember that you become far less effective as a coach when you are very emotional (e.g., angry or anxious) because at such times it is harder to be consistent. Plan ahead for ways in which you can give yourself a "time-out" from interactions with your child when those interactions provoke strong emotional responses in you. When you take time away, tell your child what you are doing and let them know that you will come back a little later. Similarly, when you work on your child's anxiety program, it is important to do so at a preplanned time when you are both calm and relaxed. You should not try to teach your child new lessons on the run when they are crying with fear at going out the door. Finally, when you do find yourself escalating, try to get away and gather your thoughts. Get a partner, friend, or older sibling to stay with your child and try to explain that you need to get away to calm down. Then go into another room and get your thoughts together. You'll be able to deal with your child's anxiety far more effectively when you keep your cool.

Distinguishing Between Anxious and Naughty Behavior

One of the most common difficulties parents have is drawing a line between a child's anxious behaviors and times when a child is just being naughty. Parents also often get a mixture of advice from well-meaning others who believe that all of the child's behaviors are pure naughtiness and should therefore be punished. Unfortunately, the two behaviors can look very similar, but the anxious ones don't deserve to be punished, making it difficult for parents to know what to do. Another difficulty can be that some anxious children would much rather get in trouble than face a feared situation (the type of trouble a child will get in is usually pretty predictable and therefore quite safe from the child's point of view), so they will deliberately mess up to get out of it.

There are three principles that can help you to distinguish between anxious behaviors and naughty behaviors:

- Even if a child is anxious at the time, any form of verbal or physical aggression is not acceptable. That means that swearing, calling people names, hitting, and throwing things should all lead to immediate consequences. In the real world, these behaviors are not excused just because someone feels bad; therefore, allowing children to act like this without consequences will in the long run disadvantage them. They need to learn to deal with their emotions appropriately, even when these feelings are really strong.

- You need to look at the situation in detail to see if there is a reason why your child might be avoiding a task. For example, if you have asked your child to go and brush their teeth and this hasn't happened, stand back and look at the situation. Suppose that you know that your child is scared of the dark, the bathroom is at the end of the hallway, and at the moment there are no lights on. In that case, it is quite possible that your child is avoiding the task rather than being disobedient. However, if there are no such limitations and your child is just glued to the television, then it is probably disobedience and turning off the television immediately for ten minutes would be an appropriate response.

- You can also look at how consistently your child seems to avoid a situation. For example, if your child says they are too scared to go into their room every time there is homework to do but seems quite happy to sit in there for hours at the computer, then you may assume that your child is exaggerating their fears.

Children who get out of activities by complaining that they are afraid, often do look quite happy when they succeed—that is, do not have to do the task. This can fool people into thinking that this is just manipulative behavior. However, it is important to look at what you know of your child's fears and worries to see if this behavior makes sense from that point of view. If you worried about that thing, would you be willing to do the task? If the answer is no, it points to an area where you need to apply anxiety management skills. If the task is not associated with a known fear, then it is probably safe to insist that your child complete the task without working on the anxiety.

Managing Naughty Behavior

Although this is not a course that will help you deal with deliberate naughtiness or disobedience, we encourage the use of nonphysical punishment when a child's behavior gets out of hand. Again, these punishments need to be used consistently and with emotions in check.

TIME-OUT

This is a very useful form of "punishment," especially for younger children. Before using time-out, the terms need to be carefully discussed—that is, why a time-out is necessary, what behavior will result in a time-out, where the time-out will be (choose a boring place like the bathroom or an entryway), how long your child must stay in time-out (generally five to ten minutes for primary school children), how they must behave while in time-out (the time doesn't start until your child is quiet), and what you want to see at the end of a time-out (completion of a task, an apology). You and your child should also agree on what will happen if they do not adhere to the time-out agreement (e.g., loss of a privilege until the time-out is completed).

As an example, it may be that you and your child agree to use a time-out when your child starts shouting. If they shout, the time-out is five minutes in the bathroom. The time does not start until your child is quiet. After five minutes of time-out, the child can come back to the conversation and explain (in a reasonable tone) what they are upset about. After using time-out, parents should find the next opportunity to praise their child for good behavior—in the example above, the parent would praise the child the next time that the child talks calmly.

Hayley's Example

Hayley has recently been aggressive when she becomes highly anxious. She will yell that she hates people and has hit both her mom, Maggie, and her dad, Dan, several times when they have tried to insist that she complete a task. Her parents are at a bit of a loss as to what to do with her when she is like this but have tended to try to comfort her and have never had her do the task that caused the problem. The last straw came when Hayley's little brother hit his mother and got upset when he was sent to his room because Hayley has never gotten in trouble for hitting. Maggie and Dan decided to make a house rule that any aggressive behaviors from any of the children would lead to an immediate time-out. They sat the children down and made up a list of aggressive behaviors, including hitting, throwing objects, and screaming at a person, that would no longer be allowed in the Jones household. They explained to the children that if they did these things, they would have to sit quietly in the bathroom for five minutes. The five-minute period wouldn't start until the child was quiet, and when time was up (which a parent would announce), the child would have to say what they would do differently next time.

The first time-out was used three days later when Hayley hit Dan when she didn't want to eat her vegetables. Dan immediately took Hayley to the bathroom and told her that she should sit quietly for five minutes. Hayley yelled and hit the door, and each time she came out, Dan or Maggie would take her straight back to the bathroom. It took twenty minutes before Hayley was quiet and Dan was able to start the five minutes. At the end of the time, Dan went and opened the door and asked Hayley what she would do differently next time. Hayley replied, "Not get mad" and she then went back to the table and started to eat her cold vegetables.

The next time Hayley was sent to time-out it only took her five minutes to sit quietly. Over several weeks, the number of times Hayley was sent to time-out dropped from five in the first week to once in a two-week period. Maggie and Dan finally felt like they could work on Hayley facing her fears without someone getting hurt.

Removal of Privileges

If further punishment is necessary beyond a time-out agreement, then removing a privilege is the next best thing. When a privilege is removed, it needs to have a meaningful and fairly immediate impact. For example, telling a child in October that there won't be any Christmas presents will not work nearly as well as telling the child that they cannot watch a favorite television program in half an hour. Privileges should never be removed for more than a few days as the impact will be lost, and it is likely that it will be too difficult for you to follow through and not give in. As with all our other strategies, communication is essential, and children need to know clearly why they lost the privilege and when they can get it back.

Natural Consequences

Sometimes the things that anxious children do to express their anxieties have a natural consequence. For example, a child who decides to back out of going to a party should be responsible for phoning and saying that they cannot attend. If there are natural consequences to an undesirable anxious behavior, then allow your child to experience that consequence; do not protect them from it. In Hayley's example above, having to eat her vegetables cold was a natural consequence of her behavior.

What to Do When Your Child Becomes Frightened

You may be wondering at this point, how do I stop my child from feeling anxious at those times when they suddenly become very scared and refuse to do something? The simple answer is you don't! It is not possible to take away all of a child's anxiety. We all feel anxious at times, and we all need to learn how to deal with it. Even though it's really hard to see it in our own children, as parents, we sometimes have to accept that our children will feel anxious. When children get really scared for some reason, it is usually important to give them lots of contact, comfort, and security. Also, as we discussed earlier, it is very important for you to stay cool and calm so you don't add to the problem. Finally, we describe here a very structured way of helping your child to control their panic and begin to find potential solutions.

A Problem-Solving Approach

Use of a problem-solving approach in handling children's anxiety has two advantages. First, it encourages a collaborative approach to solving the problem where both you and your child can influence the outcome. Second, it encourages children's independence in managing their own anxiety by giving them some of the responsibility. There are six steps to the problem-solving approach.

- **Summarize what your child has said.** Check the accuracy of your understanding of the problem—that is, make sure that you know what your child actually means. Don't try and argue; rather, communicate your empathy with your child in a sympathetic but calm way.

- **Identify what can be changed.** Ask your child what they can change—the situation, their reaction, or both.

- **Ask your child to brainstorm all the possible ways in which their anxiety might be reduced.** Make sure you don't just take over the task for children. Rather, help them to come up with their own suggestions of ways to reduce the anxiety and feel better. Naturally, you will need to guide younger children more than older children, but it is important to praise children of all ages for the ideas that they've generated. Even if the ideas are not actually very useful, praise them for their effort. The fact that they're engaging with you in the process of trying to constructively reduce their anxiety is a very positive and important step. Encourage your child to think of their detective character and to use detective thinking as one option.

- **Go through each idea or strategy that your child has come up with, one by one.** For each idea, ask the child, "What would happen if you did this?" If the child doesn't know, gently point possibilities out (for instance, you might say, "I wonder what would happen if you did _____ to make yourself feel better. What do you think?"). Your overriding goal is to encourage your child to find solutions that involve approaching the situation rather than avoiding it. Praise your child for trying to come up with outcomes for each strategy.

- **Ask your child to choose the idea (or combination of ideas) that is most likely to get the best result.** Remind your child of the evidence from detective thinking. You may find it helpful to have your child score each idea on a scale of 1 (not at all helpful) to 10 (very helpful) to help them choose the strongest strategy.

- **Later, once your child has implemented their plan, evaluate its success.** Discuss it with your child and consider what was successful, what was difficult, and what your child learned that could be used next time.

Hayley's Example

Hayley's parents, Maggie and Dan, are going out to dinner to celebrate their wedding anniversary. Hayley is extremely worried about the potential of an accident happening while they are out. She is crying and clinging to her parents, begging them not to go.

Step 1: *Maggie and Dan sit down with Hayley to find out what the problem is.*

Maggie: Hayley, we can see that you're very upset about the idea of us going out. Can you tell us exactly what it is that is worrying you?

Hayley: I don't know. I just don't want you to go.

Dan: Okay, we know that you don't want us to go. But we need you to tell us why. What is it that you are afraid will happen if we go out?

Hayley: You might be in an accident and be hurt.

Maggie summarizes and checks her understanding of what Hayley has said.

Maggie: So, you don't want us to go out because you think that we might be in an accident and get hurt. Is that right Hayley? Is that why you're so upset?

Hayley: Yes.

Step 2: *Maggie and Dan present Hayley with her choices.*

Dan: Okay, Hayley, your mother and I are going out tonight. And it's really up to you how you deal with that. You can keep on doing what you're doing right now and feel really bad. Or you can try to do something to cope with the bad feelings that you're having. Mom and I would really like to help you cope with the bad feelings. Are you willing to give that a try?

Hayley: I want you to stay with me at home. If you stay, I won't have any bad feelings.

Maggie: Hayley, you've heard your dad. We're not going to stay at home with you tonight. The decision you have to make is what you're going to do about how you're feeling right now. How about you work with us and we'll try and come up with a plan to make you feel better?

Hayley: I guess…

Step 3: *Maggie and Dan prompt Hayley to generate some suggestions as to how she might cope with her anxiety (that is, what she might do to make herself feel better). Hayley is praised for her effort.*

Maggie: Okay, Hayley. We need to think of as many things as possible that you could do that might make you feel better. What do you think you could do?

Hayley: What do you mean? I don't understand.

Dan: Well, for instance, you're worried about us going out because you're saying to yourself that if we go out, we might have an accident. Maybe instead, you could watch a movie and take your mind off your worries. Do you see what I mean?

Hayley: I could take your car keys and hide them. Then you wouldn't be able to go. Or I could have a giant tantrum and try to stop you from going.

Maggie: Well, that's one idea. At this stage, we'll write down all the ideas and then we can decide on one later on.

Hayley: I could go and watch my movie to take my mind off things.

Dan: Great, Hayley. What else could you do?

Hayley: I could write down that thing about you and Mom being good drivers so that I can remember it later.

Maggie: You mean your detective thinking—that's really excellent, Hayley. You're trying really hard and coming up with some good ideas. Can you think of anything else?

Step 4: *After brainstorming a number of ideas, Maggie and Dan prompt Hayley to identify the likely consequences or outcomes of each of the strategies she has come up with.*

Dan: Right. Now Hayley, we've got a few different ideas written down here about what you might do to make yourself feel better about us going out. Let's go through them one at a time and find out what would happen if you actually did each of these things. First of all, there was the idea that you hide the car keys. What do you think would happen if you did that?

Hayley: You might stay home?

Dan: You know, Hayley, I think that if you did that, it's probably more likely that we'd send you to your room and call a taxi to take us out to dinner.

Hayley: Yeah, I guess.

Dan: How about your idea about watching a movie? What would happen if you did that?

Hayley: I'd have fun, and I wouldn't be thinking about you and Mom.

Dan: How about your idea of writing down that your mom and I are good drivers? What do you think would happen if you did that?

Hayley: It would remind me that you probably wouldn't have an accident, and I might feel better.

Maggie: Okay, that's the end of our list. Well done, Hayley. You're doing a really excellent job of helping yourself to feel better.

Step 5: *Maggie and Dan prompt Hayley to choose the best solution.*

Dan: Okay, now the last thing we need to do is to pick one of these ideas. Have a look at the list and the things that would probably happen if you chose each idea. Which one do you think would be the best for you?

Hayley: Well, that's easy. It would be my idea of watching the movie. Plus, I could also write down something about you and Mom being good drivers, to remind myself not to worry.

Maggie: I think that's an excellent choice. Your dad and I are very proud of you for being able to figure out how to cope with your worry in a helpful way.

Step 6: *Assuming that Hayley handled her anxiety in a useful way and allowed Dan and Maggie to go out without further difficulty, they would praise her efforts the next morning and evaluate the usefulness of the strategies. They should also organize a special reward to acknowledge her bravery, such as playing a favorite game with Hayley.*

Maggie: I'm so proud of the way that you handled yourself last night, Hayley. Not only did you deal with your worries, but you did the things that we agreed to and got through the night without even calling us.

Hayley: Yeah, Sally [the babysitter] and I made some popcorn to watch with the movie. The movie got a bit scary, and we both hid under the pillows!

Maggie: It sounds like you had a great time. What did you learn from what we did?

Hayley: That if you find something good to do, eventually the worries don't bother you so much.

Maggie: What about the detective thinking?

Hayley: That helped when I thought about you guys at bedtime. I started to get worried again, but I just said to myself, "Dad's a good driver, and they're only ten minutes down the road."

Maggie: Very well done. You even came up with some evidence of your own. Is there anything that you would do differently next time?

Hayley: Yeah, I'd get some chocolate to go with the movie!

That evening Dan went bike riding with Hayley to reward her for her efforts the night before.

The completed problem-solving worksheet from this situation would look like this:

STEP 1: WHAT IS THE PROBLEM?

Mum and Dad are going out and I don't want them to go.

STEP 2: WHAT CAN YOU CHANGE?

I can change my reaction, they are going out even if I don't want them to.

STEP 3: BRAINSTORM IDEAS FOR SOLVING THIS PROBLEM.	STEP 4: WHAT WOULD HAPPEN IF YOU DID THIS IDEA?
Take the car keys and hide them.	I'll get in trouble and they will get a taxi.
Watch a movie to take my mind off of it.	I'd have fun and wouldn't be thinking so much.
Write down some evidence for my worries.	I wouldn't be thinking about accidents and I might feel better.
Have a big tantrum.	I'll get sent to time-out and end up more upset.

STEP 5: WHICH IDEA IS BEST? WHICH IS SECOND BEST?

I'll use 2 and 3. First do some detective thinking and then watch a movie.

STEP 6: EVALUATE HOW YOUR IDEA WORKED. WHAT WOULD YOU DO NEXT TIME?

My worries stopped once I started to enjoy the movie and as a reward I got to go bike riding with Dad. My solutions worked well. I'll think of some movies I want to watch next time Mom and Dad go out.

PARENT ACTIVITY: Problem Solving

For the situation your child most commonly gets anxious in, jot down some ideas for each step of the problem-solving procedure. Try to preempt any difficulties that you might have at each step. (Visit http://www.newharbinger.com/49913 to download this worksheet.)

STEP 1: What is the problem?	
STEP 2: What can you change?	
STEP 3: Brainstorm ideas for solving this problem.	**STEP 4: For each idea—what would happen if you did it?**
STEP 5: Which idea is best? Which is second best?	
STEP 6: Evaluate how your idea worked. What would you do next time?	

HELPING YOUR CHILD BECOME RESPONSIBLE FOR SOLVING PROBLEMS

Do you remember that being too directive (in other words, taking over responsibility for a child's problem and the solution of this problem) was identified as an unhelpful strategy for managing children's anxiety? When it comes to problem solving, children are definitely going to need their parents' help as they get used to this new way of thinking about and coming up with solutions to problems. However, ultimately, we want to get to a point where children can engage in the process of problem solving themselves, with minimal input from you. This way, they will be able to use the strategy in situations where they are not with you (by the way, this is a good way to explain to children why they need to be able to do it by themselves).

So, we need to be careful that we don't encourage children to become too dependent on parents for using problem solving. Once you have used the strategy together several times, encourage your child to use it on their own. It's a good idea to have them practice using this strategy on their own at a time when they are calm. It can also be a good idea to use a hypothetical or made-up situation the first time you have them do problem solving on their own. For example, you could ask them to fill in the Problem Solving Worksheet for the situation of being unfairly accused of talking in class by the teacher. Another tip when it comes to problem solving is to ask your child to pay attention to how other children solve problems or deal with difficult situations. For example, you could ask your child to discover successful ways that classmates use to join in group activities. This "investigating" approach can be used to find solutions to many different challenging social situations. Make sure you provide lots of praise for effort as your child gradually becomes better and better at using this strategy themself.

PARENT ACTIVITY: Responding to My Child's Anxious Behaviors

Having read all of this information on managing your child's anxiety, you need to start putting in place the ideas that you think are most appropriate for your child and family. There are two different approaches provided. (Visit http://www.newharbinger.com/49913 to download the worksheets for this activity.)

The first form is useful once you have identified the parenting "traps" (that is, the unhelpful strategies you are using) that you have fallen into in particular situations where your child is regularly anxious. Record what you intend to do differently when interacting with your child, and then your daily success in changing your interactions. Consider recording both your comfort in changing your reaction and how your child responded. Do not try to change many things at once; focus on one or two situations at a time.

The second is a monitoring form that you can use to follow your attempts to respond to your child's anxious behaviors that happen unexpectedly. Over the coming weeks, keep track of which of the helpful and unhelpful strategies you use. This will help you to become aware of where you need to change in your own interactions with your child.

Both of these tasks will help you to increase your awareness of how you can change your responses to your child's anxiety and, when making those changes, how their behavior shifts.

Changing My Approach

Situation where my child is anxious	
What parenting trap am I currently falling into?	

What will I do instead?	What will I say next time?

How successful was I?
Sunday:
Monday:
Tuesday:
Wednesday:
Thursday:
Friday:
Saturday:

Responding to Anxious Behaviors

What is it that my child did?	What action did I take (suggested strategy, praise, or consequence)?	What happened when I did this (what was my child's response)?

ACTIVITIES TO DO WITH YOUR CHILD...

CHILDREN'S ACTIVITY 13: Rewards

Begin by getting your child to tell you what a reward is. Make sure that you remind your child that rewards are not only for success but also for effort. Next, brainstorm as many rewards as you can together. (Visit http://www.newharbinger .com/49913 to download this activity from the Activity Book.)

To help you come up with a long list, here are some suggestions:

- going out for lunch
- pizza delivered
- sleepover
- extra-late bedtime Saturday night
- magazine or comic
- special activity (e.g., movie, miniature golf)
- planning and preparing dinner
- going on a family picnic
- visiting grandparents
- doing craft
- inviting friends over
- mystery trip
- going to a community activity
- new clothes
- trip to a bookstore
- having a movie night
- chore-free pass

- pieces of a construction set
- school effort awards
- bike ride with parent
- tokens that can be saved for big rewards
- having a TV in the bedroom for a night
- making a home movie
- planting our own garden
- camping out
- bubble bath
- swimming
- stickers
- playing board game or cards with parents
- kite flying
- "I'm proud of you" card
- poster for bedroom
- jigsaw puzzle

Once you have a large list, have your child identify rewards that they would like to work toward. Ask your child for ideas of fun things to do with the family, things they would like to hear (such as praise from Dad), activities to do at home, and material goods to work toward. You can also encourage them to say nice things to themselves. Let your child identify unrealistic and realistic rewards at this stage; you can negotiate which rewards are used when you work on creating stepladders in the next chapter. Remind your child that rewards can be for success or for big efforts.

CHILDREN'S ACTIVITY 14: Learning to Solve a Problem

This activity is about learning how to solve a problem using a structured worksheet. This activity will probably not be appropriate for very young children. You will need to create a worksheet of your own based on the example from earlier in the chapter or use the one provided in the Activity Book. (Visit http://www.newharbinger.com/49913 to download this activity.)

Explain to your child that problem solving can be used when they aren't sure of the best thing to do in a situation. Using Hayley's example described earlier, show your child how it is possible to brainstorm solutions for a problem and then evaluate what would happen if you did each possible solution so that you can choose the best one to try. Have your child think of another solution that Hayley might have considered, and work out what the likely consequences would be to that solution.

Explain the six steps of problem solving, including the following:

1. Write down the problem.

2. Work out if you can change your reaction, the situation, or both.

3. Brainstorm solutions.

4. Work out if each idea would lead to a good or bad outcome.

5. Choose the idea (or a combination of ideas) that would work best.

6. Put the plan in place and afterward evaluate how well the plan worked. If it didn't work, you go back and try some of the next-best possible solutions. Once you have worked out the best plan, agree on what you will do next time.

Using a blank worksheet, choose a problem that has recently been faced by your child, or create a hypothetical problem (e.g., getting invitations from two friends for the same day and having to resolve how to deal with this while not wanting to hurt either person) and have your child work through the problem-solving steps. To start with, choose a simple problem that is not too closely related to your child's current anxieties. Be sure not to become critical of your child's suggested solutions or past behaviors—never use the words, "Well, wouldn't that have been a better way to behave than bursting into tears yesterday?!" Your only response to your child's ideas should be praise and encouragement for the effort.

Once your child has gotten the idea, you can try to use problem solving as a skill to help manage anxiety in difficult situations.

CHILDREN'S PRACTICE TASK 3: Problem Solving

The focus of this practice task is on getting your child to practice the structured problem-solving approach in situations where they are anxious. For example, if they left their spelling book at school and they are worried that they will get in trouble for not doing their homework, you could then work together to use the problem-solving strategy to find the best solution (you might consider ideas such as don't do homework, have a parent write a note, call a friend, go to school early, etc.). Encourage your child to lead the process with your support and encouragement. Practice first on situations that are at the lower end of the worry scale. Once they have used problem solving successfully a few times, you can use the approach with higher rated worries. (Visit http://www.newharbinger.com/49913 to download this practice task from the Activity Book.)

As situations arise, your child should also continue to practice using detective thinking (and parents should reward such efforts).

CHAPTER HIGHLIGHTS

In this chapter, you learned...

→ the unhelpful strategies when parenting anxiety:

 → giving your child excessive reassurance

 → being too involved or directive when your child attempts activities

 → permitting your child to avoid age-appropriate activities

 → becoming impatient with your child

→ the helpful strategies when parenting anxiety:

 → rewarding brave, nonanxious behavior

 → ignoring anxious behavior

 → prompting your child to cope constructively

 → modeling brave, nonanxious behavior

→ ways to distinguish between anxious behaviors and naughty behaviors, and useful ways for responding to naughty behaviors

In this chapter, you and your child learned that:

* providing clear and consistent rewards for your child can help to support and increase brave behaviors;

* effort is as important as achievement when facing fears; and

* how to use collaborative, structured problem solving as a way of dealing with difficult situations.

Your child will need to do the following:

* Practice using structured problem solving in situations where they feel anxious (starting with low-anxiety situations and then more challenging situations).

* Continue to practice detective thinking. Your child should do this with respect to any situation that makes them even a little anxious and should also be encouraged to use the detective thinking technique as much as possible throughout the day whenever they notice anxiety increasing.

CHAPTER 5

Facing Fear to Fight Fear

Detective thinking will have taught your child different ways to think about things that worry them. This is an important first step in managing anxiety. However, learning new ways of thinking about a situation is not enough by itself to overcome worries and fears. Detective thinking is not much use if the old ways of behaving don't change as well. It is now time for your child to try out their new ability to deal with fears and worries in real situations. For very young children, this may be one of the only techniques that you use.

Understanding Stepladders

Stepladders are a way to help children overcome their fears by facing up to the very things they are scared of. It's mostly a commonsense procedure, and you will probably find that you have tried something like it before. The difference here is that we will put it into an overall anxiety management plan, and we will show you how to be more structured in the way you approach this strategy. Stepladders are carried out in a step-by-step fashion so that it isn't overwhelming for your child. In this way, your child will experience difficult situations gradually and learn to cope with them. Being encouraged to try things that are frightening, and learning to cope, will give your child confidence and help to break the pattern of automatically responding with fear and worry.

Avoiding Fears Doesn't Help

There is an old story of two men walking along the street, one man stopping every few steps to bang his head on the sidewalk. Finally, his friend can stand it no more and says, "Will you stop hitting your head on the sidewalk?" The first man answers, "I can't; it keeps the crocodiles away." His friend says, "But there are no crocodiles here!" The first man smiles and says, "See?"

Anxious children will avoid many apparent dangers that just aren't very likely to happen when we look at them rationally. However, by continuing to avoid, the child never learns that their behavior has nothing to do with the outcome. For example, just think of a child who is frightened of being killed while sleeping and so wants to sleep with their mother and father every night. We all know that the chance that the child will be killed while sleeping is almost zero. But by sleeping with their parents every night, the child never actually learns this. Convincing the child that they won't be killed is the goal, and using detective thinking is the first step. But this is not enough. The child must actually face the fear to *really be convinced* that being killed at night just won't happen.

Avoiding things actually strengthens the anxious beliefs, making it increasingly difficult for children to do things. Most anxious children have developed ways to avoid situations where they might become anxious. Sometimes these avoidance strategies can be very subtle and so habitual that even parents can be unaware of them. Stepladders give your child opportunities to practice different ways of behaving and learn that they really are able to cope with the fear.

The same ideas apply to all types of fears, whether they are fears of being separated from parents, fears of specific objects (e.g., heights, spiders), or excessive worrying about social situations or performance in a school test. The particular things being faced up to might differ, but the basic principles remain the same.

Let's look at an example of how you might try to overcome a fear of your own using stepladders. Suppose you were afraid of public speaking and you wanted to become more comfortable with this so that you could take a promotion at work that involved giving talks to large groups of people. Naturally, you would begin by doing your detective thinking—what is it that you are worried about, what is the evidence that this would happen, and so on. But this technique alone would not be enough. You would also need to face your fears. To begin with, you might decide to present a short speech to your family. This would perhaps be a little frightening because it might seem silly, but it shouldn't be too hard. Once you have done this step (probably more than once), you might decide that you are now ready to present a short talk to a group of friends. After this, you might practice doing readings and introducing speakers at your local club. The whole time you are doing these steps, you are practicing your detective thinking. After a few weeks of practicing these easier steps, you should find your confidence starting to build. Your next step might then involve presenting a few practice talks to your work colleagues. At the same time, you might join a public speaking club and practice giving weekly talks to the club members. Finally, you grab that promotion and begin to give talks as part of your new job. Even here, you could break things down by organizing your schedule so that your first talks are to smaller and less important groups and your later talks are the really tough ones. By gradually and systematically building up to your final goal in this way, you will become used to public speaking and will learn that you can cope and that the terrible things you may have imagined before are just not very likely. Over a period of weeks (or even months), you will find yourself becoming less and less worried about presenting in public.

Exactly the same principles apply when you begin to do stepladders with your child. For example, let's think of a child who is afraid of going to sleep in the dark and wants the lights on in their room every night. To do stepladders, you might first get the child to go to sleep with a fairly bright light on in the hall. If this is not too big a step, the child will most likely agree. After several nights, you might get the child to go to sleep with a light on in the room across the hall. Then, after a few nights, the child might agree to try a small, fairly dull lamp in the hall outside. Eventually, the child could try going to sleep with the only light being a very faint one in a distant room. Finally, the child will go to sleep without the light on at all. At each step, the child will undoubtedly be a little anxious. But by gradually reducing the light in this way and having small enough steps, the child can reach the final goal without ever having to face extreme fear.

How Do Stepladders Work?

Stepladders are a step-by-step way to learn that the danger that the child is afraid of almost certainly won't happen. Or even if it does happen, it probably won't be as bad as they expected and they can cope with it. Through this description, you can hopefully see that using stepladders is simply a "real life" extension of detective thinking. In detective thinking, you have been helping your child to find logical evidence that their anxious prediction almost certainly won't happen, or if it did happen, it probably won't be as bad as they were expecting. In stepladders, you will simply be asking your child to face their fears to learn these same lessons through direct experience. With your help, your child will work out a step-by-step plan to face each of the fears or dangers that they expect. Your child will attempt each step in turn, beginning with the least difficult and working up to situations that are the most worrying.

Every step of a stepladder is more proof to your child that the bad outcome they were predicting won't happen, or if it does happen, they can cope. They will feel proud of their success as they conquer each step but will need your encouragement to keep going. A system of rewards can be negotiated between you and your child to provide extra incentives to keep trying. To remind yourself about the ways to use rewards, see the section "Rewarding Brave, Nonanxious Behavior" in chapter 4.

Children learn from stepladders that even if they feel worried, they can cope. During a stepladder, children will have to experience some situations that make them feel worried. This is important because it helps children learn that although they may have started off feeling uncomfortable and worried, the bad outcomes they feared did not actually happen. By doing this, your child learns that they can tolerate some feelings of worry and that these won't stop them from doing things. After all, none of us can go through life without ever feeling anxious.

Practice is the key to success. It is not enough to practice a step just once. Your child will have to repeat each step over and over until the situation no longer causes a lot of anxiety.

It is important to point out that **stepladders is the most important technique in the entire "Helping Your Anxious Child" program.** Even if your child has struggled with any of the other techniques, this is the one you need to focus on the most. Facing fears through stepladders is also basically the same for any age of child—from 4 to 94!

How You Can Help

Anxious children lack confidence in their ability to manage certain situations. They may believe that they are less capable or weaker than other children. And of course they commonly expect to find dangers in a wide variety of situations—we refer to this as their "anxious prediction." Children's past experiences may make them reluctant to try something new or something they may have "failed" at before. You are going to have to encourage your child to try to do things that will not be easy. You will need to be sympathetic and understanding, but at the same time, you will have to be tough and consistent. This won't be easy. But remind yourself that it is for your child's good in the long run. At times, it may help to read over chapter 4 on parenting an anxious child.

BELIEVE THAT YOUR CHILD CAN DO IT

You may be worried about your child's capacity to tolerate anxiety and discomfort. For example, you might feel that your child is more sensitive than other children. Children can pick up subtle messages from parents about how capable they are or how difficult a certain task may be. For this reason, it is important that you don't let your doubts show. Be positive about what your child is trying to change.

ARE YOU WORRIED TOO?

As a parent, it can be very difficult to know when to be sympathetic and help children out and when to ask them to try a little harder. This can be extra difficult for parents who may have similar fears. You know that it is good for them to do it, but you may also feel empathy with the worries your child has and feel inclined to protect them. If you feel like this, it's understandable. But you will have to try and separate your own concerns from those of your child. It may help to do your own detective thinking about the problem. As we discussed in the previous chapter, it is also often a good idea to model for your child how you are coping. You can do this by setting your own stepladders so that you and your child can work on them together.

When your child begins to do stepladders, you may well find this quite difficult to face. There will be times when you will be sending your child out to face some pretty difficult situations and possibly to become quite frightened. At these times, many parents feel guilty and torn. If this is a risk for you, you need to try and put some safeguards into place to help you through this part of the program. First, remind yourself that encouraging children to face their fears is good for them and is the only way they will overcome their fears. Next, brainstorm some ways in which you might help yourself feel better at those times when you feel bad. For example, you might write out a Detective Thinking Worksheet for your own beliefs and worries at these times and read over it to remind yourself of the more accurate beliefs. Or you might make sure you have plenty of work to get into to distract yourself from your guilty thoughts. Alternatively, you might be able to ask for support from your partner or a good friend. These people might be able to remind you that you are doing the right thing and that your child will not "break" or "hate you" for what they are going through. In short, these feelings are completely understandable but need to be overcome for the good of your child.

BE CLEAR ABOUT WHAT YOU EXPECT

It's important to be clear in your mind about what are reasonable expectations for children of your child's age and for your child particularly. Your child will be best helped if you are clear on what you expect them to be able to do and how much you will help. For example, it would be unrealistic to expect a six-year-old child who is afraid of being away from Mom to stay home alone in the evening. But it would be quite reasonable for a fifteen-year-old to do this. In a similar way, there might be different expectations for children in different areas. For example, expecting your child to walk home alone from the bus stop might be quite reasonable in certain neighborhoods but not in others. Talk to other parents or your child's teacher if you are unsure about what you should reasonably expect from your child. In other words, you will need an objective and realistic view about what are the real possible dangers for a child given your child's environment and age. In addition, if you have a partner or someone else who also cares for your child, make sure you sort out these expectations together so that you are in agreement about what your child should be able to do. It is very difficult for children to learn that something is not dangerous if they are getting different messages from their caregivers.

How to Use Stepladders with Your Child

Developing stepladders with your child is usually fairly straightforward. But it can be tricky at times, and, as with any skill, there are some systematic steps you can follow that can make it more likely to work.

Step 1: Explaining Stepladders to Children

The first step in facing fears with your child is to explain clearly and simply the purpose of the exercise. It's important that your child is a willing and active participant in the process, or you will be fighting an uphill battle. Naturally, the way in which you explain stepladders and how much your child needs to "buy into" the process, will vary depending on your child's age.

A useful way of explaining stepladders to children is to tell them a story of a child who is scared of something very straightforward (like a fear of dogs or a fear of heights) and ask them to suggest some ideas on how they could help that child overcome those fears.

A good example is to describe a child who is frightened of swimming in deep water (but is able to swim). Ask your child what they might suggest to that child about how to go about getting used to going into the water. Most children are pretty good at coming up with a commonsense plan. Hopefully, your child will be able to come up with a plan where the other child would begin with a low-fear step (for example, going into water up to their knees). If your child does not come up with a sensible approach, you will need to prompt gently until they get the idea. The next suggestion might be for the child to gradually begin to move deeper and deeper into the water. This should allow time for the child to relax and get used to each step. Hopefully, children will understand that the frightened child will need to experience a little bit of fear, but by moving through each step gradually and getting used to each step along the way, that child will eventually reach the final goal without too much discomfort. If you are using the Activity Book (available at http://www.newharbinger.com/49913), the story about Molly and her fear of heights will help you to structure this introduction.

Step 2: Making a Fears and Worries List

Once your child understands the idea of stepladders in principle, the next step is to apply these ideas to their own specific difficulties. To begin, you and your child will need to sit and brainstorm all the different things that they are afraid of. A good question to begin might be this: "What are some things that you don't like to do because you get scared?" You will create a Fears and Worries List that is a record of a number of different situations and activities that your child finds frightening and usually avoids. For example, items such as approaching big dogs, meeting new people, and spending time away from you, could all be included. For some children, there may only be one type of fear, while for others there will be many. No doubt, you will have many suggestions and you will need to make sure that your child covers as much as possible. But it's important that your child is involved in the exercise, so encourage them to come up with the ideas first, if possible. Try to make this a fun game, seeing how many things you can list. Children may need to be reminded of specific situations where they may have been anxious rather than presented with a general concept such as fear of separation. It's also important that this is not seen as a list of failings but as a list of things they would like to be able to do.

At this stage, the idea is to get your child involved and brainstorming. Therefore, don't worry if the suggestions are not realistic or even sensible. They can be fixed later. Also, don't worry if the list does not cover everything. The list can be added to later—it is a working reminder of what your child wants to change. As the items are generated, you will divide the list into things that are really hard, moderately hard, or not too hard. It is often a good idea for your child to give a worry rating for each item, although this is not essential at this stage. The most important point of this exercise is for you and your child to get lots of examples of the types of things that they avoid doing because of anxiety. Giving worry ratings to each item might simply help you to make sure that fears are roughly sorted.

You might find that your child isn't able to come up with fears or may even suddenly claim now to have no problems at all. It is not uncommon for anxious children to deny any difficulties, and it usually happens because your child wants to appear "perfect" both to you and to themself. If you believe that your child is avoiding acknowledging their fears, don't nag. Begin by suggesting one or two recent situations that were difficult. Focus on the lower-level fears and remind your child that you will tackle those first and then come back to the list later. Some children may avoid some areas of difficulty, such as social fears, but focus on others. Acknowledge that your child is working on one area and plan to try the other, more difficult problems later. As your child succeeds on easier problems, they will gain the confidence to try to beat other worries. If your child still denies having any difficulties, challenge them to try certain things anyway. For example, you might say something like "I think you are a little afraid of X, so why don't we put this down, and if you are not, then you can prove to me that I am wrong." Finally, for some children who are very young or very concrete in their thinking, they might find it too hard to come up with their own items. For these children, it is perfectly okay for you to plan most of the list for them.

Lashi's Example

Lashi had many worries—and they seemed to be getting worse, upsetting everyone in the family. Lashi and her mother made a list of the main things she worried about. Her mom chose a quiet time when she and Lashi could talk about the worries. At first, Lashi thought everything worried her equally, but when talking with her mother she was able to sort the worries into groups.

Fears and Worries List

THESE THINGS ARE REALLY HARD TO DO	Staying with a sitter while Mum goes out for the night	9
	Having an injection	10
	Mum being late home or being late picking me up	9
	Hearing noises outside when in my room at night	10
	Sleeping in my own room	8
THESE THINGS ARE HARD TO DO	Going to school	6
	Going to the doctor with Mum	5
	Hearing strange noises at night	7
	Being in the dark	6
	Staying over at Dad's place	5
THESE THINGS MAKE ME A LITTLE WORRIED	Being in another room at home	2
	Going to a friend's house after school	4
	Visiting Granddad and Grandma with Mum	1
	Visiting Dad's place for the afternoon	2

Using this list of fears and worries, Lashi and her mom could choose which worries to start with to make step-by-step plans to fight her fears. The fears seemed to fall into three main groups, each with a slightly different type of danger that Lashi expected: (a) being away from Mom (Mom will be kidnapped and I will never see her again), (b) being in the dark (there are burglars and other bad people who will kill me), and (c) going to the doctor, particularly getting an injection (it will hurt too much for me to bear). Together Lashi and her mom made three separate stepladders, one for each type of anxious prediction.

PARENT ACTIVITY: Exploring Your Child's Fears and Worries List

As part of your anxiety management session this week, your child will be creating a Fears and Worries List. It can be helpful for you to think through what might appear on that list before the session. (Visit http://www.newharbinger.com/49913 to download this worksheet.)

THESE THINGS ARE REALLY HARD TO DO	
THESE THINGS ARE HARD TO DO	

THESE THINGS MAKE ME A LITTLE WORRIED	

How might these fears be grouped together—that is, how do the situations fit into a common theme, or in which ones is your child predicting the same bad outcome?

_____

_____

_____

_____

Step 3: Working Out a Step-by-Step Plan

Once you have listed as many fears as possible, the next step is to organize the fears into a practical plan. The aim is to have one or more stepladders—that is, lists of fears that are practical and organized so that they contain a number of steps going from the easiest to the hardest. But don't get too hung up on making this perfect. As long as the generally easier ones are tried first and the generally harder ones are left until later, that will work perfectly well.

You will find that some of the fears that you have recorded on the Fears and Worries List are already small practical steps in and of themselves. For example, the item from Lashi's list "Visiting Grandpa and Grandma with Mom" is rated as a low-level worry and is practical and doable. On the other hand, some of the items on your list will be much broader and larger. For example, from Lashi's list, the item, "Being in the dark" is quite vague and broad because Lashi's level of fear might be very different depending, for example, on whether she was inside or outside, which room she was in, what time it was, how dark it was, and so on. The items that are practical and doable, can be left as is. However, the items that are broad and a little vague need to be rewritten so that they are much more specific. This might involve breaking them down into several smaller steps. For example, the item, "Being in the dark" could be broken down into several different items such as "Being in my room with the light down low," "Being in my room with the light off in the early evening," "Being in my room later at night with the light off," "Being in the far room with the light off," "Standing outside the back door with the light off," and "Standing at the end of the garden with the light off."

When you have a detailed list consisting of specific, practical tasks, your child can place them in order of difficulty from easiest all the way up to the hardest. As mentioned above, this doesn't have to be perfect—just a rough direction. Once they are organized, you and your child will have your first stepladder.

If your child has lots of different fears, you will find it easier to create several stepladders. Each stepladder would contain items that logically go together and are relating to the same anxious predictions. For example, you might have one stepladder for being away from parents, another for mixing with people, and a third for sleeping in the dark.

In creating stepladders, you'll need to make sure that you and your child have come up with steps that are not too far apart. The idea is that eventually your child will begin with the first step on the ladder and practice that item until they are relatively comfortable with it. Then, your child will need to move on to the next item up the stepladder, and so on. If the steps are too far apart—if the next step is too much of a jump for your child—they will not be able to do it and could lose confidence.

The best way to create smaller steps to reach a goal is to think about several different ways that a child can face a situation. For example, a situation such as "asking directions from a stranger on the street" can include many different features that will result in quite different levels of anxiety.

Directions could be asked from a male or a female, from an older person or a younger person, or from a person alone, a couple of people, or a group of people. Each of these variations would most likely produce different levels of anxiety for a shy child, and each child will be different. By brainstorming about these variations, you can produce a large number of steps that your child can then put onto a stepladder.

Another important consideration in creating a stepladder is to choose items that are doable. After all, your child is eventually going to be asked to do each item on the list. Look over the list and remove any steps that are off track or perhaps not even possible. For example, if dealing with a fear of heights, climbing to the top of Mount Everest might really help, but it's not very likely to happen.

On the stepladders in the children's Activity Book, there are ten steps, but you can have more or less than that. There is no set number of steps to be included, but there should be enough steps to provide plenty of opportunities for practice. It is more effective to have a greater number of smaller steps to reinforce the learning than only a few large ones. Large steps and big jumps in the level of difficulty between items must be avoided. Each step should be very clear, with details of time to be spent, the place, and what is to be achieved. Use everyday activities to give your child opportunities to really do lots of practice. Tasks that are too elaborate or difficult to organize, demanding special efforts from parents, will rarely be done despite good intentions.

Lashi's Example

Lashi and her mom came up with a number of different areas that she was frightened of, including sleeping over at various people's houses (including her father's), sleeping by herself at night in the dark, staying home with a sitter while her mother goes out, and going to school. To help organize all of her fears more easily, Lashi and her mother decided to create separate stepladders for each of these different areas. We show, below, part of Lashi's stepladder for learning to stay home while her mom goes out.

Lashi's goal: *To stay at home with a sitter at night*

Lashi's anxious prediction: *"If mom is away from me, she might get hurt or killed and I will never see her again."*

- *Stay home with Dad while Mom goes out for ten minutes.*
- *Stay home with Grandma while Mom goes out for thirty minutes.*
- *Stay home with Dad while Mom goes out for the afternoon.*
- *Stay home with Grandma while Mom goes out for most of the day.*
- *Stay home with a sitter while Mom goes out for the afternoon.*
- *Stay home with a sitter while Mom goes out for most of the day.*
- *Stay home with Dad while Mom goes out for the evening (a few hours).*
- *Stay home with Grandma while Mom goes out for the night (until late).*
- *Stay home with a sitter while Mom goes out for a few hours in the evening.*
- *Stay home with a sitter while Mom goes out for the night (until late).*

Ethan's Example

Part of Ethan's shyness also extended to a perfectionistic streak. Ethan was so worried about what others thought of him that he tried not to make any mistakes. As a result, he often worried extensively about whether he had said or done the wrong thing and he often redid his schoolwork many times in order to get it just right. Below is part of one stepladder that Ethan made up to tackle this problem.

Ethan's goal: *Not to be bothered by making mistakes at school*

Ethan's anxious prediction: *"If I make a mistake, people will think I am stupid or will get angry at me."*

- *Intentionally call Mark (a close friend) by the wrong name.*

- *Don't brush hair before school.*

- *Draw a messy line on a schoolwork page and leave it there.*

- *Don't check an essay for mistakes before handing it in.*

- *Make a deliberate mistake in a science project.*

- *Intentionally hand in an essay with several spelling mistakes.*

- *Answer a question in class when not 100 percent sure of the answer.*

- *Intentionally return library books three days late.*

- *Deliberately give the wrong answer to a question in class.*

- *Don't do the correct homework.*

Ethan is very shy, so one of his worst fears was speaking in front of other people. The following stepladder was designed to tackle this problem. Ethan did not begin work on this stepladder until after he had done several steps on most of his other stepladders. This was both because public speaking was not a very important goal for Ethan and also because it was a harder topic to tackle than some of his other goals.

Ethan's goal: *To present a talk to the class*

Ethan's anxious prediction: *"I will give a bad talk and people will laugh at me and think I am stupid."*

- *Prepare a short talk and practice alone, but record it.*
- *Give a short talk to parents.*
- *Give the talk again to parents and deliberately leave something out.*
- *Give the talk to grandparents and mispronounce a word.*
- *Give the talk to aunts and deliberately drop notes.*
- *Give the talk to friends and family.*
- *Give a longer talk to friends and family.*
- *Ask a question of the teacher in front of the class.*
- *Read out loud in class and mispronounce a word.*
- *Give a two-minute report to the whole class.*
- *Make an announcement to the whole school.*

Talia's Example

Talia's fear of water had meant that she missed out on a lot of fun activities like pool parties and vacation activities.

Talia's goal: *To swim at the beach with friends*

Talia's anxious prediction: *"I will drown."*

- *Go to the local pool and swim across the pool at the point where I can just stand up.*
- *Go to the local pool and swim at the deep end with Dad next to me.*
- *Go to the local pool and swim in the deep end alone.*
- *Go to the beach and swim in the sheltered lagoon.*
- *Go to the beach on a calm day and swim with Dad.*
- *Go to the beach on a calm day and swim on my own up to shoulder height.*
- *Go to the beach on a rougher day and swim with Dad.*
- *Go to the beach on a rough day and swim to shoulder height.*
- *Go to the beach and swim out and back on a boogie board on a calm day.*
- *Go to the beach and swim out and back on a boogie board on a rough day.*

Hayley's Example

Although Hayley has two close friends at school, she is scared of spending time with other children in case she loses her current friends. She worries about this constantly and has missed out on activities with other children because of her fear.

Hayley's goal: *To spend time with children other than Sally and Annie*

Hayley's anxious prediction: *"Other kids won't like me and won't want to be with me."*

- *Call Jill and ask her about some homework details.*
- *Ask Madeline a question on the playground before school.*
- *Ask Jill and Madeline to join Sally and Annie in a game of basketball.*
- *Talk to Sally and Jill about their favorite activity or vacation destination.*
- *Invite Madeline over for dinner on Friday.*
- *Sit with Jill while eating lunch and then ask her to join Sally and Annie.*
- *Walk around to Madeline's house after school to see if she is home.*
- *Arrange to meet Jill and Sally at the mall to have lunch.*
- *Invite Madeline, Jill, Sally, and Annie to go to the movies.*
- *Go to a party when Sally and Annie won't be there.*
- *Accept an invitation to visit someone else's house.*
- *Invite Madeline and Jill for a sleepover.*

Ang's example

Ang's very young age meant that Ang's mother made up most of his stepladder; his strong levels of inhibition meant that his steps were quite small and they proceeded slowly. Here is the first part of Ang's stepladder to start to speak to other people.

Ang's goal: *To be able to speak with other children and nonfamily adults*

Note: *Because Ang is so young, he hasn't been able to tell his mother what he is worried about when he talks to others. But from things he has said and the way he acts, Ang's mother has made a good guess about his anxious prediction: "When I talk to others, my voice will sound funny and they will laugh at me."*

- Answer yes/no questions from Aunt Jasmine when she visits our home.
- Answer yes/no questions from Mr. Sun in our home.
- Say good morning to daycare teacher.
- Answer one question from another child at daycare (teacher to monitor).
- Tell Aunt Jasmine about one thing that happened at daycare.
- Ask teacher to go to bathroom at daycare.
- Tell Mr. Sun about one thing that happened at daycare.
- Say good morning to downstairs neighbor.
- Say good morning to people using a silly voice.

There are several other types of stepladders that will be discussed in the next chapter. These are slightly trickier to create, but they help with fears that involve doing things to reduce worry, like when a child wears only certain clothes or washes their hands a lot. If these types of fears are the only ones that your child has, then you might want to read the next chapter now. However, it is preferable if the first stepladder you attempt to create is for a concrete fear where your child is directly avoiding an activity. This is because the stepladders for these types of fears are easier to design and are easier for your child to understand.

PARENT ACTIVITY: Creating Your Child's Stepladders

Although you will be creating stepladders with your child's help, it is useful to think through the possible stepladders and steps in advance. (Visit http://www.newhar binger.com/49913 to download the worksheet for this activity.)

Based on the Fears and Worries List, how many stepladders do you think your child will need? Think about some ideas *before* you work with your child to create their stepladders. For each of the possible stepladders, you should list your ideas for possible steps—but remember that (if they are old enough) your child should feel involved in which of these steps are entered on the final stepladder and the order in which they'll be listed.

How many stepladders will your child need? _____

Remember a stepladder will contain different situations that all relate to the same worry.

Stepladder 1 Possible Goal _____

Stepladder 1 Worried Thought_____

Brainstorm Potential Steps

Stepladder 2 Possible Goal _____

Stepladder 2 Worried Thought _____ .

Brainstorm Potential Steps

Ways of creating more steps:

- Find other situations or tasks that involve the same fear and that are motivated by the same anxious prediction (e.g., talking to relatives at the dinner table and giving a presentation to the class might both be motivated by the same anxious prediction—"I will say something stupid and people will laugh at me"—so they can go into the same stepladder).

- Change the number, age, gender, or familiarity of the people present while doing a step (e.g., spending time in the playground with the sixth-grade children versus spending time in the play-ground with classmates from fourth grade; saying hello to a kid I know from class versus saying hello to a kid I don't know from the school).

- Change items by the location of the task (e.g., asking for help at the corner store versus asking for help at the customer service desk of a shopping mall).

- Change the amount of time spent in the situation (e.g., staying at after-school care for a half hour versus staying at after-school care for the afternoon).

- Change the amount of preparation before going to an event (e.g., being told on the previous Wednesday what will be happening on the weekend versus being told on Saturday morning what is hap-pening on the weekend).

Step 4: Motivation and Rewards

Asking children to do stepladders can be like asking someone to have a tooth removed without anesthetic. Stepladders will be hard work for your child, and some steps can be quite frightening. By developing good stepladders with small steps, you can reduce the fear. But it isn't possible to get rid of it entirely. Your child is going to have to face fear to overcome fear.

We all need encouragement to help us to do unpleasant or difficult things. As an adult, you can recognize the value of unpleasant things; for example, if you have to undergo a painful operation, you would do it because you realize that it will help you in the long run. But children are not as good at recognizing what is good for them. One of the biggest differences between adults and children is that children have very little understanding of the future and the concept of time. Telling children "You have to go through this pain now because it will be good for you later," just doesn't make the same sense to them as it generally does to adults.

For this reason, one of the really important parts of stepladders is to give your child rewards when they successfully complete a step (and to use backup rewards to encourage ongoing effort when your child tries a step but is unsuccessful). Giving rewards after each practice increases your child's motivation because it balances the unpleasantness of facing fears with a positive experience.

Over the years, we have occasionally come across some parents who do not feel that they should reward their child for doing stepladders exercises. After all, other kids can do these things without problems, so why should your child be rewarded for doing something that other kids do so easily? The point is that all children are different. For whatever reason, your child doesn't find these things easy, even though other children might. To put it in context, imagine forcing yourself to sing a song on national television or climb into a pit full of snakes. The level of fear you might feel doing these things is no more than what you are going to ask your own child to face. It is necessary for your child to do these things so that they learn to overcome these fears. But it won't be easy. Offering rewards for your child's attempts is the only way you will motivate them to try these things, and it will also communicate to your child your pride at what they are doing. A reward is not a bribe. Bribes are things you give someone to make them do something that is of benefit to you. A reward is simply a motivator to encourage your child to do something that will ultimately benefit them. A reward is also a signal of your delight and approval in your child's behavior.

We covered all of the important facts about how to give rewards in chapter 4 about parenting an anxious child, so we will not go through it again here, but we urge you to reread the section, "Rewarding Brave, Nonanxious Behavior" to remind yourself of the important points. Here are some of the main points to remember:

- Rewards do not have to be financial, but can include fun activities.

- Rewards do not have to be large, but need to be relevant to your child.

- The reward should be an appropriate size for the difficulty of the step.

- Rewards need to be given as soon as possible after your child has done what they agreed to do.

- You need to be consistent—give a reward if your child has earned it, but don't give it if the step wasn't attempted at all.

- Reward your child for doing the step whether or not they were scared.

Step 5: Doing Stepladders

Once you and your child have brainstormed a series of situations that your child is frightened of, organized these situations into one or more stepladders, and decided on a few rewards for the first few steps of the stepladders, your child will be ready to begin facing their fears.

To begin stepladders, your child should pick the first step of one or two stepladders. You and your child will set a date and time that they will try the first step. How much you leave this up to your child's control will depend on the age of your child, the type of step, and what point you are up to in the program. For an older child, you may simply decide that they need to do the step "sometime this week." For a younger child, you might need to set the precise day and time, and you might need to be present. It is also a good idea to be more specific about practice early on in the program, for example, actually set a specific date and time for it—then you can loosen up a little and leave more control to your child later on, as they build confidence. However, the control and timing will depend mostly on the type of step. Some steps will need to be set at a particular time (e.g., if the step involves you going out and leaving your child with a sitter), whereas others can be done more flexibly (e.g., leaving it up to your child to decide when to call for information on the telephone). Some tasks will need to be set up so that a situation occurs "unexpectedly" (e.g., the step is answering the door when someone knocks, and you as the parent quietly ask a neighbor to pop by unannounced). Don't forget to reward your child when they have done the practice.

To help your child to get the most out of the stepladder, your child will keep a record of the week's plans and all of their practices (see "Children's Practice Task 4: Fighting Fear by Facing Fear" at http://www.newharbinger .com/49913). This helps to make sure the practice is done and to let you know when practice is slowing down. It will also provide a great record of achievements that your child can look back on when their motivation begins to drop. This record also encourages children to think about what strategies they will use to manage their anxiety. And it allows you to track success and difficulties that may need troubleshooting.

Things to Remember

The process of conducting an effective stepladder program involves challenging anxious predictions, being realistic, responsive, and repetitive, and rewarding effort and success.

Challenge Anxious Predictions

- Work out or guess your child's anxious prediction—in other words, the type of danger or "bad outcome" that your child is expecting.

- Then brainstorm lots of different ways that your child can challenge or test out that prediction.

Choose Realistic Goals

- Choose goals that can be achieved and are appropriate to your child's developmental level and capabilities. The shy child may never become Mr. or Ms. Personality of the class but can aim to be able to speak up in class, give a talk, call to ask a friend over, and speak to the school principal.

- Your child does not have to be totally free of anxiety. A certain amount of anxiety is realistic in certain situations and may even help children to perform better. Your child needs to learn that they can tolerate a certain level of anxiety and to go ahead and "just do it."

- Finally, remember that anxiety is a natural emotion that is designed to protect people from real dangers. This program focuses on reducing *excessive* and *unrealistic* anxiety. You should not try to develop stepladders for fears that might be quite realistic—such as encouraging your child to play with guns, or encouraging your child to swim in water that is beyond their ability.

Respond by Adjusting the Stepladder If Difficulties Occur

- You need to monitor your child's progress and adjust the steps in response to the progress being made. It may be necessary to slip in new items to bridge a gap between the steps if there is reluctance to move to the next one. Sometimes the step can be altered by adding different people or varying the place where the task is to be performed. Further ideas are discussed in chapter 7 on troubleshooting.

- Moving through the items too quickly may mean the steps are not difficult enough. It may also be a form of avoidance since some children will just "grin and bear" a situation without learning that the situation itself is not too bad. You should talk to your child after each step and find out their attitude toward the situation. Doing stepladders should eventually produce an attitude like "The 'bad outcome' I have been so worried about, isn't going to happen" or "I can handle that" instead of "If I just hang in there, I can get through this." In other words, the key is to help your child to change their underlying anxious prediction.

- Where there are difficulties or things do not go well at the first attempt, this too is a valuable opportunity to encourage your child to persist, to learn that a "failure" is not a disaster, and to look at how they might do it differently next time. When a child tries and doesn't succeed, you should still provide some form of backup reward for the effort. Remind your child that not everything has to be perfect every time.

Repetition Is the Key to Long-Term Results

- It is important to remember that the best results and most long-lasting benefits from the program will come from lots of practice and repeating steps over and over until your child feels confident. You will know when your child has practiced a step enough because you will get the feeling that your child could suddenly do that step again anytime without warning and not get thrown at all. Look for a feeling such as "I'm bored doing this step."

- Repeating the steps strengthens children's learning of new ways of doing things by giving them more success and a growing feeling of mastery over the fear. Your child has probably had many experiences of feeling like "a failure." Trying the steps several times proves to children that they can do it and is essential to overcoming these well-established expectations.

- At the same time, don't be too rigid with the "order" of steps. As long as you are not forcing your child into a step that is too hard, jumping around the ladder a little is not a bad thing. The main point is that your child learns that "the bad outcome that I have been expecting will almost certainly not happen to me, or even if it does happen, I can cope." So giving your child every opportunity to test out their anxious prediction—by changing up the place, time, people, etc.—will help them to really learn that lesson.

Reward Effort and Success

- Maintain the reward program consistently throughout the stepladders process.

- Keep up the praise and the rewards. Anxious children need reinforcement of their efforts to encourage them to keep going in the face of frustration.

- Good intentions to reward children for progress can be easily overlooked after some progress. However, the reward program and parental praise should be continued right through all of the steps of each stepladder. Age will also affect this. Younger children will need more praise and rewards for longer, while older children and teenagers will begin to enjoy being more independent and confident as these experiences will feel good.

As your child progresses up the first stepladder, you will be able to start on another of their stepladders. Children can usually work on two or three different stepladders at the same time.

ACTIVITIES TO DO WITH YOUR CHILD...

CHILDREN'S ACTIVITY 15: Fighting Fear by Facing Fear

Remind your child that anxiety often changes what we choose to do or makes it much harder to give things a try. Then tell your child that fears can be stubborn and that they don't go away until you stand up to them and have a go. (Visit http:// www.newharbinger.com/49913 to download this activity.)

Tell the story of Molly, whose best friend is moving and is having a party in a restaurant at the top of the tallest building in the city. The problem is that Molly is scared of heights. First, ask your child what Molly might be scared of—in other words, what bad thing might Molly think will happen to her (e.g., the building will collapse; I will fall; I will get dizzy and faint)? Next, ask your child to come up with ideas of how Molly could check out whether her bad expectation is really true. Encourage your child to come up with the idea of breaking the fear down by slowly having Molly go to higher and higher places to eventually prove to herself that the bad thing she expected (e.g., the building will collapse) is not going to happen. Repeat the activity of solving someone else's problem until your child seems to have a good grasp of the basic idea of breaking fears down and facing small amounts of fear at a time to check out their anxious predictions. You can use the following problems:

- Jeff won't play in the park or the yard because there might be a spider there and it will bite him.

- Adriana is afraid of the dark and still sleeps with the light on because she is thinks there might be ghosts.

Explain to your child that with your help, they will be starting to face fears. Some children will be concerned about what they will be expected to try and how difficult it may be. When talking with your child, emphasize these things:

- You can create your own stepladders. All steps are negotiated, starting off with things you can almost do already, so it won't be too difficult. The harder steps will only happen once your confidence starts to improve, and then those steps won't seem so hard.

- Each step will be done a few times until you feel confident doing it.

- When doing steps, your anxiety will drop if you stay there long enough and also the more times that you do the step.

- You will be earning rewards as you move up your stepladders.

CHILDREN'S ACTIVITY 16: Making a Fears and Worries List

Similar to what you did earlier, help your child to create their own Fears and Worries List. It may be helpful to read through Lashi's example, found earlier in the chapter, before beginning so that your child understands that some fears listed will be ranked as only a little scary and others will be ranked as very hard to do. (Visit http://www.newharbinger.com/49913 to download this activity.)

CHILDREN'S ACTIVITY 17: Making Your Stepladders

Continuing with Lashi's example, show your child how Lashi's fear of being away from her mom was turned into a stepladder. Emphasize that Lashi helped to plan these steps, that there were rewards for doing each step, that each step was repeated until Lashi wasn't really worried anymore by that situation, and that it was not until then that Lashi would move on to the next step.

Help your child to create a first stepladder by following these steps:

- Set a goal that is practical and work out what bad outcome your child is expecting to happen (anxious prediction).

- List all the possible steps you can think of to break the worry down. Remember, you can make lots of steps by changing the time of day, the duration, or the people involved, or by thinking of other situations where your child worries about the same bad thing happening.

- Give each step a worry rating (although this is not absolutely necessary).

- Choose enough steps from your list so that almost all of the possible worry ratings have a step next to them—in other words, no really big jumps.

- Write your steps roughly in order from easiest to hardest to create a stepladder. If you like, you can simply put them into groups—easy steps, moderate steps, hard steps—rather than an actual ladder.

- Discuss what reward will go with each step (small rewards go with the little steps, and bigger rewards go with the harder steps). Make sure your child is really involved in this part —that will help them to be more motivated.

When you complete the stepladder, praise your child for taking the first steps toward facing their fears. (Visit http://www.newharbinger.com/49913 to download this activity.)

CHILDREN'S PRACTICE TASK 4: Fighting Fear by Facing Fear

Using the first stepladder (and any future stepladders that you create), your child now needs to commit to starting the first step. (Visit http://www.newharbinger .com/49913 to download this practice task from the Activity Book.) Talk about when, where, and how the first step on the stepladder will be attempted. Tentative plans for facing the second and future steps can also be made. Generally, your child's fear will need to come down at least a bit on easier steps before they move on to harder steps, but as we said earlier, this doesn't have to be too rigid. Make these initial plans with your child and then follow through during the week. It is a good idea for the very first step to be pretty easy. This will make sure your child starts with a win and gets a reward, and that will help build their confidence and motivation.

A table with column headings—"What step will I do?," "When will I do it?," "What strategies will I use?," "What did I learn?," and "What reward did I get?"— can be very useful for keeping track of stepladder progress. Below these columns you can make a space to record the worry ratings from before and after each step is completed. The strategies column is designed to remind your child to use other anxiety management skills, such as detective thinking, during the stepladder practices. Once you have the plans written down, you will need to follow through with attempts at the steps at the planned time. Ideally, your child will attempt a step or two every day (although remember that your child may need to do the same step several days in a row, before they are ready for the next step).

In addition to having your child plan and record attempts at steps, it is also useful for parents to record the successes, challenges, and difficulties you experienced. To help with this task, a table is provided for you to use in the parent activity below. You can use these notes to work out any patterns to the difficulties your child is having. These patterns may help point to a solution. You can also use them to remind yourself of successes that your child is having over time.

PARENT ACTIVITY: Monitoring Progress

It is important to monitor both your progress and your child's progress in implementing the agreed-upon steps. Use this table to record successes, challenges, and difficulties. (Visit http://www.newharbinger.com/49913 to download this table.)

Stepladders in Practice

What step was being attempted?	What problems were encountered?	What successes were achieved?

CHAPTER HIGHLIGHTS

In this chapter, you and your child learned...

→ to fight fear, you have to face fear, and

→ the best way to face fear is to break the fear down into small steps, with each step being a little harder to do than the last.

→ To create a stepladder, you need to do the following:

  → Set a practical goal and identify your child's anxious prediction.

  → List all the possible ways you could break the worry down into small steps (each step should test the same anxious prediction).

  → Give each step a worry rating (this can often be useful, but is not absolutely necessary).

  → Choose steps that are practical and that cover low to high worry ratings.

  → Write the steps in rough order from easiest to hardest.

  → Set a reward for each step.

  → Steps can be broken down by varying the type of task attempted, the people (or type of person) present, the location of the step, the amount of time in the situation, or the amount of preparation allowed before completing the step.

  → It is important to plan when you will do steps and to keep track of successes and any problems faced.

Your child will need to do the following:

*   Create their first stepladder(s) with the help of a parent or other adult, depending on their age.

*   Attempt the first step or the first few steps on their stepladder(s) a number of times.

*   Use detective thinking as a strategy to reduce anxiety when attempting a step (if old enough).

CHAPTER 6

Simplifying Detective Thinking and Creative Stepladders

At this stage of the program, your child should be working on challenging themself by facing fears, gradually moving up a stepladder or three, and combining this with detective thinking. In this chapter, we will give your child a way to make the detective thinking quicker and easier. We will also introduce some stepladder approaches that address the unnecessary things children do to try to control their fear. Remember that detective thinking is not a technique we normally use with very young children, but stepladders most definitely is, so pick the sections from this chapter that are relevant to your child's age.

Rapid Detective Thinking

As your child gets better at detective thinking, it is helpful to simplify the process so that there is no need to complete an entire Detective Thinking Worksheet every time they get worried. With new worries, particularly ones that are very distressing, the full process (in other words, using the complete original form) is important. However, you will also find that a lot of your child's worries are the same old ones going around again and again. In these cases, once your child has used the detective thinking successfully a number of times, they will be able to switch to using simple prompts to be reminded of the evidence.

Although there are many types of evidence you can look at when you do detective thinking (such as past experience, alternative possibilities, etc.), we have found that many children will have one or two particular types of evidence that really work best for them. They also often have one or two calm thoughts that can be used in many situations.

Discovering which thoughts and questions are most useful for your own child is a good way to make detective thinking work more quickly. Once your child has found one or two good questions and one or two good thoughts, they should record them on "cue cards" that can be used as a reminder of how to think or what to ask when they start to feel nervous. This will make it easier for your child to manage anxious feelings independently.

Here are some examples of questions and thoughts that may trigger rapid detective thinking:

Your child may discover that asking "What happened last time?" is the best way to change most of their worried thoughts into calm ones.

Others may find that thinking about past experience doesn't usually work too well, but answering the question "What is another explanation?" works better.

Your child may find the question "What would Janice think?" (where Janice is a particularly confident friend) useful to ask when about to talk in front of other people. If your child has this question written on a small card in a pencil case, they can use it as a reminder just before answering a question in class.

Some children find it useful to ask themselves what their superhero character would think in that situation.

On the other side of the card, your child might write a detective thought, such as "Lots of kids get some answers wrong, and it doesn't matter."

By creating cue cards, your child has two prompts that can help when they are feeling worried. Importantly, your child can use these prompts without help from you or other adults, and these prompts can become a shortcut to helping remind your child of their calm thought quickly and easily.

Cue cards work best for those children who discover patterns to their worried thoughts and find the same (or very similar) thoughts or evidence coming up again and again. These shortcuts work better after your child has done the full detective thinking several times so that they really believe their calm thought and understand the evidence that it has come from.

Those children who have not been doing the full detective thinking but have been creating or choosing a calm or helpful thought to replace their worried thought can adapt the points above to trigger their calm thinking. There may be a few particularly important calm thoughts that your child gets the most benefit from. These can also be listed on a cue card to help remind your child to use these important thoughts.

Developing Creative Stepladders

Stepladders are the most essential tool for overcoming fears and combating worry. Some fears are very concrete and are easily broken down into a series of steps. For example, a fear of dogs can be manipulated by changing the size, distance from, and activity level of a variety of dogs. Similarly, fears of separating from a parent can be manipulated by changing concrete factors such as the length of time away, the time of day, or the person doing the caregiving. However, some fears are much harder to break down into steps because they are not as concrete, and so working out how to manipulate steps can sometimes be quite difficult. In this section, we will look at ways of addressing some of the more complicated and less obvious sorts of fears.

What You Need to Know to Create Successful Stepladders

As a first stage in developing stepladders for these less obvious fears, there are two questions you can ask yourself to help to make the source of the fear more concrete: "What is your child really afraid of?" and "What is your child avoiding?"

WHAT IS YOUR CHILD REALLY AFRAID OF?

This may sound like a silly question, but consider this. You have a friend who is afraid of flying. That's how she describes it—"a fear of flying." If you wanted to work on a stepladder for this person, you might start with her reading about planes, then going to the airport, then walking on a plane, then taxiing in a plane, and finally going on a flight. Now this might work, but if it didn't, you would need to consider that fears of flying can actually involve several very different fears (we also refer to these as "anxious predictions"). Some people who are scared of flying are actually afraid of the flight itself—that is, they are afraid (predict) that the plane will crash. But others are more afraid of having to sit in those cramped seats, and they really have a fear of small spaces (they may predict that they will suffocate or run out of air). Others are actually afraid of the fact that the plane is flying so high, and they have a fear of heights (they might predict that they will fall or pass out). So, if your friend was actually afraid of being up that high, reading about planes and being on the plane while it's on the ground would not be of any use. When it came to taking off for the first time, however, she would still be terrified because she wouldn't have done any gradual steps to address her real fear of heights. Obviously, to create an effective stepladder you need to know what it is that the person is *really* afraid of—in other words, you need to know the type of danger or "bad outcome" that they are predicting, otherwise you might do a lot of steps but not get anywhere.

With children, working out what they fear (or predict) in a situation is important, but it can also be difficult if they can't tell you what their prediction is. This may be particularly tricky with younger children, or children who are less verbal. At times, you will need to experiment with different steps that cover different things that they *could* be afraid of until you find the ones that *do* cause their worry ratings to rise. It will be a matter of trial and error. A related "trick" might be to ask your child a set of hypothetical questions. Ask your child to close their eyes and imagine being in a situation that you will describe and then have your child tell you how frightened they would be. Then you can change the situation in various ways to work out what sorts of things make a difference to the level of fear. For example, with the situation we described above with your friend's fear of flying, you could have asked her to imagine sitting near the window or sitting near the aisle. If she was afraid of crashing, this really wouldn't make much difference, but if she was afraid of small spaces, she would probably be far more anxious jammed in next to the window. Similarly, if she told you she was more frightened looking out of the window than looking at the seat in front of her, it might tell you that she was afraid of heights since looking out of the window would make her much more aware of how high the plane was.

When working out what questions to ask your child, make sure you think of the situation from a child's-eye view. What a child understands the situation to be will be very different from your understanding of it. For example, say you are about to take your child on their first trip to the snow. Your child has never seen snow but loves vacations so is excited. As you start driving up into the mountains, your child starts to get upset while looking out the window. Your child starts crying, and you have to turn back. To you, there is not much that is frightening about driving in this area; you've done it before. To your child, these are the new things that they are dealing with: high rocks on one side of the car and a big drop on the other; signs that warn of falling rocks; strange-looking clothes and equipment; the noise from the chains on the car's wheels; and snow—which doesn't always look like the pictures in the travel brochures. There are a lot of things here that a child could be frightened by, while from your adult point of view, these things are normal. Take a moment to look at the world from your child's point of view—it can help you to work out what your child still needs to face.

WHAT IS YOUR CHILD AVOIDING?

Once you know what it is that your child fears, you then need to consider one step further and establish what your child avoids because of the fear. This can be particularly difficult if what they mostly do is worry about things. A child who's a worrier may avoid going into an unknown situation by asking many questions so that situation won't be an unknown anymore. You might just think of that child as a worrywart, but to help you develop stepladders, you need to think in terms of avoidance and realize that your child is avoiding anything that they do not know or cannot plan for. Trying to work out or even guess the anxious prediction they are making will also help. For example, the child we just described might have a very general prediction that if I don't know what's going on, I will get hurt—as a result they "avoid" not knowing what is going on.

In a similar way, your child might be very perfectionistic and work really slowly or check their work many times. But you need to think about what your child is avoiding—most likely it is the possibility of making a mistake; their anxious prediction might be "If I make a mistake, it will show that I am stupid." Or consider that the child who always sticks to the rules, tells others to stick to the rules, and who always does the "right thing" might be avoiding getting into trouble. There are a lot of possibilities for each fear. The key is often to look at the motivation for different actions. If you are unsure of what avoidance is going on, for each of your child's actions ask yourself, "What bad outcome is my child trying to prevent?"

When you know what the "bad outcome" is that your child predicts and what your child has been doing to stop that "bad outcome" from happening (avoiding), then you will be able to begin to create stepladders that are more precise. The techniques listed below can help you to create appropriate steps when the fears are harder to grasp.

Response Prevention

We all understand avoidance when it involves *not* doing something. For example, children who won't go to school because they are afraid of leaving their mothers are pretty easy to understand. But in some cases, avoidance might involve actually doing one behavior in order to avoid another. This is often much harder to understand and identify.

A good example might be the child who is afraid of burglars breaking in at night (anxious prediction). This child might check and recheck all the locks on the doors and windows every night before going to bed. In this example, the child is *doing* something—going around the house and checking. But notice that this behavior is still a type of avoidance—the child is avoiding the possibility that a burglar might break in.

A child who is afraid of germs provides a more complex example. This child might predict that if "I touch something dirty, I will get germs and get sick," and they might avoid touching certain dirty objects. This is obvious avoidance—the child is *not* touching. But that child might also wash over and over again, just in case they have touched something dirty. In that case, the child is also *doing* something—washing. But not doing something (not touching dirty objects) and doing something (washing repeatedly) are both types of avoidance—they are both aimed at stopping the predicted "bad outcome" (getting sick) from happening.

When a fear causes your child to do something to avoid it, like checking that the doors and windows are locked, you need to gradually get your child to *stop* doing that behavior. When your child builds a stepladder, stopping that particular behavior should be included among the steps. This is called *response prevention*—in other words, *stopping your child from doing an action that they think is protecting them from their anxious prediction.* This type of stepladder is very commonly needed for children who have obsessive-compulsive disorder. But it is also very useful for children with many other fears, such as those who are very perfectionistic or those who seek a lot of reassurance, or even children with some unusual fears such as fears of illness or fears of death. When you are trying to create stepladders for these issues, you are trying to change the way something is done or reduce the number of times it is done.

Kurt's Example

Kurt is afraid of having germs on his hands because he expects that this will cause him to get very sick. Because of this fear, he spends a lot of time washing his hands many times during each day. When he washes his hands, he has to do it in a certain way because he thinks that this is the only way that will protect him from the germs. Kurt first washes his hands all over, then the bottoms of his arms, then his hands again. After this first wash, Kurt washes the taps to make sure that he won't get germs from the tap when he turns it off. Once the tap is washed, he washes his hands again, then turns the tap off and dries his hands on a clean towel that he pulls out of the cupboard (which he opens with his feet). The whole process takes between three and eight minutes, and at the moment, Kurt has to wash like this many times each day. In the following stepladder, each step builds on the last, so when he moves on to step 2 he continues to do step 1 at the same time.

Kurt's goal: *To not (overly)** wash my hands for a whole day*

Kurt's anxious prediction: *"Not washing my hands thoroughly after I touch something will give me germs, which will make me very sick."*

- *Use the hand towel that is on the hook to dry hands.*

- *When washing, do not wash arms; stop at wrists.*

- *After washing taps, only rinse hands again; do not use soap.*

- *Do not wash taps, just hands.*

Note: *These first few steps are showing Kurt that he doesn't have to wash in a ritualistic way to get rid of the germs.*

- *Do not wash hands before eating a cookie (in the house).*

- *Open and close every door in the house, and then eat a sandwich.*

** A note about medical reasons for washing: The COVID-19 pandemic showed the world the importance of regular washing and good hygiene, and most started washing hands more than they used to, during that time. Clearly, there are certain circumstances such as future pandemics, going into areas with high infection, and so on, when careful, extensive washing is necessary. However, it is very important to distinguish between normal, healthy handwashing (e.g., systematic scrubbing for 20 seconds, or use of sanitizer after attending potentially infected areas) and the excess washing, usually accompanied by fear and distress, of young people with obsessional fears. In this example, Kurt's family allows him to wash (briefly) when it is warranted for genuine, health reasons, but they stop all additional cleaning.

Note: *These steps are showing Kurt that even when he touches things he doesn't get enough germs to make him sick.*

- *Play basketball, take shoes off, and then make and eat lunch with Mom.*

- *Go to the toilet and then eat tacos and lick sauce off fingers.*

Note: *This step is showing Kurt that if he eats, even with (some) germs on his hands (from the toilet), he still doesn't get sick.*

- *Only wash hands when having daily shower (and when warranted by the circumstances such as a pandemic—limited to 20 seconds).*

- *Go for forty-eight hours without washing at all (genuinely warranted washing permitted, such as pandemic or illness, determined by parents).*

Children with obsessive problems need to do more in their stepladders than most of us would usually do in our daily lives because their anxious predictions are often quite complicated and hard to disprove. For example, for Kurt's fear of germs, one step might involve urinating a few drops on his hands and then not washing it off. Most of us would never want to do this, but it is not actually dangerous, and to really and deeply prove to themselves that their expectation is wrong, children with these obsessive types of fears will need to practice these types of tests until they no longer scare them.

Here is another example of a stepladder for a child who has to check three times that all of the doors and windows are locked before going to bed:

Goal: *To go to bed without checking locks*

Anxious prediction: *If a lock is left open, someone will break in and hurt me.*

- *Check all locks but only check twice.*

- *Check all locks but only check once.*

- *Check the locks in a different order than usual.*

- *Only check the door locks.*

- *Have someone else check the locks, but I am allowed to ask about each door.*

- *Have someone else check the locks, but I can't ask about them.*

- *Go to bed and not check at all.*

- *Go to bed after deliberately leaving the doors unlocked.*

In both of these stepladders, three things are done: first, the order in which a routine is done is changed to prove that nothing bad will happen if things aren't always done in a particular (rigid) way; second, the child is prevented from doing the routine as often as they are used to in order to prove that even if you don't check all the time, nothing bad will happen; third and most importantly of all, the child intentionally does the thing they have been trying to avoid to prove that even if something goes "wrong" (e.g., a lock is left open or I get germs on my hands), nothing bad ends up happening. This type of approach can also be used for reassurance seeking and perfectionism.

Hayley's Example

Here is an example for a stepladder that is aimed at reducing the number of questions Hayley asks about homework:

Hayley's goal: *To complete homework within twenty minutes*

Hayley's anxious prediction: *If I don't check and recheck, I will make mistakes and get into trouble.*

- *Do homework with Mom, answering each question before asking her about it.*

- *Do homework with Mom, completing five questions before asking her to check it.*

- *Complete whole sheet, keeping questions to the end.*
- *Complete whole sheet; Mom can check but only to correct spelling.*
- *Complete sheet; only do one rough copy.*
- *Complete homework directly on worksheet.*
- *Complete homework in forty minutes and cannot check the answers.*
- *Complete homework in twenty minutes without checking.*
- *Only complete ten minutes of homework and hand it in.*
- *Intentionally make three mistakes in homework and hand it in.*

There are many times when stepladders will include steps that prevent a response; some examples of such steps might be not sleeping in a parent's bed, stopping a child from constantly organizing their belongings, covering mirrors so a child cannot check how they look before going out, and not allowing a child to talk endlessly about worries at bedtime.

Exposure to Consequences

Remember back at the beginning of chapter 5, we explained that practicing stepladders is an extension for your child of their detective thinking. They should be learning, through their own practice, that the worried expectations they have are almost certainly wrong and most of these "bad outcomes" will never actually happen to them. But there is a second part to the worries of most anxious children. Not only do they overpredict how *likely* a bad outcome will be, but many children who worry also overpredict how *terrible the consequences* of a feared event will be. This overpredicted fear leads them to avoid taking the risk of having the catastrophe happen by avoiding the original task completely or by doing whatever they can to reduce any possible risk. For example, a child may go to great lengths to find out what friends will be wearing when they all go out to make sure that they won't look different. Up until now, you have probably been helping your child to learn that the "bad outcomes" they are predicting probably won't happen. The next step will now be to make sure that some of your child's steps actually force them to face their anxious prediction to learn that it actually wasn't so bad and they can cope with it (we have already included some of these steps in our earlier examples). Note that if your child is very young or is a particularly concrete thinker, you might need to go gently with this section and not push it too hard.

These extra steps in a stepladder are particularly important for children who have social fears, generalized worries, or obsessive-compulsive fears. These types of anxiety disorders are more common among older children, so much of this chapter is slightly less relevant to parents of young children. However, there may be times when young children also need to be exposed to feared consequences in a gradual way. To conquer these fears, children need to be directly exposed to the potentially bad outcome so that they learn that *even if it happens, it really isn't that bad* and life will go on. For example, a child who is socially anxious might need to learn that *even if* I do something really silly in front of others, they won't hate me and will probably forget about it very soon; a child with general worries and perfectionism might need to learn that *even if* I make some mistakes on a class test, it won't be the end of the world; and a child with obsessive washing and fears of germs might need to learn that *even if* I have some germs on my hands, I almost certainly won't get sick, and *even if* I get sick, my body will soon recover.

Here is an example of a stepladder for a girl who is overly conscientious about her appearance because of an expectation that if she looks different, other kids will look down on her and not like her.

Goal: *Not to be bothered by how I look when I go out*

Anxious prediction: *If I look different to the other kids, they will think I am weird.*

- *Go to school with socks scrunched down, not folded down.*

- *Go to school with a bit of hair not in ponytail.*

- *Go to stores without smoothing or brushing hair.*

- *Go to school with shirt not tucked in.*

- *Go to friend's house in clothes that I wore yesterday.*

- *Go to stores, with friends, wearing last year's styles.*

- *Go to school wearing regular clothes on sports day.*

- *Go to picnic wearing jeans and dad's grungy T-shirt.*

- *Go to school event wearing jeans and dad's grungy T-shirt.*

- *Go to stores in a tracksuit with messy hair.*

As you can see, in this example the girl intentionally created her anxious prediction ("I will look different") in order to test out the consequence ("other kids will think I am weird"). The "problem" clothes were very individual to this girl and what she saw as appropriate. Consequently, much negotiation was needed as to what risks would be taken. While trying the stepladder, her parents developed awareness of small avoidances, like spraying perfume on clothes that had already been worn. New steps, therefore, had to be developed (where she did not use the perfume) and then implemented to help her progress.

A second situation where exposure to consequences can be appropriate is for children who avoid making mistakes. These children might check their work repeatedly or do the work very slowly. Getting them to stop checking (response prevention) or to do their work faster is a great first step, but it is not enough. All this will teach them is that they are pretty careful kids and so, even if they don't check, they probably won't make a mistake (i.e., the first half of their anxious prediction). But to really overcome their anxiety, they need to also learn that even if they do make a mistake, it is not the end of the world (i.e., the second part of their prediction—the consequence). Therefore, their stepladder has to include actual mistakes in it—in other words, they need to be exposed to the consequences of making mistakes. An example of a stepladder about learning to accept making mistakes was included in Ethan's examples in chapter 5.

An example of how to gently expose to consequences for young children can be seen in Ang's example in chapter 5. Notice that in the very last step of this ladder, Ang was supposed to say good morning to people using a silly voice. This is an example of exposure to consequences because Ang will be learning that even if I do sound silly, most people will just ignore it or smile and nothing bad happens. However, another step on that ladder required Ang to ask the daycare teacher to go to the bathroom. After Ang had successfully done that step a few times and was building his confidence, his mother asked the teacher that next time Ang asked, the teacher should say, "No, you can't go right this minute." Then after a few minutes, the teacher could allow Ang to go. In this way, Ang was exposed to the consequence of not getting his way immediately and drawing the attention of the class to himself, but only after he had mastered the earlier steps.

When including consequences in stepladders, it is especially important to include detective thinking about the implications of what really could or did happen. This is important to make sure that children recognize the objective evidence because otherwise the level of worry may not reduce. Sometimes children might believe that something really terrible happened when in fact it wasn't so terrible at all. For example, Hayley has a stepladder where she faces the fear that she will get in trouble if she breaks a rule. She had a step where she had to "forget" to take library books to school on library day. Hayley came home and described getting in terrible trouble for forgetting her books. To look at this in more detail, her parent encouraged her to do detective thinking. When they looked at the evidence of what really happened, Hayley said that the teacher told the class that everyone who didn't return books couldn't borrow new books this week. By going through the detective thinking after the step, Hayley was able to realize that although she wanted to borrow a new book, it really wasn't a tragedy that she couldn't do so.

In Ang's case, his parents didn't do formal detective thinking with him due to his young age. However, after the teacher had said that he couldn't use the bathroom immediately, when he got home that afternoon, his mother sat and talked about what had happened and made sure that Ang understood that even though he couldn't use the bathroom immediately, he was not in trouble, no one laughed at him, and it all worked out okay in the end.

Exposure at School

Many fears that children have (especially social fears) can be even more intense when they are at school. Consequently, the stepladders for these fears need to be completed at school. This can raise some difficulties, including checking whether steps have been completed, providing immediate rewards, and dealing with the many unknown factors introduced by other children.

CREATING STEPLADDERS FOR SCHOOL

Stepladders that are done at school need to be simple and doable by the child on their own. It is usually only possible to do a single step each day (although that step could be done more than once during the day). As a reminder, it is useful to write the step for the day on a piece of paper that is put into the child's school bag or into their homework diary. Steps should specify what a child will do (e.g., ask for a ball), who they will do it with (e.g., ask the gym teacher), and when it should be done (e.g., at recess). School stepladders often require research from parents about what is possible in the school setting. For example, say you are trying to reach the goal of not worrying about breaking school rules and the step is to walk outside the appropriate play area. You will need to know where "out-of-bounds" is and to specify this in the step. Otherwise there may be confusion as to whether your child achieved the step or not.

INVOLVING TEACHERS

When attempting school-based stepladders, most teachers are often more than willing to assist. It can therefore be useful to have a meeting with your child's teacher and/or school counselor if any of the stepladders are going to happen at school. School staff can help with things like reminding your child to try the next step, helping you to know what is possible within the school, and providing a check on whether your child did their step. Teachers will also have ideas for steps that you may not have thought possible.

However, whether or not to warn the teacher or to involve them in a particular stepladder is a complex issue and will depend on the particular expectation that your child is testing and how far they have come in their anxiety management. For example, let's imagine that your child will be testing an in-class behavior like answering a question (the teacher will need to be ready to call on your child when they put a hand up) or perhaps deliberately making a mistake or breaking a rule like talking to a friend in class. If your child is still early in the program and they are only just starting to build their confidence, then you might want to involve the class teacher in the stepladder to make sure that everything goes calmly and smoothly. For example, you might warn the teacher that your child is going to raise their hand to answer a question or that your child will be making an intentional mistake and ask the teacher to please be gentle and forgiving at this stage. However, later in the program, as your child starts to build their confidence, you will want your child to experience the normal consequences of their actions like being slightly criticized for their laziness or even being put on detention. After all, you want them to experience the consequences that they are worried about and learn that they can cope. Therefore, whether and how much to involve the classroom teacher will depend on what you want your child to learn and how far along they are in the program.

Teachers may also be able to help monitor step completion. For example, say a step for a socially anxious child is not tucking in a shirt for the whole day. You may inform the class teacher by way of a short note in the morning that this is today's step and ask that they let you know whether it was completed. That way the class teacher is aware, but your child still has to risk being scolded by other teachers for being messy. By having the teacher let you know about step completion, you can be confident that your child is progressing or know where you need to adjust steps.

Occasionally, you may come across a teacher who is less than willing to be involved with implementing stepladders. That teacher may feel that there is no problem, that it is not the teacher's or school's responsibility to help, or worse, think that you, as a parent, are the problem. In this case, it may be better not to involve that teacher and either rely on your child's integrity or find a more sympathetic teacher or perhaps the school counselor to support your efforts from within the school.

REWARDS AT SCHOOL

Remembering that rewards are more effective when delivered quickly, it may be useful to create rewards that can be given at school wherever possible. Special snack-time treats that can be handed out by the teacher for step completion, or tokens that can be exchanged for rewards when your child gets home are effective. It may also be possible for your child to work toward school rewards like certificates. The most important thing is that the rewards are consistently given.

OTHER CHILDREN

When completing steps at school, other children, or at least their reactions, might become involved. This can bring in an element of extra risk in completing the step. When preparing your child for a step that might involve things going badly, such as getting teased after answering a question incorrectly, it is worth talking about some of the outcomes that might happen and what that means before the step is attempted. This can be incorporated into the detective thinking about the worst possible consequences. At times, steps may involve social skills that your child is not yet particularly confident at using, like being able to handle teasing. If this is the case, then developing these skills before attempting the step that uses them will be important. Developing social skills and assertiveness are covered in chapter 8.

Overlearning

When you take a fear to its extreme and really challenge the consequences, it can help consolidate the learning that takes place when you complete a stepladder. By doing the worst possible feared event, or by doing what seems very much out of the ordinary, your child can gather very convincing evidence that even when the very worst occurs, nothing much happens that will be important after some time passes. In the stepladders described in the section "Response Prevention" above, each last step is something that most people would not normally do—like not washing for two days. However, if your child does do any of these last steps, they certainly won't be concerned about the original thing that was feared. This is called *overlearning,* and other examples of it include having a child who fears doing something embarrassing wear their pajamas to a shopping center or having a child who fears making mistakes deliberately answer every question wrong in a test. This last one will require you to also let go of the need for your child to achieve their best all the time. The lesson to be learned by doing this final step is that even when you really do "mess up," the worst that happens is a bad grade on the test and perhaps a not-so-good end-of-term report on that subject—the world certainly doesn't end and the child won't get held back, both consequences a child might have feared before working on stepladders. Your child might also learn that mistakes can be overcome, so it is worth persisting. Overlearning is not a necessity for learning to manage anxiety, but it can bring about significant change in your child's fear and worry levels. The sense of freedom a child can get when they manage to do something "really crazy" is definitely worth the effort.

Spontaneous Practice

As your child gains more confidence and becomes used to the idea of taking steps, you and your child will come across opportunities for what we call *spontaneous practice*. "Spontaneous practice" refers to opportunities to practice facing fears that were not actually part of your child's stepladder but have just come up in your child's daily life. For example, if your child is shy and has a fear of meeting new people, you may be sitting in a park one day and notice another child shooting a basketball alone. Although this specific situation may not be on your child's stepladder, you could encourage your child to grab the opportunity to join the other child as a way of facing the fear of meeting a new person. If your child is hesitant, don't forget to help with their detective thinking and come up with a good reward for doing the spontaneous practice. In some cases, these opportunities may even be a few steps higher than your child is currently at on their stepladder. If your child is willing to try, they should be encouraged and rewarded. However, if your child is really too worried, don't force the issue—it may simply be too soon.

Other Resources

Use resources in the community, family, and school system to provide a wide range of stepladder situations. Most people are willing to assist children who are learning new skills and readily understand the basic concepts involved once they are explained. Encourage grandparents and others not to be too helpful and to allow the child to experience some anxiety to overcome fears. Even store clerks, park attendants, or bus drivers can be relevant in certain situations.

PARENT ACTIVITY: Facing a Fear of Your Own

As we discussed in the section "Modeling Brave, Nonanxious Behavior" (chapter 4), a great way of modeling anxiety management to your child is to actively face your own fears. It is even better when you get your child to help you design your stepladder or to find evidence. Take a simple fear of your own and work with your child on facing this fear. Use the same steps and materials that you are familiar with. Allowing your child to help you face a fear helps to make worry and fear seem normal, it shows the benefit of managing fear, and it gives your child a great boost in confidence—being the "expert" by helping Mom or Dad to do something is a powerful experience. It is a good idea to pace each other—set your goals together earlier in the week and then go over your achievements at the end of the week. If you do this, you can both monitor your efforts and get special rewards (maybe one of your chosen rewards can be your child making you a cup of tea in the morning—the more you involve them the better). (Visit http://www.newhar binger.com/49913 to download the worksheet for this activity.)

ACTIVITIES TO DO WITH YOUR CHILD...

CHILDREN'S ACTIVITY 18: Detective Thinking Cue Cards

Assuming that your child has had several weeks of practicing detective thinking, work with your child to identify the most useful thoughts and questions that help them to think more logically and accurately when anxious. Have your child write these on a small cue card to be carried in difficult situations. Your child may need to write out more than one card—for example, one to carry in a pencil case at school and one to have beside the bed at night. Each card will be specific to the situation that causes anxiety. (Visit http://www.newharbinger.com/49913 to download this activity.)

CHILDREN'S ACTIVITY 19: Revising Your Stepladders

After completing *two weeks* of working on stepladders, children and parents will both have a better understanding of how the facing-fear process works. This is a good time to revise your child's stepladders. With your child, examine the first stepladder to look for these common problems:

- *The steps are not practical.* Are the next steps tasks that can be done within the next few weeks? Do both you and your child know exactly what the tasks involve?

- *The steps are too big or too small.* You want to make sure the worry ratings are not too far apart nor too close together. Over time, worry ratings can change, so it is worth checking fear levels for upcoming steps. If the next task seems very easy to your child, just one attempt at the step may be enough before they move on to the next one. If the next task seems very difficult, then new intermediate steps should be added.

- *There are too many goals.* Each stepladder should work on one type of fear or worry. When there are too many goals on one stepladder it can slow you down.

If you identify problems, work with your child to change the steps to overcome the problems. (Visit http://www.newharbinger.com/49913 to download this activity.)

CHILDREN'S ACTIVITY 20: Creating New Stepladders

It is very likely that you will need two, three, or more stepladders to work through your child's different fears. Create stepladders for the next most important fears that your child needs to face. Make sure that your child has the greatest say in which fears are most important. Granted, they may not be your highest priorities, but it is highly likely that what your child chooses will be the fears that are giving them the most trouble. There will be time as your child's confidence grows to get to other fears that cause you concern.

Use the same process as the one that you used to create your child's first stepladder (see "How to Use Stepladders with Your Child" in chapter 5):

- Set a goal and identify the anxious prediction.

- List all the possible steps and variations.

- Rate these on the worry scale.

- Choose a set of steps that covers the full range of the worry scale and write these in order onto a stepladder.

- Assign rewards for each step.

- Finally, make plans to start on the first steps of the new stepladder.

(Visit http://www.newharbinger.com/49913 to download this activity.)

CHILDREN'S PRACTICE TASK 5: Doing Steps

Children need to keep working on their stepladders. Write down plans for what step will be done, when, and the skills that will be used to help your child to cope. You should try to make these plans at the beginning of each week to ensure that progress continues to be made. Remember that decisions on the steps that will be faced should be led by your child. If progress seems too slow, then the step choices can be discussed, but children should still feel that they are in control of the process. If your child really seems to not want to do the step, then this reluctance may suggest that the step is too large and an intermediate step should be designed. While practicing steps, your child should use the new cue cards and, when needed, should continue to use detective thinking and problem solving to reduce feelings of anxiety. (Visit http://www.newharbinger.com/49913 to download this practice task.)

CHAPTER HIGHLIGHTS

In this chapter, you learned…

→ to try and work out your child's anxious predictions to help guide you to the most precise and effective stepladders;

→ how to create stepladders that address particular actions your child might use to reduce fear of something (such as checking homework too often or washing hands constantly); These stepladders might include "response prevention"—that is, stopping your child from using actions that their fear encourages them to do;

→ how to create stepladders that expose your child to feared consequences, such as looking different or making mistakes, to help your child learn that they will "survive";

→ what to consider when stepladders need to be completed at school, including how to involve teachers, give rewards, and anticipate the reactions of other children; and

→ how to take advantage of spontaneous practice to help your child face their fear.

In this chapter, you and your child learned…

* to identify the calm thoughts and evidence-finding questions that are particularly useful for your child;

* to review stepladders regularly for steps that are not practical, too big, too small, or that do not fit well together; and

* to continue to create stepladders for each of your child's anxious predictions.

Your child will need to do the following:

* Practice more steps from the first stepladder and begin steps from any new stepladders.

* Start using cue cards to shortcut detective thinking and continue to use the full detective thinking process when facing a new or difficult worry.

* Continue to use problem solving when an anxious situation arises.

CHAPTER 7

Troubleshooting Stepladders

Learning to manage anxiety can be challenging. Stepladders are the most important component of overcoming anxiety. However, there are many ways in which stepladders can be difficult. We don't mean that you can harm your child. Rather, there are some ways of doing stepladders that are really effective and other ways in which they may be less effective. We now discuss some of the problems you might come across when using stepladders and some ways of overcoming these problems.

Getting Stuck

With the gains they are making, regular praise from others, and the chance to earn rewards, most children enjoy stepladders and make rapid progress. However, some children may find the going tough, and things may not go as smoothly as you would like. Children may get stuck on a step and refuse to try the next one, they may move through the steps very slowly, or they may want to give up on the stepladders altogether. If this is the case for your child, there are several things you can try.

First, summarize the progress that your child has made so far by repeating the last few steps that they have successfully done. Use this opportunity to really praise your child for their efforts and the gains that have been made. You may need to repeat this process several times to build up your child's confidence in their capacity to face fears.

Next, revise the detective thinking skills in relation to the new step. In particular, look carefully for any underlying worries your child may have. There may be unforeseen worries that your child has not admitted to that need to be dealt with before your child can move on.

Then, brainstorm ways in which the next step can be broken down into slightly smaller steps. This is especially important if your child has been moving along well and all of a sudden has become stuck. In this case, it is very possible that the next step is just too big a jump. Create variations of the step by changing where it is done, who is present, how long the situation lasts, or use any other element that you can change to make the step easier. For example, if the step that is too hard is taking a message to the school principal, you may be able to make an easier step by asking which other teachers in the school would be less scary to approach, and then have your child deliver messages to the teachers in their order of scariness. If your child unexpectedly finds a step too hard, rather than abandoning the step attempt, ask your child, "What's a small step that you could do right now to make it a little easier?" This might lead to an idea to role-play a step, or a way to break the step down to get a quick smaller step done. For example, if the step was to order a milkshake, a small step might be buying a bottle of water (as this might be less worrisome as it is less likely that the clerk will ask questions). Once the water is purchased, and the child has had a small success, they can try the original planned step again as they are likely to feel more confident.

Finally, if your child is "stuck" and progress has stalled, ask yourself whether you have been holding up your end of the bargain. Have you been rewarding your child as promised? Have the rewards been consistently delivered? Have they been given immediately? Have you been praising your child and putting effort into the program? You need to be very honest with yourself about the answers to these questions. If you are not consistent and do not support and reward your child as promised, you cannot expect them to take the program seriously. If this is the case, it is never too late to get back on track.

It is sometimes the case that children just run out of steam with the process of stepladders and get bored with the same old rewards that are being offered. The initial excitement that often comes with starting a new activity, picking rewards, and working on something together might just have worn off for the moment. If this is the case, it is often possible to get your child moving again with a bit of a reward kick start. Discuss the rewards you have set for each step with your child and see whether there are any that they might want to change. Perhaps setting the next one or two rewards as slightly bigger ones might provide the motivation needed to get your child going again.

Need for Reassurance

We discussed the issue of reassurance seeking in chapter 4. While seeking excessive reassurance can be a problem in many areas of an anxious child's life, it may become especially apparent during stepladders. When you do stepladders, you may find that your child constantly asks questions such as these: "What is going to happen?" "Exactly what time will you be back?" "Will you be okay?" Being a loving parent, it is very hard to ignore these requests for reassurance. But it is very important not to give in by providing too much reassurance for your child during stepladders. This does not mean that you need to be nasty or hard, but rather that you gradually need to encourage your child to rely more and more on their own judgment. At first when they ask such questions, encourage them to tell you what they think the answer is. If they have the wrong factual information, you can provide the correct information. If their answer is unrealistic, you can encourage them to work though detective thinking. If seeking reassurance is a persistent problem for your child, you may need to include it in the stepladder. For example, you may encourage your child to play at a friend's house as one step, allowing some reassurance questions, and then the next step might repeat the process but without allowing any questioning. It may be a good idea to go back to chapter 4 to reread the section "Ignoring Behaviors That You Don't Want."

Lashi's Example

*Lashi had been working on one of her stepladders for going to sleep in
her own bed with the light off. She was doing very well, was finally able
to sleep in her own bed all night, and was allowing her mother to turn
off all the lights in her part of the house. But there was still an anxious
habit that needed to be addressed. Every night when Lashi went to bed,
she would call her mother to her room four or five times before she
finally went to sleep. At these times, Lashi would ask a bunch of
questions such as "Are you staying home tonight?" "Have you checked
the doors and windows?" and "How long will you be up?" Lashi's
mother was answering all of these questions because she was so pleased
with Lashi's progress. But she soon realized that she was going to have to
work on this reassurance seeking because it was stopping Lashi from
getting to sleep. Lashi and her mother discussed how they could include
these questions in Lashi's stepladder. They decided that at first, Lashi
could call her mother into her room twice before she went to sleep. After
that, her mother would ignore her. At the next step, Lashi could only call
her mother into her room once after going to bed. Then Lashi and her
mother would go through Lashi's detective thinking before Lashi went to
bed, but she could not call her mother after going to bed. Finally, Lashi
was rewarded only for going to bed without any reassurance from her
mother either before or after going to bed.*

Dealing with "Failure"

Anxious children seem to have more sensitive "failure" detectors than
other children, so the importance of a minor setback in doing a simple task
will be greatly magnified in their eyes. This can be a blow to their confidence and may increase the level of anxiety about attempting any further
steps or even things they found quite easy to do before. Many anxious children easily slip into negative self-talk such as "I'm hopeless; I knew I couldn't
do anything right."

If your child tries one of their steps and suddenly finds that it is too hard, or the outcome is not what they expected, they may see this as a complete failure. If this happens, it's important to encourage your child to do some detective thinking about the importance of the success or failure of these efforts. Role reversal is a particularly good source of evidence to use. In other words, ask children to imagine what they would say to someone else who was in the same position. Try to point out that there is no real failure in doing stepladders. Each attempt is an opportunity to learn. If they were not able to do that step, it simply means that the step was too hard and they need to break it down into smaller, easier steps. If something unexpected happened, like a friend said no when invited over to play, focusing the detective thinking on whether the no meant "I don't like you" or whether there is another explanation, such as the friend was already busy that day, will help your child to evaluate their "failure" more fairly.

On the other hand, some anxious children actually get worried about being successful because then they might have to do even better next time. In other words, for some kids, doing a good job makes them feel under more pressure for next time. If this is true for your child, you may find that they play down or even completely deny their successes. This tends to happen with very perfectionistic children, in particular. You will need to stress to your child that doing stepladders is what counts—not winning or being the best. Again, remind your child that there is no way to fail stepladders—they just need to do them. You may also want to include some stepladder exercises aimed at reducing any perfectionism, such as making deliberate mistakes, looking messy, or learning something that they are not naturally good at.

Taking On Too Much

A different sort of problem arises if your child is trying really hard to please you and to be the "perfect child." In this case, you may find that your child will choose stepladder steps that are just too hard. Sometimes it is so easy for you to get caught up in the excitement that you begin to encourage your child to take on harder and harder steps and the process might begin to go a bit too quickly. It is important to praise your child for their enthusiasm. Having a child who wants to try hard is wonderful. But you also need to remind your child that everyone is individual and that there are no prizes for being the first to finish. Encourage your child to try each step at least once rather than skipping steps. For the top steps on a ladder, repeating the steps is particularly important as it is only with repetition that your child will have the opportunity to believe that what they predicted would go wrong does not happen, not just once, but every time they try the step.

Speeding Through

In some cases, children can have a sort of breakthrough—in other words, by facing one or two situations that they may have avoided for years, they get a sudden burst of confidence and lose their fears very quickly. If this happens, it can be wonderful.

However, other children complete individual steps too quickly—that is, the actual attempt at the step is done as quickly as is possible, such as running down the hall grabbing the toy from the dark room, and running back to the light again. This may be a sign that they are not learning anything from the step. On the one hand, it may mean that the steps are just not challenging enough for your child. If this is the case, you will need to sit down together and come up with some more difficult steps. On the other hand, the steps may be so difficult that your child is not willing to stay in the situation long enough to learn that nothing bad will happen. Or it may be that your child is "cheating" a little and not fully engaging in each step. If this is the case, you need to encourage your child to redo the steps but include more detail in the instructions you give. For example, you may need to specify how long your child stays in the situation (enough time to find five different toys), or teach them such things as where to sit and how much to say so that the conversation lasts.

Ethan's Example

One of Ethan's big fears was going to parties and having to mix socially with other kids. After doing stepladders for a while and gradually building his confidence, an opportunity came up when he was invited to a party at a friend's house. Even though this was pretty scary for Ethan, his parents encouraged him to put it on his stepladder and give it a try. When Ethan came home after the party, his father asked him how it went. "Fine" was all he said. Something in his tone made his father think that it all seemed too easy. So he asked Ethan to sit down and tell him exactly what he had done at the party. Ethan looked sheepish and admitted that he had gone to the party as they agreed but had spent the entire evening sitting in a corner watching everyone. Ethan got his reward, as agreed, for going to the party, but his parents suggested that next time he would need to make sure he mixed with some of the kids. When the next party came up, the step was not only to go to the party, but to make sure that Ethan spoke with at least three different kids while there. This time when he got home, Ethan said that it had been pretty hard, but he was also surprised at how much he had in common with one kid there and they had actually gotten along quite well.

Ups and Downs

During the stepladders process, there will be some days that seem better than others and progress will not always be smooth. You should act as a coach to encourage your child to do the best they can do on any given day and to keep trying the next day. On bad days, it may be better to repeat a step already achieved than to try a new, more difficult step. Rewarding good attempts as well as success at achieving the step will encourage your child's ability to persist and to tolerate what they see as failure.

Worried Sick

Most parents and therapists would agree that anxious children and adolescents "wrote the book" when it comes to excuses and explanations about why they can't do something. A common, and sometimes the most difficult, problem for parents to deal with is complaints of illness at times of stress. Headaches, sore stomachs, and "feeling sick" are difficult to deal with when you are not sure of the cause. And sometimes parents or caregivers disagree with each other about the reason for the complaints.

Consultation with the family doctor is a necessary first step to exclude physical problems. This is especially important if there is disagreement between you and other adults over the cause of the complaints and the most appropriate way to manage them. Once physical causes have been ruled out, anxiety management skills can be applied.

When your child complains of aches or sick feelings, first, acknowledge that the physical symptoms are real and are unpleasant but that they are not in danger. Encourage use of relaxation (see chapter 9) to reduce physical tension and complete detective thinking with a focus on evidence that the "tummy ache" is not dangerous and is something that they can cope with and push through. Then create stepladders where the steps ask a child to complete activities even though they have a "tummy ache." When making a stepladder for a child that includes steps where a child persists despite being uncomfortable, the steps should be ordered not only on how much worry is expected but also how much pain/discomfort the child is anticipating.

It is important that there is a consistent approach taken by everyone involved. In families where the parents are separated and the child moves between two households, these issues will need the involvement and agreement of all the adults involved in the child's care. In addition to parents, teachers, school administration, and the school nurse will also need to be on board.

In families with a history of physical illness, where there may be strong anxieties about physical pain, those worries will need to be dealt with first. If this applies to your family, you may need to work through your concerns about this issue. Try to use detective thinking about your own concerns about your child's health. Look at the realistic consequences of both encouraging your child to challenge their fears and of allowing the avoidance to continue and perhaps worsen.

Lashi's Example

As Lashi moved through the program, Lashi's mother decided that it was time that she started to go out and leave Lashi at home with a sitter. On the first night that she was getting ready to go out, Lashi began to cry and throw a huge tantrum. She became so worked up that she vomited. Lashi's mother ended up canceling the sitter and staying home. Lashi began to experience stomachaches and feel sick every time her mother wanted to go anywhere and even on some days when she had to go to school. Sometimes Lashi got so worked up that she would, again, make herself physically sick.

As a first step, Lashi's mother took her to the doctor to get a full checkup. "All clear" was the doctor's diagnosis: "This is a healthy little girl." After that, Lashi's mother told her that when they worked on the stepladder, they would do whatever they had agreed on whether or not Lashi felt sick. Lashi's mother contacted the school, and they agreed that if Lashi felt sick at school, she could go to the nurse and rest for a while and then she would go back to class. Lashi's mother would not come and pick her up unless she had a fever.

Soon after, Lashi's mother was asked to a party. Lashi and her mother discussed the situation and decided that this was a reasonable step for the stepladder. However, on the night of the party, Lashi began to feel sick and have pains. Lashi's mother told her that she understood how hard it all was and that she really felt bad about her pain, but that she was going to go to the party anyway. She gave the sitter detailed instructions about how to handle Lashi and to call her only if Lashi had a fever. That night was hard for both Lashi and her mom, but in the morning Lashi got a big reward for doing her step from the stepladder.

Lashi's mom went out on two more occasions with the same results. It was not easy, but they both stuck with it.

Finally, on the fourth time, Lashi was not sick when her mom went out. Even though she was still scared, she did not throw up and did not complain of stomachaches. To celebrate, Lashi got an extra reward in the morning.

Smart Tricks

People can reduce their fear by using behaviors such as carrying a lucky charm or special toy, by wearing certain lucky clothes or taking a mobile cell phone, by humming a song or chewing gum, or by going through a particular ritual such as insisting on a certain bedtime routine which includes particular words that must be said when saying good-night. These tricks are used to either decrease the risk of something going wrong or because of a superstitious belief that the item will help. All these methods of avoidance are used by adults, including sports stars and actors, and they are often used by anxious children.

These beliefs and behaviors can act as subtle ways of avoiding facing up to the feared situation. If your child uses any of these subtle types of avoidance, the big risk is that they may not believe that a success is due to their own ability. Instead, your child may attribute success to the special object or ritual.

To properly overcome anxiety, your child needs to experience the fear, use the detective thinking techniques to assess the real level of danger, and then experience the situation to learn that there was no need for that level of concern. Your child must be able to credit their subsequent lack of fear to a real lack of danger, not to the magical protective powers of a lucky charm, a crystal, or special socks.

Children with separation fears are increasingly reliant upon having instant access to their parents (e.g., via the mobile cell phone), and this is a subtle type of avoidance. In other words, separating from a child but having them in regular possible contact with you through the phone does not allow the child to learn that their anxious prediction was wrong. You may find that your own anxieties can play a part in this overreliance on immediate contact as well. Look carefully at the line between safety issues and the convenience of being in reasonable contact with each other, on the one hand, and a subtle avoidance of dealing with fears about separation, on the other.

Safety strategies and superstitious behaviors are especially common in children with obsessive-compulsive fears. These children have often developed very subtle rituals and magical ways of doing things that they believe can protect them from danger. For example, your child might count to a magic number under their breath, might touch things in a particular way, or might move in a certain pattern. These things may be very hard to see, and as a result you will probably not be aware of all the rituals that your child does. It is important to regularly ask your child about these types of activities. The best question is to ask your child after every step of the stepladder, "Is there anything you could have done differently that would have made it harder?" If they report using a smart trick, make sure that doing the step again without the rituals or objects is part of the stepladder.

A special example of subtle avoidance might be found in children who are taking medication for their anxiety. If your child is on antianxiety medication while doing stepladders, it is very possible that they will think, "The only reason I could do that was because my medication helped me through it." In this case, your child may not be building their own confidence but instead will be learning that they can only cope with the help of a drug. Use detective thinking and add evidence gathered from your child's doctor about what the medication actually does (e.g., helps the body to create the chemicals it needs to make different emotions) and what it does not do. Help your child discover that it is still them who chooses to do the step, who makes the decisions along the way of what to say and do, and who shows independence and confidence.

The existence of lucky charms, aids, or medication is not a major problem. It simply means that the stepladder steps will need to be repeated at some point without these things. In the case of charms or other aids, you can actually organize the steps so that they are each done the first time with the aid and then repeated without it. In the case of medication, your child may need to complete all or most of their anxiety program while taking the medication. Then, when improvements seem to be going very well, you may want to begin to reduce the medication under the guidance of the prescribing physician. Once the medication has been stopped, you will need to go through a few of the stepladder steps again, just to convince your child that they really are in control.

Talia's Example

Talia had been working on her stepladder of going swimming for some time and was getting really confident in the water. Talia's dad really wanted to be involved and had taken a very active part in the whole process. As part of his involvement, Talia's father had been going with her to all of the steps of her stepladder. Each time Talia went into the water, her dad would stand outside and watch her. Talia regularly waved to her dad and would look at him a lot. On one occasion, Talia was at the beach swimming and having a great time. Her dad decided to go off to get ice cream. When he returned, Talia was out of the water and crying. She screamed at him, "Where did you go? I might have drowned!" Talia's father suddenly realized that by being with her for all of her steps, Talia had learned to use him as a safety cue. As a result, Talia's anxious prediction that she would drown if she went into deep water had never really been tested because her dad was always there to protect her. Talia and her dad discussed the problem and decided that she needed to start over and redo most of her stepladder but this time without her dad being there. Going through the stepladder the second time was much faster, and it wasn't long before Talia's confidence in the water was sky high.

PARENT ACTIVITY: Reviewing Early Attempts at Facing Fears

Visit http://www.newharbinger.com/49913 to download this worksheet.

Looking at your records of your child facing fears, list the successes they have had.

_____

_____

_____

What rewards did your child receive for these successes?

_____

_____

_____

What rewards did your child receive for putting in effort on the not-so-successful attempts?

_____

_____

_____

What types of problems did your child have in completing their steps?

_____

_____

_____

What could you do to overcome these problems?

_____

_____

_____

Could you see any behaviors, magical objects, or ways of doing things that your child might have used to help them get through the activity? Did you ask your child what could have made the situation more frightening?

_____

_____

_____

What steps might you need to add to ensure that they face their fear?

_____

_____

_____

Obstacles to Your Child's Progress

In addition to difficulties that your child may face when attempting to manage anxiety or when working on steps, there are also other difficulties that could undermine your child's progress. Some of the possible obstacles are discussed below.

Not Enough Time for Stepladders

Insufficient time is a very common problem because most family members have very busy lives. Continuing improvement will require the prioritizing of stepladders, detective thinking, and other new skills so they can be structured into your and your child's life. Eventually, the time required for consistent practice will decrease. Remember, the more practice there is, the more the skills will be used naturally in other areas of life. Your child will experience less anxiety and they will be able to use anxiety management skills independently. We encourage families to reduce another of the child's commitments while working on stepladders. This may mean reducing the number of extracurricular activities for a few months.

Alternatively, if your child practices some steps after school, that may mean, on that day, they do not need to do all or part of their school homework or a chore. Similarly, be fair to yourself. If you have spent time in the afternoon helping your child complete steps, reward yourself with a takeout dinner. The idea is to balance the amount of hard work that is needed each day so that the fun and relaxing times are not lost to the stepladders (even if that means that the bed sheets don't get changed this week).

Limited Parent Motivation to Create Opportunities for Steps

To maintain motivation for anything, we need to provide ourselves with incentives to keep going. You need to reward yourself for your efforts in helping your child manage their anxiety. Reviewing your child's records about the successes they are having can help maintain your motivation. Success increases motivation; you may need to remind yourself of the small successes that will eventually make up the big success that your child is working toward. You may want to look back at "Children's Activity 3: My Goals" in chapter 1 to remind yourself (and your child) of the changes your child is aiming for. Your motivation may also increase if you use the anxiety management strategies to address any of your own unrealistic anxieties, if relevant, because you will get firsthand experience of the positive effect of the practice.

KNOWING WHEN TO PUSH (ANXIETY VERSUS DISINTEREST)

Knowing when to push will involve trusting what your child is telling you. Older children will often be able to tell you when their refusal to do a task or enter a situation is due to anxiety or disinterest, but you may need to ask them. But sometimes children will say that they aren't interested in something when they are really stopped by fear. For example, a child who is invited to a party where there are other kids they don't know well might say that the party will be boring or uncool, when really it is worry that is getting in the way. You will need to think carefully about whether your child really isn't interested in these things or is simply anxious. Your child may have particular cues that are familiar to you that tell you when they are feeling anxious and worried or simply disinterested. Get to know these cues to help you distinguish between anxiety and disinterest. You may find it useful to look at the cues you discovered in the first weeks of the program.

If you do find that reluctance to do a task or enter a situation is due to anxiety, try to problem solve what might be getting in the way (e.g., the steps may be too big). Remember to reward your child when you are gently pushing them, and combine steps with rewards regularly. Finally, if you are not sure whether your child is anxious or really is bored with doing something, it may be best to challenge your child to do it anyway. Tell your child that if they are bored with the step, this will be the easiest way ever to have earned a reward.

You may also need to ask yourself whether you might have some worries about how much to push your child to try something a bit harder. Often there may be a "soft" and a "hard" parent, disagreement between you as parents, or one parent opting out of the treatment plan. These can all reduce your child's enthusiasm and send mixed messages about whether your child really needs to face their fear. Try to talk these issues over and agree on a joint strategy to help your child. If you find it hard to be "tough" and push your child, you may need to try some of the detective thinking on your own worries. As long as you continue to show your child that you love them, some pushing will not cause your child to hate you or to become mentally scarred or damaged. Remember that being a little tough now will help your child become more confident in the long run.

Taking Over Because It Is Easier or Faster

There will be times when you are tempted to take over. Try not to give in to this temptation! Remember to challenge your own anxious prediction—ask yourself what will really go wrong if you don't step in and help out this minute. Children need a clear and consistent message that it is okay for them to face their fears and that they can do so independently. Remember that when your child does something that is close to what you want, this should be praised or rewarded too.

Parent Anxiety, Beliefs, or Expectations Getting in the Way

Some parents find that their own unrealistic anxiety gets in the way of allowing their children to participate in stepladders or other everyday activities. You may worry that your child won't be able to cope, that the situation is unsafe, that your child will miss out on something important if you do not step in, or that you will damage your relationship with your child if you ignore their feelings. Anxious children can be very sensitive to their parent's concerns. If you are personally worried about the next step or are not totally convinced about the value of stepladders, you may accidentally be giving your child subtle messages that are interfering with their progress.

If this is true for you, we encourage you to apply the anxiety management strategies that you have taught your child to your own worries. Modeling your own efforts to face your own fears will be a powerful message to your child that they can also manage anxiety.

One of the biggest difficulties for anxious parents will be trying to decide what is a reasonable thing for their children to do alone and what is really dangerous. For example, should you let your child walk home from school, stay home alone, go to that party, and so on? This is a time when getting feedback from other parents can be really useful. Talk to other parents whose children are in the same situation and get their opinion. And don't forget to do your detective thinking—look for evidence about what sorts of things are actually likely to go wrong.

Your own beliefs and expectations about different situations can be difficult to recognize because often they have been around for a very long time and they influence what you do without you thinking about it. A simple example of how a belief influences the way we behave would be that we automatically make coffee each morning because we believe that we won't be able to function without it. Your beliefs and expectations can influence your child's progress. For example, if a parent believes that authority figures are "superior," they may not expect a child, who gets anxious when speaking to the principal, to face this fear. Similarly, a parent may expect a child to be "perfect" at particular tasks such as schoolwork or sports because that parent believes that when their child makes a mistake, it reflects negatively on the child and on their parenting ability. This parent might not want their child to make mistakes as part of a stepladder that aims to reduce the child's need for perfection.

Being aware of such beliefs or expectations is the first step to reducing their impact on your child's progress. Try to problem solve ways to reduce the influence of your beliefs and expectations on your child, such as doing your own detective thinking about that belief or, if your child's fear also reflects a fear of your own, doing the stepladder tasks with your child. If you feel that your anxiety, beliefs, or expectations are a significant obstacle to your child's progress and it is too difficult to manage independently, it is worth seeking help from a professional who can work through the issues with you.

ACTIVITIES TO DO WITH YOUR CHILD...

CHILDREN'S ACTIVITY 21: When the Going Gets Tough

Talk with your child about the common difficulties that can occur when facing fears. These include steps that are too hard or too easy, steps that haven't been described well, having really worried thoughts when facing a step, not staying in a situation long enough for fear to start declining, moving on to the next step before the previous one was mastered, forgetting where you are on the stepladder, not giving yourself rewards, and using tricks to reduce the amount of worry experienced during the step (such as listening to music or going somewhere, but only with a friend). Help your child to identify possible solutions to these problems in the following ways:

- Use coping skills in preparation for each step.

- Be persistent and do a lot of practice.

- Keep records (as much to make sure that you follow through with rewards as anything else).

- Do each step until it is, or nearly is, boring.

- Revise steps so that they always feel challenging but not impossible.

Visit http://www.newharbinger.com/49913 to download this activity.

CHILDREN'S PRACTICE TASK 6: Doing Steps

Once again, work with your child to create written plans on what steps will be attempted in the coming week(s). Also remind your child to use their cue cards during steps and, when needed, to use detective thinking and problem solving as ways of managing anxiety. (Visit http://www.newharbinger.com/49913 to download this practice task.)

CHAPTER HIGHLIGHTS

In this chapter, you learned possible solutions to some of the common difficulties that can be faced when working through stepladders include the following:

→ revising stepladders and rethinking rewards when you get stuck;

→ reducing reassurance to ensure that children learn they can cope alone;

→ using detective thinking to deal with "failed" steps;

→ making sure steps are not too big or too small;

→ accepting that there will be good days and bad days;

→ persisting despite physical symptoms of illnesses; and

→ being vigilant about finding safety strategies that children may be using to reduce the anxiety that they experience during steps.

Some of the obstacles that can interfere with progress include the following:

* not dedicating enough time to working on stepladders;

* not providing enough opportunities to do steps;

* being unsure of when to push your child to try the next step;

* taking over because it is easier; and

* demotivating children with your own anxieties or beliefs.

Your child will need to do the following:

* Identify any problems or difficulties that they have had when working on their stepladder and revising the steps to fix the problems.

* Continue to work on steps from their stepladders, using other anxiety management skills to help with any fears or worries that arise. (By now, you should really be encouraging your child to move on and up the higher steps.)

CHAPTER 8

Social Skills and Assertiveness

Developing social skills and assertiveness is very useful, particularly for children who have social anxiety or socially based worries. If this is not your child, if they are generally confident, can ask for help, and tell people to stop if needed, then you do not need to complete the activities in this chapter. Instead continue to work on the core skills of detective thinking, problem solving, and stepladders.

The Importance of Social Skills

Most anxious children are perfectly competent at making friends and interacting with other people. However, some anxious children find it hard to interact with others in a successful or skilled manner. Sometimes this can make other children and even adults react negatively to these children by ignoring them, rejecting them, or even teasing them. As you can imagine, if this happens, it makes it even more difficult for an already anxious child to learn to be more confident.

Ethan's Example

Ethan spends most of his spare time alone. Even at school, you will find him on his own. He rarely speaks to his classmates. At lunchtime, he usually goes to the library and sits alone, reading a book. Sometimes he walks around the school and stops to watch some of his classmates playing soccer. They never ask him to join in. In fact, they don't notice that he is there. Ethan would love to join in, but he can't think of how to ask and he is afraid that they will laugh at him or refuse to let him play. He returns to the classroom after lunch and sits at the back of the class hoping not to be called upon to answer any questions. He doesn't speak to the other students. He really likes the girl who sits in front of him in science class. He would love to talk to her, but he can't think of what to say and is afraid that he would get it wrong and feel stupid. The teacher is going around the class asking everyone to give an idea for the school festival. Ethan thinks it would be a good idea to run a coconut stall where you win a prize for knocking the coconut off a stand. Ethan's turn comes. He looks down at his desk and mumbles, wishing that he could disappear. He tries to explain his idea to the teacher, but his voice is too quiet and no one can hear him. The teacher moves on to the next person in the class.

After school, Ethan walks home alone. One of his classmates goes home the same way. Ethan notices that the boy has dropped his school folder and the pages are flying around. Ethan wants to offer to help but is not sure what to say. He walks past, leaving the boy to pick up the papers on his own.

The next day, Ethan is standing in line at the school cafeteria, waiting to buy some lunch. Another boy pushes in front of him, leaving Ethan feeling angry. He would love to tell the boy to go back to the end of the line, but he does not say anything.

Why Are Social Skills and Assertiveness Important?

Children need to be successful in a wide range of situations with other children and with adults, including parents and teachers. For example, with other children, they need to be able to hold conversations, ask to join in games or activities, and invite other children to play or to come over for a visit. They need to be able to ask questions, listen to what other children say, ask to take a turn in a game, give compliments, offer toys or items to other children, and assert their rights if they are unfairly treated. All these activities are important if children are to make friends and be accepted into their peer group.

Children also need to be able to handle adults. For example, they need to be able to ask for help when they need it, offer to help, express their point of view, pick the right moment to interrupt, answer questions, and start and maintain conversations with adults. When you think about it, there are an enormous number of social tasks that children have to be able to perform in a competent way. By the time children reach adolescence, there are an even greater number of social situations that they have to learn to handle, including romantic relationships, getting through job interviews, and keeping a job.

The skills that we need in order to perform these social tasks successfully are called *social skills*. Our research shows that some anxious children perform more poorly than other children on many social tasks. There are two possibilities as to why this might be the case. It might be that some anxious children are too afraid to use their skills. In other words, they might know what to do, but their anxiety stops them from doing it. Alternatively, some anxious children may not have developed their social skills because they have less experience and practice at interacting with other children. Many anxious children avoid interactions with others and therefore have less opportunity to practice how to interact with other people. Whatever the explanation, our research has shown that there are significant benefits to teaching anxious children social skills in order to improve their relationships with others. Anxious children also tend not to be very assertive. Assertiveness is the ability to express your needs, to assert your rights with other people, and to stick up for yourself in a way that produces a positive outcome.

The Building Blocks of Social Skills

There are five main areas of social skills: body language, voice-quality, conversation, friendship, and assertiveness. These skills generally build on each other, with the skills listed first being needed before the latter skills can develop.

Body Language Skills

Eye contact: Child looks others in the eye during conversations to show that they are listening and paying attention but does not stare excessively.

Many anxious children avoid making eye contact and tend to look down or away when talking to others. This may be seen by others as indicating unfriendliness and lack of interest. It's also a problem if children make too much eye contact during conversations and stare at others too much, as this makes other people feel uncomfortable.

Posture: Child sits or stands in a way that's appropriate for the situation.

Some postures, such as being slumped, hunched up, turning away from the other person, or being excessively rigid and upright, may create a poor impression on others.

Facial expression: Child's facial expressions are appropriate to the situation. They smile and have a friendly face when talking generally with others and use sad and angry facial expressions occasionally, appropriate to the situation.

Facial expressions communicate how we are feeling. Bored, angry, or fearful facial expressions or lack of smiling may be seen by other children and adults as a sign of unfriendliness.

Voice-Quality Skills

Tone and pitch: Child's speech is usually friendly, expressive, and pleasant to listen to. The child can use different tones of voice to communicate different emotions.

If a child's voice sounds boring, aggressive, fearful, whining, or is unpleasant to listen to, then this may lead to misunderstandings with other people who may misinterpret the tone of voice, thinking the child unfriendly, aggressive, or uninterested. Children need to be able to use a friendly tone of voice in most situations.

Volume: Child's volume of speech is appropriate for different situations.

Children need to be able to speak up so that they're heard and yet not to speak so loud as to be inappropriate. Many anxious children speak too quietly, which interferes with their communication with others.

Rate: Child speaks at an appropriate rate—not too quickly and not too slowly.

Very slow speech may sound boring. Very fast speech is hard to follow.

Clarity: Child speaks clearly and is easy to understand.

Conversations are difficult if a child's speech is hard to follow. Some anxious children tend to mumble and have difficulty speaking clearly enough that others can understand them.

Conversation Skills

Greetings and introductions: Child says "hello" or other greeting when meeting people they know. For older children, the ability to introduce themselves to others is important.

Most children know what to say when they greet someone, but they may be too anxious to do so or they may not do so in a socially skilled way. In all conversation skills, children must remember to use the basic skills of eye contact, appropriate facial expression, and clear, audible speech.

Starting conversations: Child is able to start a conversation by asking simple questions or making simple statements.

Some anxious children avoid starting conversations with others. They tend to be quiet most of the time, particularly with people they don't know well. This makes it difficult for them to form friendships with other children.

Holding conversations—answering questions: Child listens to what the other person has said and answers with some detail rather than with very brief answers.

Some anxious children give very short answers when other people ask them a question. The information that they give does not convey the message that they would like to continue the conversation or are interested in the other person.

Holding conversations—asking questions: Child asks appropriate questions of the other person to allow the conversation to continue. The questions are likely to be of interest to the other person.

Children need to be able to ask questions in order to continue a conversation. Not asking questions often gives the impression that they are not interested and don't want to mix with the other person.

Holding conversations—taking turns: Child takes turns in conversations, listens to others, and then replies with an appropriate comment or question.

Two-way conversation skills are important if children are going to form friendships. Sometimes anxious children tend to interrupt or talk over the top of others in their attempts to get their answers out at all costs.

Choosing topics of conversation: Child picks appropriate topics of conversation.

It is important that children can pick conversation topics that the other person is interested in and that are appropriate to the situation. Anxious children often have difficulty thinking of things to talk about. They need to learn about the types of things that other children are interested in if they are going to form friendships.

Using polite conversation: Child uses polite speech and says "please" and "thank you" as appropriate.

For most children, this is not a problem, but we mention it because the rules of polite communication are an important factor in determining the impression that children make upon adults (e.g., teachers) and peers.

Friendship Skills

Offering help or items: Child offers to help other children or adults, or offers to lend or give items where appropriate.

Forming friendships requires that children can show kindness to others. One part of this is to be able to offer to help others when they need it. Friendship involves giving and receiving help of various kinds. Some anxious children will stand by and do nothing when they really want to help. This may then be misinterpreted as unfriendliness and lack of caring.

Offering invitations: Child invites other children to join in with activities or to come over to their house.

Friendships involve spending time together and making an effort by showing that you would like to make friends. Offering invitations to others and initiating activities is part of this process.

Asking to join in: Child approaches other children to ask to join in their activity.

Many anxious children are reluctant to ask other children if they can join in their activity. Often they really want to join in, but they stand on the edge of the activity watching because they may not know what to say or may be too afraid to try for fear of looking foolish or being rejected.

Expressing affection: Child expresses affection toward children and adults where appropriate, either using speech or physical gestures such as holding hands, hugs, gentle touches, and pats on the back.

The ability to show affection is important in forming friendships with peers. This can be something very simple and physical and does not have to be verbal.

Giving compliments: Child gives compliments to others (adults and children) when appropriate.

The ability to give positive feedback to other people is an important part of friendship. It shows interest in the other person and makes that person feel good. This is just as important in children's friendships as it is in adult relationships.

Showing caring when others are hurt or upset: Child tries to help others and to care for them when they are hurt or upset.

Children need to be sensitive to other people and to show that they care when others are hurt or upset. Children cannot always do something to help, but they may try to check that the other person is okay and try to comfort that person in some way, which might be physical (e.g., a gentle touch), a spoken comment, or by asking someone else to help.

Assertiveness Skills

Sticking up for one's rights: Child is able to stick up for their rights without causing harm to other people.

There are many situations in which children have to learn how to stick up for themselves. There will be times when other children or adults try to take advantage of them, do not attend to their needs, or try to pressure them into doing something that they don't want to do. Anxious children tend to be unassertive and have difficulty sticking up for their rights. However, if children are too active in asserting themselves, then this may become aggression. In all instances, it is important that children deal with these situations in a way that does not cause harm to other people. Assertiveness requires communication of clear messages, in a loud, strong voice (but not an aggressive one). It requires being able to say how one feels and exactly what one does or does not want to happen. If a problem is too difficult to solve, the child may need to actively seek help from an adult.

Asking for help or information or expressing needs: Child is able to ask for help or information and can inform others when they need something.

At school, it is particularly important that children can ask for help, clarification, or information from their teachers when they need it. Problems may arise if children remain silent when they need help. Children also need to be able to request help from their peers.

Saying no: Child is able to refuse unreasonable requests and to say no when they wish to do so.

It is important that children are able to say when they don't want to do something. They need to be able to say how they feel and to refuse unreasonable requests from others. Some children may find themselves doing things that they don't want to do or having things taken from them because they have not clearly stated how they feel or clearly communicated the answer "no."

Dealing with teasing: Child is able to deal successfully with teasing from others.

All children have to deal with teasing. They need to be able to put a stop to excessive teasing and to learn not to become too hurt by it. Of course, if it is very frequent and severe, you and your school will need to become involved. Children need to know that it is okay to tell a trusted adult what is happening and to ask them for help in dealing with excessive teasing.

Dealing with bullying: Child is able to stop attempts at bullying by others, either by using their own strategies or by seeking the help of others.

As with teasing, all children will encounter incidents of bullying at some point in their lives. However, no child should have to put up with bullying, and below we will discuss various ways in which children can put a stop to it. Again, parents and schools need to become involved if the bullying continues. Children need to know that it is okay to tell a trusted adult what is happening and to ask them for help in dealing with bullying.

PARENT ACTIVITY: My Child's Social Skills

Observe your child carefully over one week and check their performance against the social skills building blocks. Performance does not need to be perfect, but make a note if you think lack of a skill is causing problems in your child's relationships with others. Remember the social skills that children use are different from the ones that adults use. Try to think about whether your child's skills seem comparable with those of other children of a similar age. It may also be helpful to talk to teachers about your child's social skills with peers and in class, as this may differ significantly from home. (Visit http://www.newharbinger. com/49913 to download the worksheet for this activity.)

Which of the following social skills does your child need to work on?

Body Language

☐ Eye contact

☐ Posture

☐ Facial expression

Voice Quality

☐ Tone and pitch

☐ Volume

☐ Rate

☐ Clarity

Conversation Skills

☐ Greetings and introductions

☐ Starting conversations

☐ Holding conversations

☐ Answering questions

☐ Asking questions

☐ Taking turns

☐ Choosing topics of conversation

☐ Using polite conversation

Friendship Skills

☐ Offering help or items

☐ Offering invitations

☐ Asking to join in

☐ Expressing affection

☐ Giving compliments

☐ Showing caring when others are hurt or upset

Assertiveness

☐ Sticking up for one's rights

☐ Asking for help or information or expressing needs

☐ Saying no

☐ Dealing with teasing

☐ Dealing with bullying

Teaching Social Skills

There are many ways in which you can teach social skills to your child. The strategies that you use for teaching will depend on how much difficulty your child has in using social skills. Some children have just a few areas of difficulty. Others may have poor performance in many of the skills described in "The Building Blocks of Social Skills" section above. For those children who have just a few areas of difficulty, we use a strategy called *incidental teaching.*

Incidental Teaching

Incidental teaching involves using opportunities that occur in everyday life to teach a particular skill rather than having special teaching sessions that are dedicated to training your child to use social skills. Incidental teaching involves

- identifying social situations in which particular social skills are needed;

- explaining to your child that a particular skill is needed in that situation and how it should be performed;

- explaining why it is important;

- checking that your child has understood what is needed;

- prompting your child to use the skill;

- praising your child for attempting to use the skill and describing what they did well; and

- giving your child gentle feedback about ways in which the skill could be improved.

When you use incidental teaching, it is important that you keep things really simple and stick to one skill at a time. Children become confused if they have to concentrate on too many things at once. When an appropriate situation arises, decide which skill is most important. Make sure that the skill is not too difficult and that your child has learned simpler skills first. Incidental teaching of social skills can easily be included in your child's stepladders.

Hayley's Example

Hayley's parents noticed that she rarely made eye contact with other children or with her teachers. Hayley tended to look down or away when other people spoke to her. Hayley and her father had to attend a parent-teacher evening at the school. Her father suggested that Hayley work on making eye contact with her teacher during the interview. Hayley and her father discussed why it was important to make eye contact and how this influenced the impression that people make on each other. Hayley understood what was required and laughed when she found herself making eye contact with her father. Just before going into the classroom for their interview, Hayley's father prompted his daughter to remind her to use eye contact with the teacher. During the interview Hayley tried hard, and her father noticed Hayley making occasional eye contact with the teacher. Once they were alone again, her father told Hayley how well she had done and how he had noticed the big improvement. They talked about how it had felt and about other situations in which eye contact would be important.

Helping Children Who Need More Intensive Teaching

Some children will need more intensive teaching in order to learn to be more socially skilled. Here are some guidelines about how to teach social skills to your child using a more structured approach. The teaching methods are basically the same as for incidental teaching. For each skill, you will be using the following teaching methods:

- instruction and explanation

- practice and prompting of the skill

- feedback

- praise

For some children, it can be difficult to know which skills to teach and where to start. We believe that children need to work on each small skill and then gradually put them all together to create a good performance. That is why we talk about the social skills building blocks. We suggest that you start with body language skills, and when your child is good at these, move on to conversation skills, and so on.

When you are teaching social skills to your child, they may feel a bit uncomfortable and embarrassed, so it is helpful to use games and enjoyable activities. Humor is also a good way of reducing anxiety and making the sessions enjoyable. However, it is important to laugh with your child and not at your child.

GIVING INSTRUCTIONS

Ideally you should focus on just one skill at a time, and that skill becomes the theme of the session. When you teach a skill to a child, you need to begin by giving information about the skill. In particular, you need to give information about the following:

- Exactly what is involved in the skill—how is it performed?

- Why is it important—what happens if the skill is not used?

Having discussed the skill, it is important to then demonstrate how the skill is performed. You can regard yourself as a bit like a coach in a sports situation. You can demonstrate the skill yourself or find some real-life examples to show your child. For example, you could watch other people in a shopping center or on television and discuss how they are using the skill.

It often works well to show what happens when the skill is *not* used. This can produce some comical situations. For example, you can hold a conversation with your child without using any eye contact. You can then discuss why eye contact is important and how your child felt while you were doing this. Another activity might be to sit in a café together and look for people who don't use social skills well. A fun idea, especially with younger children, is to watch their favorite television show with them and see who can pick out examples of good and bad skills the quickest.

The instructions phase is more difficult with younger children. It basically consists of giving prompts or requests for use of the skill (e.g., "I am going to ask you a question, and when you give your answer, I want you to use a loud, clear voice so that I can hear what you say. Can we try that now?"). With younger children, you can also demonstrate skills by using puppets (e.g., two puppets can be used to show how to say "hello" and ask questions of each other). You can also use puppets to demonstrate appropriate eye contact and voice volume. Keep asking your child what they think of the puppet that didn't use the skill and how they would react to that puppet.

Often the main problem is that children simply do not realize that they are not using their social skills. Helping them to check themselves to make sure that they are using their skills is important. It is also helpful to remind them that using good social skills helps children to make friends. This may help to motivate your child.

PRACTICING BODY LANGUAGE AND CONVERSATION SKILLS

Once you have explained to your child how a skill should be performed and the possible downsides of not doing so, it's time to practice using the skill. To begin with, it is best to practice in the safety of your home where things can't go too wrong. And in the same way that you need to practice hitting a tennis ball in order to become a good tennis player, progress in social skills will only be made with regular practice. Ideally, your child should practice every day.

In the teaching of the simpler social skills, such as body language or conversation skills, we suggest that you practice using short conversations together. One fun way to do this is to develop a set of practice cue cards.

Conversation topics are written onto the cue cards and prompt a short talk between you and your child during which each skill can be practiced. For example, one time you might use the cue cards to work on eye contact—your child would pick a card from the top of the pile and start a short conversation with you while making sure they keep good eye contact. On a different occasion, your child might pick another card and this time focus on increasing voice volume.

Here are some examples of cue cards that you might find useful while you practice the social skill:

- What is your favorite movie? Now tell me what the film was about.

- What is your favorite book? Now tell me all about the story in the book.

- Tell me about your favorite hobby.

- Pick someone in your family. What exactly does this person look like?

- Tell me about what you did last weekend.

- What is your favorite TV show? Explain to me why you like it.

- Ask me some questions about when I was a child.

- Ask me about people in my family.

- Ask me about where I would like to go for a vacation.

When you are teaching a new skill, it is important to stick to one skill at a time. Only move on to teaching the next skill when your child is able to perform the first one reasonably well. When you do move on to a new skill, keep prompting your child to remember to use the body language and voice skills that they have already learned. For example, when you are teaching your child to ask questions when they meet another child for the first time, here are some prompts you can give: "Pick a topic they might be interested in, make clear eye contact, use a friendly facial expression, and ask your question in a clear, loud voice."

Also, spend some time talking with your child about how to choose appropriate topics for starting up a conversation. For example, topics might include a TV program, a sports team, the local news, movies, pets, hobbies, or asking about other people (e.g., their family, their opinion, their favorite activity). Together with your child, you might like to make a list of topics that children at school tend to talk about in their free time.

When your child has learned the basics of body language and conversation skills, you can move on to teach more complicated social skills relating to making friends and assertiveness. In addition to the teaching methods that we have already described, there are two additional techniques for coaching your child in more complex social skills. These teaching methods involve problem solving and role play.

ROLE PLAY

Role play involves creating an imaginary situation in which you and your child act out a scenario. The idea is for your child to practice their social skills by attempting to deal with a pretend situation. The aim in role play is to make things as realistic as possible. Before children can start to practice in real-life situations, it's best for them to practice in the safety of their home, with someone they trust (you).

Here are some examples of situations that you can role-play with your child. In the more complex situations, you may need to problem solve the scenario first. Choose from the following scenarios to role-play with your child:

- *Starting a conversation.* A new student starts in your class. You decide to ask this new child what their name is and where they come from. (Parent plays the part of the new student.)

- *Starting a conversation.* The teacher asks you to do an errand with a student who you don't know very well. You have to walk over to the school office together. (Parent plays the part of the other child.)

- *Maintaining a conversation.* You start at a new school and are sitting in the playground. Another student comes over and sits down in the next seat and asks you how you like the school. You have to answer and then ask them a question. (Parent plays the part of the other child.)

- *Asking to join in.* The teacher instructs all the children in the class to find a group and help to produce a poster for the school open house. You look around and see that the other kids have already gotten into groups. Problem solve how you might go about joining one of the groups. Role-play how you might approach a group of classmates and ask to join in. (Parent plays the part of another child in a group.)

- *Asking for information.* A parent tells you to go into the local store and buy some tomato sauce. You can't find it and have to ask the store clerk where it is kept. (Parent plays the part of the store clerk.)

- *Asking for information.* You don't hear what the teacher says when they give an instruction in class. You have to ask the teacher to repeat the instruction. (Parent plays the part of the teacher.)

- *Offering help.* A classmate drops their homework papers all over the ground, and you decide to offer to help to pick them up. (Parent plays the part of the other child.)

- *Giving a compliment.* You want to give a compliment to the student sitting in the next seat in class. The other student has done some really excellent artwork. (Parent plays the part of the other child.)

- *Offering an invitation.* You have won a couple of free tickets to go to the movies. Problem solve how you might invite someone from your class to go along to the movies. Then role-play the chosen response. (Parent plays the part of the other child.)

- *Offering an invitation.* You have a birthday party coming up. Brainstorm how you might go about inviting some classmates or other children. Then role-play how to offer the invitation. (Parent plays the part of a classmate.)

- *Owning up.* You borrow a ball from a kid on your street and then lose it. Brainstorm possible solutions to this problem and decide upon the best solution. Imagine that you decide to tell the other child about having lost the ball and explain that you have brought a new ball to replace it. Role-play this situation. (Parent plays the part of the other child.)

- *Apologizing.* You drop your parents' favorite plate in the kitchen, and it breaks. You are clearing up the pieces when one of your parents walks in. Brainstorm this situation and work out the best solution. Imagine that you decide to apologize to your parent and role-play this scenario. (Parent plays the part of the parent.)

- *Asking for information.* Your teacher assigns some work in class, and you do not understand what you are supposed to do. Brainstorm different solutions to this problem. You wait behind after class and ask the teacher to explain. (Parent plays the part of the teacher.)

- *Saying no.* Another child is trying to convince you to loan out your favorite possession. You are worried that they will break it and know that you should say no. (Parent plays the part of the child trying to borrow the item.)

- *Sticking up for yourself.* A parent yells at you for breaking a window, but you didn't do it. Brainstorm possible solutions to this problem and decide upon the best solution. Imagine that you decide to explain that you did not do it. Role-play this situation. (Parent plays the part of the parent.)

- *Dealing with teasing and bullying.* Specific strategies are discussed later in this chapter in the section "Dealing with Teasing and Bullying."

GIVING FEEDBACK AND PRAISE

When children are learning new skills, they can only improve if they're given feedback about whether their performance is correct or whether some changes need to be made. When children start to practice their new skills, they may not be very competent at first. It's really important that you look for good things in their performance and give them plenty of praise for trying. They must not feel as if they've failed. You should praise early attempts even if they are doing only a little bit better; expect them to get better and better over time. In particular, you need to focus on the good things about your child's performance and tell your child what they did well (e.g., "That was a great try. I really liked the way you smiled when you told me your name"). If you are giving feedback about something that needs improvement, this should be phrased in a gentle and encouraging way. For example, if your child is not making eye contact during a conversation, you could say, "Well done. I really liked the questions you asked. Now try that again and see if you can look at me just a little."

Practicing in the Real World

Once your child is able to use these new social skills at home in practice sessions with you, they will need to practice them in real-life situations. For example, they can practice their skills at school, when you have visitors to your home, when out shopping, during out-of-school activities, or at other people's homes. It is important that you set some small homework tasks for real-life practice after each session. These tasks need to be simple and relatively easy to perform. There is no point in children trying something far too hard and then failing miserably. They will not be likely to try again in the future, and their worst fears will have come true. You might want to talk to your child's teacher and explain to them about the program you are doing. The teacher might have some good ideas about very simple social tasks that your child could try. Some teachers might even organize a small group situation for your child where practice would be easier.

Some real-life tasks in which to practice specific body language or voice skills in the real world could include the following:

- Say good morning to the teacher.

- Say hello to a particular child (preferably pick a sociable, friendly child to begin with).

- Ask a question of a relative when they come to visit.

- Practice asking questions with a brother or sister.

- Ask a particular child what their favorite TV show is.

- Ask a particular child whether they have any pets.

It is a good idea to organize these practices into a stepladder just like you are doing with your child's feared situations.

Only one task should be set after each home practice session. It is helpful to write the task down on a card and put it somewhere visible to remind you both. The card should describe what the task is and with whom, where, and when it is to be performed. Then the card should have a space to record when the task was completed and any difficulties encountered. The practice cards can be used with most children over the age of seven, depending on reading and writing abilities. With very young children, you may need to prompt the practice of skills by attending playgroups or activities with them.

It is also a good idea to prepare children for ways of handling situations in the event that they do not work out well. For example, it can be devastating to ask to join in a group for the first time only to be rejected by the group. You need to prepare children to use their detective thinking to handle things if their early attempts are not very successful. It is also important for you to help children set realistic goals that are within their capabilities. Many anxious children will be only too ready to interpret a reasonable attempt as failure. If possible, you might want to ask the help of a teacher who can prompt your child on the first couple of occasions. Teachers may also be able to observe from a distance and increase the chance of a successful outcome by discreetly arranging the situation.

Combining Social and Anxiety Management Skills

Once your child begins to practice these skills in real-life situations, it is important to remember that this part of the social skills program should fit together with the anxiety management methods that your child has learned, including detective thinking and stepladders. In many cases, learning to deal with new social situations should become part of your child's stepladder. Your child should not be pushed to tackle a social situation when it is still too difficult for them, though. If a particular social skill is still too difficult, remember to break this goal down into smaller, simpler steps. For example, if your child is working on the skill of eye contact, a mini-stepladder might look like this:

Mini-goal: To look a person in the eyes while doing the following tasks

Mini-steps:

- Talk to my teacher for thirty seconds; look at her at least three times.

- Pick up a takeout meal that my family ordered and look at the person when I pick up the order.

- Talk to my neighbor for two minutes and keep good eye contact with her.

- Talk for a minute with my sports coach; make eye contact.

In addition, many of the stepladders that you and your child have planned will include social contacts. It is very important to remind your child to use these opportunities to practice their social skills.

Creating Social Opportunities

In addition to teaching social skills, parents can help by setting up opportunities for children to practice their social skills. Anxious children often avoid places such as clubs where children have the chance to interact with each other. For example, many anxious children protest at the thought of going to a social or activity club, church groups, study groups, chess clubs, or sports clubs. It is a good idea to make a list of all of the social clubs and activities for young people in your area or at their school. Libraries, government services, other parents, or the Internet might provide some of this information. Together with your child, you can work out which club or activity would be of greatest interest. You may find quite a bit of resistance to the idea from your child. However, it is really worth encouraging your child to attend events where they would be with other children. You might be able to help by arranging contacts with another family whose child belongs to a particular group. Remember, if it seems too frightening for your child to do this, then it is a useful thing to do. However, you will need to create a stepladder with attending the club or group at the top and break it down into smaller steps.

Dealing with Teasing and Bullying

Sadly, anxious children who are quiet, unassertive, and possibly awkward can sometimes become a target for bullies. Luckily, most anxious children are not teased or bullied, but if they are, this can really add to their worries and can lead to poor self-esteem and depression. It is important to explain to your child that they must tell you if they are being bullied. If you discover that your child is being teased or bullied, acting quickly and calmly to help your child deal with the problem will be very important.

How to React as a Parent

Bullying and teasing are an unfortunate part of the reality of childhood. As a parent, your first instinct when hearing about bullying will probably be to get angry and you will want to step in and see that the bully is appropriately punished. However, this will not necessarily stop your child from being picked on in the future, and it probably won't make your child feel better about themself. When you realize your child is being teased or bullied, you need, first of all, to show concern and sympathy for your child—they may not want you to do anything (yet), but may just want to talk it through. Do not let *your* hurt, pride, or anger get in the way of helping your child to solve *their* problem. Make sure you give your child permission to swear and say things that they would not normally be allowed to say at home so that they can talk about all that is happening. Talking about it will help to take the hurt and shame out of the teasing.

In the case of teasing, often you will need to help your child to work out whether the other child is trying to be friendly and fooling around (even though that child's behavior has been hurtful) or whether the other child is being cruel. If it's the former, then you need to help your child to learn to laugh along or to be honest that the teasing has upset them (in other words—to be assertive). If it's deliberate cruelty, then you need to help your child to work out a different way of reacting so that they can take control of the bully's game. In some instances, bullying takes the form of being excluded from peer activities, having possessions destroyed or hidden, or having rumors spread. In our time of social media, you also need to be aware of whether you child is experiencing online bullying. Regretfully, some children experience physical bullying—being hit, pinched, or hurt in some way—or they may receive threats rather than physical actions. All forms of bullying require firm action on your part and no child should be expected to put up with this.

It is important to involve school personnel if your child is not able to stop the teasing within a short space of time or if the bullying is online or in any way physical. Most schools have bullying policies—give the school a chance to implement their policy but ask when you should check back with them, and do so. Be persistent but never accuse any person of being incompetent or uncaring—it will not help your child's situation. Expect the school to take action, but do not be surprised if they suggest changes for your child, including how your child interacts with other children. Although teasing and bullying should not take place and the responsibility for stopping it is with the bully, bullies choose easy targets—that is, those children who are not assertive and who get upset or angry when teased. By teaching your child to outsmart the bully, you are providing them with constructive strategies for self-protection.

How to Outsmart a Bully

Depending on the type and severity of bullying and how long it has been going on, there may be things that your child can do to reduce the problem. You may be able to help them to apply the "outsmarting-a-bully" tactics to their unique situation. Remember that every child's situation is different and what works for one child might not work for another. Our aim is to encourage children to respond in a calm and confident way that diffuses and then puts an end to a situation—even when they do feel hurt or upset.

If the bullying is not severe, then children may be able to use the following approaches to outsmarting a bully:

- Your child's motto needs to become "Do something different." Bullies tease and push to get the typical reaction of fear, sadness, or anger from their victims. Doing anything that shows the bully that the tease hasn't bothered your child will take the "fun" out of teasing. Brainstorming ways of doing things differently and practicing new responses can be helpful in building your child's confidence. For example, a child might ignore the bully, walk away, laugh at themself (it is rarely a good idea to laugh at the bully), or pretend not to hear.

- Rather than reacting to the tease in an emotional way, children can learn new responses or comebacks. For example, if a bully says, "You're a fat pig," rather than yelling, "I am not, you *!@$," a very confident child might respond, "What! I was aiming for enormous elephant this week; I'll have to keep trying." Such a response injects humor and usually confuses the bully enough to make time for the child to move out of the line of fire. For anxious children, it is unlikely that they will be able to respond with this type of humor, but they can learn to respond with a short, nonthreatening phrase before moving away from the situation.

- For example, your child could respond, "Thanks for letting me know" and keep walking or turn away. It is important that your child is not nasty, rude, or aggressive to the bully since this might simply make the situation worse. Rather, your child can diffuse the situation and show the bully that what was said doesn't hurt (even if at first it does). Other simple comebacks include "Yes, I am good at that," "You could say that," "True, I do wear glasses," or "Yeah, whatever."

- You will need to have your child practice using the comeback, particularly focusing on saying it with a neutral, bored tone. Perfect this at home before trying it with a bully. Practice in a role play and then practice spontaneously. Say a tease while eating dinner, traveling in the car, or watching TV and have your child respond. Use a lighthearted manner, slowly increasing the severity of your tone (but not aggressive or overly hurtful) so that your child gains confidence with responding to each tease. Once they feel confident and can say it instantly, have your child practice at school.

- Children need to stay close to a sympathetic audience such as friendly children or teachers. It can take some planning to work out who will be sympathetic or, for example, how to stay close to others when walking home (children might need to change their route slightly). Discussing how to limit who they are interacting with online is equally important.

- Work on assertiveness and ensure your child can give a clear and confident "No" before they move away from a situation and toward safe people or places.

- Teasing and bullying does lead to anger, hurt, and sadness. Just because we want your child to look unfazed, does not mean that the hurt and sadness don't exist. Allow your child to talk about their experiences. Listen to their story, empathize with their frustration, anger, and sadness, and celebrate their successes in shutting down teasers and bullies. If you notice that your child is believing the teases or you hear unrealistic worried thoughts when they talk to you (such as "I'm stupid and no one will ever like me"), you can use detective thinking to find evidence and a new, more realistic calm thought to have in response to the bullying (such as "My real friends like me and they know that I am smart").

- Using these techniques takes practice and planning. Even though you will probably find this very hard to do, one excellent practice is for you to role-play being the teaser so that your child can practice a new way of reacting or a new comeback until they are able to do this easily. Once your child can do these things without thinking, they can use them in real life. Try hard to keep the practice humorous so that your child does not become distressed. The aim is for them to gradually learn new strategies.

- Before your child tries the new approach, it can be helpful to discuss what to do if the bully doesn't back off. A good attitude is that if at first you don't succeed, try again—with small changes to the plan. *However, it is important to remember that if the teasing doesn't stop, or if it escalates into bullying, the school and professional help need to be involved.*

ACTIVITIES TO DO WITH YOUR CHILD...

There are no specific activities in the Activity Book to use for developing social skills and assertiveness, as each child's starting point differs. Follow the instructions in this chapter to explain to your child what the skill is and why it is needed, to practice and prompt use of the skill, to provide encouraging feedback on developing skills, and to praise and reward improvements for each skill that you identified as needing work for your child.

If your child is struggling with teasing and bullying, complete the following activity. (It is also available for download in the Activity Book at http://www .newharbinger.com/49913.)

CHILDREN'S ACTIVITY 22: Outsmarting Bullies

Talk with your child about the different ways to outsmart a bully (described above), including talking about it to someone you trust, getting an audience who may help if needed, doing something differently than you would normally, being able to say "No" assertively, and developing comebacks that you can say to end the conversation. Emphasize that when they interact with a bully, they need to seem like they are bored by and not bothered by the interaction.

Ask your child to think of some things that have been said to them (or to friends) as teases, then work together to come up with an action plan of how they will respond differently next time. Have your child practice the action plan in role plays and spontaneous practices with parents or siblings, before trying it with a bully.

CHAPTER HIGHLIGHTS

In this chapter, you learned...

→ Social skills are important, and children need to develop certain types of social skills to be successful.

→ Social skills build on each other, and children need to know basic skills such as eye contact before they can successfully learn more difficult skills such as starting a conversation or giving a compliment.

→ There are different ways of teaching social skills, such as discussing appropriate skills, and using modeling and role play. The latter can be a good way to teach children who have more extensive difficulties.

→ There are different ways of outsmarting bullies, including talking to reduce the hurt, staying close to friendly children and adults, planning ways to react differently when teased or bullied, and learning comebacks to use in response to a tease.

Your child will need to do the following:

* Work with parents to practice behaving assertively in everyday situations or, for children who struggle more extensively with social skills, practice one new social skill at a time using role plays at home and then in the real world.

* Work out an action plan for responding to teasing and bullying, practice the plan, and then implement at school.

* Continue to work on stepladders and continue to practice other anxiety management skills such as detective thinking and problem solving. (Your child should be quite a way up a few of their stepladders by now.)

CHAPTER 9

Relaxation

Learning to relax is very useful for all children, but especially for those who experience chronic muscle tension or whose bodies react intensely when anxious (e.g., racing heart, breathing really quickly, sweating a lot, or getting very shaky). If this is *not* your child, then you do not need to complete the activities in this chapter. Instead continue to work on the core skills of detective thinking, problem solving, and stepladders.

Skills for Relaxation

All children experience physical tension in their bodies when stressful things happen. Different children experience physical tension in different ways. Often it involves muscle tension and tightness, and it can affect different parts of the body, such as arms, shoulders, back, or forehead. Some children may have stomachaches, headaches, sleep difficulties, and muscle pains in response to this physical tension. Feelings like these can make it difficult for children to use good coping skills, as they become too tense to concentrate on using their skills. If your child often experiences a high level of physical tension, it may be helpful to teach them how to reduce these reactions to a level that allows them to use their other anxiety management skills.

One strategy that children can use to reduce physical tension is relaxation. During relaxation, our body's reactions change so that our heartbeat slows down, our breathing becomes calm, and our muscle tension decreases. Signs of muscle tightness, such as headaches, may also gradually disappear. An added advantage is that our thoughts become calm and peaceful, blocking out anxious and worrying issues. These reductions in body tension and worrisome thoughts produce an emotional feeling of calmness and well-being. It's difficult to feel really anxious at the same time that you feel really relaxed. Relaxation might be especially useful for those children who find it difficult to use their other coping skills.

Some of the different ways that children can learn to relax include listening to soothing, peaceful music; meditation; relaxing imagery; muscle relaxation exercises; deep-breathing exercises; yoga; and massage. This chapter aims to teach your child to relax by progressing through a series of steps that build awareness of muscle tension and then focuses on learning to relax all the muscles of the body while using calm breathing. Finally, we add a variation to the process that allows a child to rapidly relax in situations where they are anxious. We have also included some very simple meditations to calm and relax their mind. You can add these into the relaxation sessions.

Teaching Your Child to Relax

One of the best ways to teach children how to relax is to have the whole family involved in practicing and using the relaxation exercises. The method that is presented here combines a variety of techniques, and you are welcome to adapt the exercises to suit you and your family.

Before you start to teach your child how to relax, there are a few points that we need to discuss that will help you in these teaching sessions.

Relaxation Is a Skill

Like all new skills, relaxation exercises have to be practiced regularly in order to be performed well. For the first couple of weeks, you and your child will need to practice every day. To encourage you to practice regularly, we suggest you ask your child to keep a written record of their practice sessions using the Relaxation Practice Record in the Activity Book (which you can download at http://www.newharbinger.com/49913). Ask your child to complete the record every time they practice (on their own or with you). It's a good idea to keep the form clearly visible in a place where you are likely to see it each day (such as the refrigerator door). This will help remind both you and your child to do the relaxation practice.

At first, children may find it quite difficult to relax, and it will take at least a week of daily practice for your child to relax well. The practice sessions do not need to take very long, ten to fifteen minutes should be long enough. Once your child it able to do the body relaxation task quite well, then you can introduce the meditation tasks, if you both wish to do so. However, it is important to keep up daily practice of the body relaxation skills while you go through the other steps in this chapter. Relaxation can be a useful technique for children to use when they are still learning other anxiety management skills, and it can give them confidence that they have some skills to help them to cope when they have to do things that they find scary or stressful.

Pick the Right Time

There are several things that you can do to make learning to relax an enjoyable activity. It is important to pick the right time to practice. We suggest that you pick a time when there are no other important things to do, and set up a family routine that helps to make sure that the practice actually happens. For example, don't pick a time when your child's favorite TV show is on, when it's meal time, or when schoolwork needs to be done. If you are thinking of inviting visitors over, make sure that it won't conflict with relaxation practice. Many families decide to get up ten to fifteen minutes earlier each day to do their relaxation practice. Others may set aside time before their child goes to bed. Before bed is often a convenient time, but you need to make sure that your child isn't too tired and therefore unable to concentrate on learning the skills. Using relaxation as a way to get to sleep is fine, but practicing relaxation needs to be done at a time when your child can concentrate.

Make the Time

It is easy to allow relaxation practice to be pushed out by other activities such as homework, sports, TV, and just general living. Setting aside a regular time for relaxation benefits the whole family. It makes everyone in the family aware that life can easily be taken over by the kind of rushing around that stops us from looking after our emotional well-being.

Create a Habit

One of the best ways of making sure that relaxation practice takes place is to make it a daily habit. Gradually, relaxation will become an automatic activity that is built into the family routine like brushing teeth. Try not to miss days, and have a stand-by time that can be used if your regular practice time is not possible.

Create a Relaxing Environment

When your child is learning to relax, you need to create an environment that will encourage relaxation. The area needs to be quiet and one where you will not be disturbed. It is important to put all phones on silent and to put all mobile devices well out of reach. The place of practice needs to be warm and comfortable. You can use a bed, a comfortable chair, or a mat or towel on the floor. But if you use a bed, make sure you and your child do not fall asleep. Relaxation practice is easier if you and your child wear comfortable, casual clothes. Some families like to put on some quiet, calming music. Children respond well to relaxation music, and it may be useful to set the scene for practice by putting this type of music on quietly in the background.

Use Praise and Make It Fun

As with all the skills in this book, you will need to use plenty of praise to encourage your child to practice. Remember to give praise for trying, not just for succeeding in relaxation. As much as possible, make relaxation time an enjoyable, fun experience. There are plenty of ways to make relaxation practice interesting, including using imagery meditations where children can imagine themselves in peaceful, relaxing situations, such as magical islands, secret gardens, sailing ships, and so on.

Keep It Simple and Short

Children tend to lose interest quickly and find it hard to pay attention for long periods. With young children, it is better to practice more often for shorter periods, such as five minutes at a time. You also need to use simple language (as we have done in the sample script below) so that your child can understand the instructions.

Teach by Example

In the "Steps to Relaxation" section below, you will find a series of exercises for learning relaxation skills. Depending on the age of your child, you will probably need to be the teacher of these skills. Some older children and adolescents find it difficult to accept instructions and guidance from their parents and prefer to read through instructions and practice the skills on their own. However, one of the best ways to teach young children how to relax is to show them how to perform each step. This involves actually demonstrating each step by doing it yourself. It is really important that with each step, you explain exactly what you are doing and why you are doing it. That way, children gradually learn to quietly say these instructions to themselves and can eventually instruct themselves to use the relaxation methods.

The Final Goal

The goal is for children to be able to use their skills to relax when they become afraid and when they try to face difficult situations. However, it is important to learn the skills really well at home first. Happily, a habit of daily relaxation for the whole family creates a calm atmosphere at home that benefits everybody.

Steps to Relaxation

There are several steps to teaching your child to relax. We have provided some sample scripts below to help you explain the ideas to your child. Of course, you don't have to read these scripts exactly, and if you want to change the words to better suit your style or use words that your child understands better, that is perfectly all right.

Step 1. Learning to Tense and Relax the Body

One of the best places to start is to learn the difference between being tense and being relaxed. The instructions for step 1 follow. The words in italic are the instructions you should say aloud to your child. You need to perform the actions you're describing as you give your child these instructions. (The words in square brackets are additional prompts for you and should not be read aloud.) Remember to use a calm, relaxed, and gentle voice while you give the instructions.

Before you start the relaxation task, explain to your child what relaxation is and how it can help with reducing body symptoms of anxiety. Guide your child through step 1, and then incorporate practice of this activity every day for approximately three to four days. You can read the relaxation script we provide below during the practice session, but also consider making a recording of the relaxation instructions (given in italics) so you don't need to read them out each time. Alternatively, older children and teens, if they have good reading skills, can read the script (in italics) aloud in their own voice and audio-record it. It can be a fun thing for them to do.

SUGGESTED SCRIPT

When we are scared or worried, our muscles often get very tight and tense. This can happen anywhere in our body, and it can happen in different parts of the body for different people. Your muscles can start to feel tight or stiff, or your fists or your jaw might be clenched. In this exercise, you will learn to find parts of your body that feel tight or tense, and then you will learn how to relax them.

Before we start, make yourself comfy and quiet, and close your eyes. If you can, lie on your back and have your hands down by your side. Otherwise, sit back in a comfy chair. Make sure that you don't have any devices switched on that can disturb you over the next ten minutes.

First of all, I want you to feel what it is like when your muscles are really tense and tight.

Watch me first. I take a deep breath...scrunch up my face...push my shoulders up into my neck...tighten up my arms and legs...clench my fists, and curl up my toes. I hold this while I count to four, and then I let go...1...2...3...4...and breathe out, like a big sigh. [Give a big, loud sigh as you breathe out]. I let all my muscles go floppy so that they are relaxed.

Now you try. Tense up first. Take a deep breath...scrunch up your face...push your shoulders up into your neck...tighten up your arms and legs...clench your fists, and curl up your toes. Even your face should be screwed up. Make your body go stiff all over. Imagine that you are a robot. Hold it there while you count to four...1...2...3...4...and now let out a big breath with a big sigh.

How did your body feel when it was really tight? Which part of your body was the most tensed up? [Listen to what your child says here and give praise for paying attention to their body signals.]

Good—it is really important that you can feel when your body is tightening up.

Let's try that again. Take a deep breath in and really try to tense up every muscle in your body: your legs, arms, fists, face, push up your toes. Count to four while you hold it tight: ...1...2...3...4. Now a big breath out, like a sigh, and let go of all your muscles in your body. Let your whole body go all floppy so that your hands drop back by your side. Let your arms and legs go limp and loose. Your body should feel just like a rag doll—all floppy, limp, and loose. Or you could imagine that you are a jellyfish, just a large lump of floppy jelly. [Keep your voice very soft, calm, and gentle while you say the next words.] Just let your body go really, really floppy. Let all tension and *tightness drift away. Relax now just for a couple of minutes. Quiet and relaxed. Just breathe nice and gently.*

[Let your child relax for one to two minutes.]

Good—now in a moment, I am going to ask you to slowly open your eyes. I will count to ten, and when I get to five, I would like you to open your eyes. Then, when I get to ten, I'd like you to slowly sit up. Ready? Okay...1...2...3...4...5. Now slowly open your eyes. And...6...7...8...9...10. Now slowly sit up. Try not to put all the tension straight back into your muscles. Try to stay relaxed. You did really well.

How did your body feel when it was floppy? Which part of your body was the most relaxed? [Listen to what your child says here and give praise for paying attention to their body signals.]

Were there any parts that were still tightened up?

Good—it is really important that you can feel when your body is tense and when it relaxes. Everybody is different, and you can learn what works best for you.

That is enough today for this first task, but we'll need to practice it a few times over the next three to four days. Then you will be able feel the difference in your body's muscles when they are tense compared to when they are relaxed. There are lots of times when we get tensed up, like when we are frightened, nervous, worried, or angry. Relaxing helps you to feel better in difficult times. Learning to relax is just like learning to ride your bike or to roller skate or anything else. You have to practice, and bit by bit, you will find that it gets easier to do.

That was a really good start. Well done.

[Talk about a good time to practice over the next three to four days, and about filling in the Relaxation Practice Record, which you can download at http://www .newharbinger.com/49913.]

It is best to practice this short task each day over the next three to four days, repeating the instructions above. It is important to practice tensing and relaxing the whole body until your child is very good at telling the difference between being tense and being relaxed. Immediately after relaxation, you might ask your child to show you which parts of the body felt the most relaxed and which still felt tense.

You should also get your child to keep a record of how relaxed they become each time they practice, using the Relaxation Practice Record in the Activity Book (which you can download at http://www.newharbinger .com/49913) or create a table with these headings: Day of the week, Where did I practice?, What parts of the body were still tense?, and How relaxed did I get? *Not at all, a bit, or very?*

Step 2. Learning to Relax Each Part of the Body

[Begin with a quick reminder about the previous step, and the quick instructions about getting comfortable, switching off devices, etc.]

SUGGESTED SCRIPT

Now that you have learned about tensing up and then relaxing your body, we're going to do that one time quickly and then learn some ways to help your body to get even more relaxed.

So, let's start to really tense up your whole body. Take a deep breath in and try to tense up every muscle that you can: your legs, arms, fists, face, push up your toes. Count to four while you hold it tight...1...2...3...4. Now a big breath out, like a sigh, and let go of all your muscles in your body. Let your whole body go all floppy so that your hands drop back by your side. Let your arms and legs go limp and loose. Your body should feel just like a rag doll. All floppy, limp, and loose. Or you could imagine that you are a jellyfish, just a large lump of floppy jelly. [Keep your voice very soft, calm, and gentle while you say the next words.] *Just let your body go really, really floppy. Let all tension and tightness drift away.*

Now concentrate on the muscles in your arms. Try to feel what the muscles in your arms feel like and let them go really limp. Check your right arm first. How does it feel? Take in a gentle breath, and as you breathe out gently, let your right arm go very floppy. Let it become heavy and droopy.

Now move your attention to your left arm. Take in a gentle breath and as you breathe out gently, let your left arm go really floppy. Let it become heavy and droopy.

Check both of your arms now. Can you feel any tightness? If you can, then try to let your arms go even floppier. Even more relaxed. Relax. [Relax quietly for a minute.]

Now let's move on to the muscles in your legs. Get your mind to think about how your legs are feeling. Check your right leg first. How does it feel? Are there any parts that feel tight and tense? Start at the top of your leg and move your attention down to your toes, letting each part of your right leg go limp...and loose...and floppy. Take a gentle breath in, and as you breathe out, let your whole right leg get really relaxed and maybe a bit heavy. Now, switch to your left leg. Start at the top and move your attention down your leg, letting each part get even more floppy until you get to your toes. Take a gentle breath in, and as you breathe out, let all the tightness and tension in your left leg drift away.

Now let's move on to the muscles in your head and face. Take a gentle breath in, and as you breathe out, let your face relax. Concentrate on relaxing the muscles in your face. Feel what your forehead feels like and let it go all limp. Now move your attention to your eyes and let them become heavy and droopy, gently closed. Relax your mouth and lips. How do your lips feel? Can you feel any tightness? If you can, then try to let them go all floppy. Even your tongue can be tense, so notice what your tongue feels like and relax it. You can relax your whole face and head now, really relax. [Relax for a minute.]

[Continue to keep your voice very calm and peaceful, speaking rather slowly. When you say words like "relax," "calm," and "floppy," make your voice sound very relaxed.]

Now we are going to relax our neck and shoulders. Breathe out gently through your mouth. Concentrate on the feelings of the muscles in your neck. There shouldn't be any tightness there. Just let your neck relax now. Take a gentle breath in, and as you breathe out, let your neck become really floppy. Really relaxed. Then your shoulders. How do they feel? Let the muscles there go all floppy.

Last of all, we can relax our chests, tummies, and backs. We will do three breaths here as you relax your chest, then your tummy, and then your back. Each time you gently breathe out, relax the muscles as you come to them.

Take your thoughts to your chest and relax down through your chest.

Breathe in...2...3...4. Relax your chest while you breathe out...2...3...4. Really relax.

Now take your thoughts to your tummy and relax down through your tummy.

Breathe in...2...3...4. Relax your tummy while you breathe out...2...3...4. Really relax.

Good, now take your thoughts to your back and relax down through your back.

Breathe in...2...3...4. Relax your back while you breathe out...2...3...4. Really relax.

Excellent. Now let your whole body relax for just a minute. Let yourself go all floppy and limp. Imagine that you are a rag doll that doesn't have any bones or *stiffness in its body. Let yourself go really limp and loose all over. Just concentrate on letting your body relax, really relax.*

Don't worry if other thoughts wander into your head. Just try to focus on letting your whole body relax. Keep your breathing nice and gentle, and each time you breathe out, ask yourself to relax a little bit more and a little bit more.

That's great. Now I'll be quiet for a couple of minutes while you continue to relax on your own.

[After one to two minutes, continue in a soft, calm, and gentle voice.]

Good—now in a moment, I am going to ask you to slowly open your eyes. I will count to ten, and when I get to five, I would like you to open your eyes. Then, when I get to ten, I will ask you to slowly sit up. Let's begin...1...2...3...4...5. Now slowly open your eyes...6...7...8...9...10. Now slowly sit up and stretch. How did that feel? How relaxed did you get? Not at all, a bit, or very? That was excellent. Well done.

[Talk about a good time to practice over the next three to four days, and at the end of each practice session, ask your child to fill in the Relaxation Practice Record (in the Activity Book available at http://www.newharbinger.com/49913). It is best to practice this task each day over the next three to four days, repeating the instructions above.]

It is important to practice going through the different muscle groups until your child is very good at relaxing all the parts of the body. Remind your child that learning to relax is like learning to ride a bike. The more you practice, the easier it will be.

Each time, start with the arms, move on to the legs, then the head and face, then neck and shoulders, and finish with the torso (chest, tummy, and back). Immediately after relaxation, you might ask your child to show you which parts of the body felt the most relaxed and which still felt tense. This will help you to identify any parts of the body that your child finds hard to relax, and then you can spend some extra time on relaxing this area in the next practice session. Although you are aiming for your child to feel very relaxed, this relaxation does not need to be "perfect."

Step 3: Relaxing Your Whole Body at Once

Once children can relax each of their body parts in turn, they can move on to relaxing more quickly by focusing on the whole body at once. Children learn relaxation skills at different speeds. Often it depends on how often they practice the skills. Some children are ready to move on to step 3 after just a couple of days of practicing step 2. Other children may need to work on step 2 every day for at least a week before they are able to relax each part of the body really well. But it is also important not to spend too many days on each step, as your child may become bored. As well as asking your child how relaxed they feel, you can check by very gently lifting up one of their arms while they are doing the task to see whether it gently falls back when you let go, or whether the arm is stiff and tense. We suggest that you and your child decide together when to move on to the next step. Following are the instructions for step 3:

SUGGESTED SCRIPT

Now that you can tell when your body is getting tense and tight, and you know how to relax your muscles, you are ready to learn to relax really quickly when you need to. This can be really useful if you are getting worried or afraid when you need to stay calm and relaxed. This time we won't be tensing up first or doing each part of your body separately. We're going to go straight into relaxing your whole body at one time.

[While you give the following instructions, keep your voice very calm and peaceful, speaking rather slowly. When you say words like "relax," "calm," and "deeper," make your voice sound very relaxed.]

Take a deep breath in. Hold it while you count to four and then let out your breath gently as you count to four. As you breathe out, let all the tension and tightness from your body drift away. Imagine that the tightness is drifting out through your fingers and toes...leaving your body feeling calm and peaceful.

With each breath in and then out, you can relax a different part of your body even further.

1. *Concentrate on your arms: Breathe in...2...3...4. Relax while you breathe out...2...3...4. Really deeply relaxing them.*

2. Concentrate on your legs: Breathe in...2...3...4. Relax while you breathe out...2...3...4. Even further relaxing.

3. Concentrate on your head and face: Breathe in...2...3...4. Relax while you breathe out...2...3...4. Relaxing your forehead, eyes, mouth, and tongue even more deeply.

4. Focus on your neck and shoulders now: Breathe in...2...3...4. Relax while you breathe out...2...3...4. Just letting any tension and tightness in your neck and shoulders drift away.

5. Think about your back, chest, and tummy: Breathe in...2...3...4. Relax while you breathe out...2...3...4. Really, deeply relaxing.

Now, go back to the top of your head and work downward, checking each muscle that you come to as you go from head to toes. Check if it feels at all tense or tight. Then, as you breathe out, say to yourself, "Relax" and let all the tightness drift away. Really relax now.

Starting at the top of your head, relax. Now relax down...through your arms and chest and down...past your back and your tummy and down through your legs, muscle by muscle, really relaxing. Relax...relax...relax. Down through your legs, past your knees and calves, through your ankles, and out through your toes. Imagine waves of tightness leaving your body through your fingers and toes, drifting out into the air, leaving your arms and legs feeling really relaxed and loose.

Let all your muscles go limp and loose now. All of them together. Let all the tightness leave your body so you feel really relaxed, further and further, deeper and deeper, more and more relaxed.

Imagine that you are that rag doll. All limp and loose and floppy. If anyone picked you up, your arms and legs would hang by your sides. There is no tightness anywhere in your body.

Good—now in a moment, I am going to ask you to slowly open your eyes. I will count to ten, and when I get to five, I would like you to open your eyes. Then, when I get to ten, I'd like you to slowly sit up. Let's begin...1...2...3...4...5. Now slowly open your eyes...6...7...8...9...10. Now slowly sit up. Try not to put all the tension straight back into your muscles. Try to stay relaxed. Good—how did you feel? How relaxed did you get? Not at all, a bit, or very?

[Talk about a good time to practice over the next three to four days. At the end of each practice session, ask your child to fill in the Relaxation Practice Record (in the Activity Book available at http://www.newharbinger.com/49913). It is best to practice this task each day over the next three to four days, repeating the instructions above.]

Step 4. Relaxing Really Quickly in Real-Life Situations

By now, you and your child (and family, if everyone is taking part) will be getting good at relaxing quickly and deeply. Once your child is able to relax quickly and effectively, they can begin to practice in real-life situations. It may take two or more weeks of practicing the first three steps above before you move on to step 4. At first, it may be too difficult to relax in stressful and frightening situations. It is best for your child to start by practicing the skills in real-life situations at times when they are not frightened. Then you can gradually teach your child to use really rapid relaxation skills in more anxiety-provoking situations.

The relaxation skills that we use in real-life situations involve very quick relaxation in a way that is not obvious to other people. These real-world relaxation skills can be used in all sorts of situations, such as in the car, at home, out shopping, in the classroom, and many other places where anxiety-provoking events occur. At first, you need to teach your child to use rapid relaxation at home, and then they can begin to apply it in other situations. It focuses on using breathing to quickly relax the muscles to provide control over the bodily symptoms of anxiety.

SUGGESTED SCRIPT

Now that you can tell when your body is getting tense and tight, and you know how to relax your muscles, you are ready to learn to relax really quickly when you need to. This can be really useful if you get worried or afraid and you need to stay calm and relaxed. When you do really fast relaxation, you don't tense up first, and you don't do each part of your body separately. You go straight into relaxing your whole body at one time.

[While you give the following instructions, keep your voice very calm and peaceful, speaking rather slowly. When you say words like "relax," "calm," and "deeper," make your voice sound very relaxed.]

Now we need to learn how to relax really quickly in situations when other people are around. Take a really deep breath and hold it tight while we count to four: Breathe in...2...3...4. Now breathe out slowly and gently...2...3...4...while you let all the muscles of your body relax together. That's good. Let's try that again.

Breathe in gently...2...3...4. Relax your whole body while you breathe out gently...2...3...4.

Breathe in...2...3...:4. Relax breathing out...2...3...4.

Let your whole body really, deeply relax.

Have a quick check to see whether any parts of your body are tight, and then relax those muscles as you breathe out. Try to stay really relaxed. Keep going with nice, gentle breathing, and relaxing.

No one knows what you are doing. They don't know that you are using your relaxation skills. But you know that you are in control of your muscles and tension. Think to yourself...I am in control...I can do this. I can relax, really relax. I can control my breathing...in...and...out...in...and...out...I can relax my muscles—really relax. No one knows what I am doing. I can relax, really relax.

Using the instructions above, try the procedure at home a few times. When you and your child have done this together, it is time for your child to practice this rapid relaxation outside the home. Decide together on some times and places to practice. A good place to start is a place where your child feels comfortable, such as when you are together in the car, sitting down in a café, or sitting in a shopping center. Remember to prompt your child to use the rapid-relaxation method and praise them for their efforts. Check how well they were able to relax.

When you think your child feels confident about using rapid relaxation, they can practice using the skills when they face frightening situations and feel tense or scared. The aim is for them to be able to use the skill themselves and to silently talk themselves through the task. This can be especially helpful as a coping skill when they come across a stressful or fearful situation when they are on their own. You can also prompt your child to use rapid relaxation as a coping skill when they are working on steps from their stepladders.

Using Meditation to Relax The Mind

Another useful strategy that children can use to help to calm themselves and to relax is the use of meditation and imagery.

Focusing on pleasant images or pictures in the mind is a useful way to relax even more deeply. Our imagination can help us feel deeply relaxed. Children often have very good imaginations and can relax beautifully with the help of imagery. When you give instructions for imagery, there are certain things that help. You need to describe scenes in a way that helps your child to conjure up the image in their mind. You need to describe exactly what can be seen in their mind—the shapes, colors, and textures— as well as the sounds that can be heard, the smells that are there, and any sensations from touch. Then you can ask your child to focus their mind on what else they can see, hear, and feel as they imagine being there in the scene. These details help to create a vivid image. Select scenes that will appeal to children and that are relaxing in content. The scenes should not be too lively or exciting. The aim is to pick scenes that are likely to produce feelings of relaxation, calmness, safety, and peace. Imagery meditations can be done sitting up or lying down, depending on where the child feels most comfortable.

The following is one example of this technique. Feel free to adapt the script to a place that your child knows and where they feel happy, calm, and safe.

SUGGESTED SCRIPT 1: *Lying Under a Beautiful Tree*

First, make yourself comfortable. Now you are going to use your imagination to relax your mind and your body. Close your eyes and listen to what I am saying. Try not to let your thoughts drift off onto other things, but don't worry if that happens. It is normal. Just try to pull your thoughts back to what I am saying.

Breathe in gently...2...3...4...and relax your whole body while you breathe out gently...2...3...4.

Breathe in...2...3...4. Relax breathing out...2...3...4.

Let your whole body really, deeply relax.

Imagine now that you are lying under a beautiful old tree in a warm, quiet place that you love. The place is very calm and peaceful. Everyone else is having a quiet time too, and nobody disturbs you. You lie in the shade on a blanket and let your body relax. Really relax. Try to imagine where you are. You can feel the warmth of the air move over your skin, and your body begins to feel calm and peaceful.

Breathe in gently...2...3...4...and relax your whole body while you breathe out gently...2...3...4.

Breathe in...2...3...4. Relax breathing out...2...3...4.

Let your whole body really, deeply relax.

You can see the sky through the leaves of the tree—it's clear and blue. You can see a bird flying way up in the sky. Watch the bird as it floats quietly above. Now concentrate on what you can hear. You can hear the leaves rustling in the gentle breeze. Another bird sings in the distance. What else can you hear? What else can you see? Now think about what you can feel with your fingers. You reach out and run your fingers through the grass. It feels cool and soft. Just imagine that you are really there, relaxing, with your muscles becoming more and more floppy. There is nothing to disturb you. You feel calm and peaceful, no worries, no problems, just really relaxed and calm...further and further, deeper and deeper, more and more relaxed.

Now spend some moments letting your muscles relax a little bit more and a little bit more. Try to keep the scene in your imagination. You are still there, lying under the tree. Just let your whole body relax even more deeply. If you have any sad feelings or worries, then let them drift away and notice how you feel safe and calm. Tell yourself "well done" for spending the time doing this meditation.

[Pause for a moment.]

Good—now in a moment, I am going to ask you to slowly open your eyes. I will count to ten, and when I get to five, I would like you to open your eyes. Then, when I get to ten, I will ask you to slowly sit up. Let's begin...1...2...3...4...5. Now slowly open your eyes...6...7...8...9...10. Now slowly sit up. Try not to put all the tension straight back into your muscles. Try to stay relaxed.

Good—how did you feel? Were you able to imagine being under the tree? Could you hear, see, and feel the things around you? How relaxed did you get? Not at all, a bit, or very?

SUGGESTED SCRIPT 2: *A Magical Place*

First, make yourself comfortable. Now you are going to use your imagination to relax your mind and your body. Close your eyes and listen to what I am saying. Try not to let your thoughts drift off onto other things, but don't worry if that happens. It is normal. Just try to pull your thoughts back to what I am saying.

Breathe in gently...2...3...4...and relax your whole body while you breathe out gently...2...3...4.

Breathe in...2...3...4. Relax breathing out...2...3...4.

Let your whole body really, deeply relax.

Imagine now that you are lying by a stream or a lake in a magical place where everyone is safe. This world is very calm and peaceful. As you lie there, your whole body begins to really relax. Your arms and legs feel limp, loose, and floppy.

You look up at the pale blue sky and you can see fluffy white clouds slowly drifting above you. You can hear the water gently lapping against the shore. Some birds are chirping quietly nearby. A beautiful butterfly flutters past you. You watch it for a few moments and it lands on some brightly colored flowers.

A gentle breeze moves over your skin and, as you breathe out, your body feels even more calm and peaceful. Now concentrate on what you can hear... [Pause for a moment.] What else can you see? What can you feel? Just imagine that you lie there relaxing, with your muscles becoming more and more relaxed. There is nothing to disturb you. You feel calm and peaceful—no worries, no problems, just really relaxed and calm, further and further, deeper and deeper, more and more relaxed. If you have any sad feelings or worries, then let them drift away and notice how you feel safe and calm. Tell yourself that you are proud of yourself for spending the time doing this meditation. Congratulate yourself—say "Well done, Me."

Now spend a few more moments letting your muscles relax even further. Try to keep the scene in your imagination. You are still there, lying by the water. Just let your whole body relax even more deeply.

[Pause for a moment.]

Good—now in a moment, I am going to ask you to slowly open your eyes. I will count to ten, and when I get to five, I would like you to open your eyes. Then, when I get to ten, I will ask you to slowly sit up. Let's begin...1...2...3...4...5. Slowly open your eyes...6...7...8...9...10. Now slowly sit up. Try not to put all the tension straight back into your muscles. Try to stay relaxed.

Good—how did you feel? Were you able to imagine lying by the water? Could you hear, see, and feel the things around you? Did you see the butterfly go past? How relaxed did you get? Not at all, a bit, or very?

Many other imagery scenes can help children to relax. Indeed, you can find many examples on the internet that your child might enjoy and find helpful. Here are some ideas that you might like to use to develop some more imagery scripts with your child—or perhaps they would like to write one of their own:

- lying on a beach

- lying on a picnic blanket next to a good friend

- sitting on the porch at Grandma's

- floating in space

- sitting in a magic garden

- watching the rain through a window

- lying in a treehouse with a friend

- watching the snow fall

- lying in front of a log fire

- camping in the country

- walking through the autumn leaves

- watching the stars

- walking through a secret garden

- lying in a warm bed, cuddled up with a sleeping puppy

Remember: When your child gets up from a relaxation or meditation practice, prompt them to complete their Relaxation Practice Record (in the Activity Book available at http://www.newharbinger.com/49913).

ACTIVITIES TO DO WITH YOUR CHILD...

Each step described above is a separate activity to do with your child. Once your child can reliably follow the instructions of one step, move on to the next. Then progress from step to step until you've completed them all.

CHILDREN'S ACTIVITY 23: Relaxation

Use the Relaxation Practice Record provided in the Activity Book (available for download at http://www.newharbinger.com/49913) or create a table with these headings: Day of the week, Where did I practice?, What parts of the body were still tense?, and How relaxed did I get? Not at all, a bit, or very? After each practice, reflect with your child on any muscles that they found difficult to relax and have them rate how relaxed they felt at the end using "Not at all, a bit, or very" as shown on the Relaxation Practice Record.

CHAPTER HIGHLIGHTS

In this chapter, you learned...

→ why relaxation is important for children who experience muscle tension and other physical symptoms as part of their anxiety;

→ that relaxation takes consistent practice, and ensuring that you first practice in a quiet and calm environment will give your child the best chance of learning the skill successfully;

→ that relaxation is taught in steps that progress from learning to tense muscles, then learning to relax tense muscles and breathe calmly, and finally rapidly relaxing by tensing, relaxing, and breathing within a few moments; and

→ that learning to relax the mind through meditation and imagery is also a useful skill for both children and adults with anxiety.

Your child and family will need to do the following:

* Learn each step of the relaxation process. Practice each step for a few days (up to a week) before moving on to the next step.

* Once rapid relaxation can be achieved at home, practice the skill in the real world—first in situations that are not stressful and then in situations where your child is worried or scared.

* Continue to work on stepladders and practice other anxiety management skills, such as detective thinking and problem solving. (Your child should be quite a way up a few of their stepladders by now.)

CHAPTER 10

Taking Stock and Planning for the Future

In previous chapters, we took you through a number of techniques or strategies to help your child manage their anxiety. Now it's time to take stock of the situation with your child and to plan for the future. Hopefully, your child has made some wonderful gains. But every child is different, and each child will respond better to some strategies than others. Taking stock will allow you to look at what has worked well for your child and what hasn't worked so well, and to think about what new directions or additional areas you might want to work on.

Bringing It All Together

In this chapter, we will briefly summarize what we have covered and then we will discuss how the various strategies fit together and how they can be combined into a comprehensive program to help your child. We will illustrate this by looking at the specific programs that we planned for the five children whom we introduced at the beginning of this book.

What We Have Covered So Far

In chapters 1 and 2, we discussed what anxiety is and how you can recognize anxiety and fear in your child. We also discussed ways in which your child can learn to understand more about their feelings. We supplied exercises to help you teach your child about the three features of anxiety: physical feelings, mental activity, and behaviors. We also introduced the idea of recording your child's anxiety using our ten-point worry scale. By this stage, your child should be getting pretty good at rating the degree of anxiety and should realize that anxiety varies from situation to situation.

We also explained to you a little of where anxiety might come from, and hopefully this gave you some understanding of why your child might be anxious. In chapter 1, we described some of the things that keep your child anxious in the here and now, and we explained the various techniques we would cover. These techniques included the core skills detective thinking, stepladders, problem solving, and parenting, and the optional social skills and relaxation.

Detective thinking helps your child change their current ways of thinking about frightening situations (as discussed in chapter 3). We suggested that anxious children (and adults) tend to think inaccurately and regularly look at the negative in situations. In particular, anxious children overestimate *how likely* it is that bad things will happen and they catastrophize about *how bad* those things will be. We provided an exercise to help your child realize that their feelings could be changed if they could learn to think differently about situations. Most importantly, we offered a way that your child could learn to think like a detective and look for evidence regarding their beliefs. The following points were made:

- Your thoughts and beliefs directly cause your feelings in a situation.

- Worried thoughts cause you to feel more anxious. Calm thoughts cause you to feel more relaxed.

- You need to act like a detective in frightening situations and look for evidence for your worried thoughts.

- There are many types of evidence you can look for. Some of the best sources of evidence come from previous experience and alternative explanations.

- Using the evidence, a calm thought can usually be found that you can use in the anxious situation.

In chapter 6, we discussed how to simplify detective thinking by using questions and thoughts that work well for your child.

Using stepladders, which we introduced in chapter 5, is the crucial technique to encourage your child to face up to their fears. Stepladders are most likely to work when they are implemented in a consistent and systematic way. There are several steps to creating stepladders:

- Brainstorm all of the situations your child fears and avoids.

- Group them together into similar or related fears (similar anxious predictions).

- Organize the fears so that your child has a series of stepladders, each made of small steps.

- Have your child begin with the first step of each stepladder and gradually work their way up to the top.

- Reward each successful attempt at a step. Unsuccessful attempts should be rewarded in a smaller way to acknowledge the effort that was put in.

There are also several ways to increase the chance that stepladders will work:

- Make sure the steps are not too far apart.

- Repeat each step several times until your child is more or less bored with it.

- Give rewards when promised, and as soon as possible after a step is completed, to keep your child's motivation going.

- Make sure that the stepladder includes the outcomes that your child is really afraid of.

There are a number of ways that the effects of stepladders can be maximized, but keep in mind that developing stepladders for some of the more subtle or complex forms of anxiety can be difficult. We discussed ways of producing more creative stepladders and fixing problems with stepladders in chapters 6 and 7.

In chapters 8 and 9, we introduced optional skills for children who need help developing social confidence and for children who find it hard to relax or experience a lot of physical tension with their anxiety.

In chapter 8, we discussed your child's social skills—that is, the way your child interacts with other people. Many anxious children have no problems with social skills, and if this is true for your child, this component can be left out of their program. But if your child does lack some social skills, it's important to address this in order to give them as many positive experiences as possible. We described a number of exercises you could use with your child to help them understand more about how to develop various social skills. When teaching your child social skills, we suggested the following strategies:

- Teach one skill at a time, explaining both why to use the skill and showing how it is performed.

- Make the lessons fun and keep them short.

- Give your child feedback and gently show them better ways to act.

- Provide opportunities for your child to get lots of practice.

- Begin with the more basic skills and gradually build to more difficult ones.

We also suggested that practicing assertive behaviors, such as standing up for yourself and dealing with teasing, will help to build all children's confidence.

In chapter 9, we introduced relaxation techniques through a stepped series of practices. These practices assist a child in learning how to control muscle tension and breathing and how to use imagery to help the body to relax. These skills are then combined to allow rapid relaxation in anxiety-provoking situations.

Finally, don't forget chapter 4 on parenting skills where we discussed both the ways in which you might accidentally increase your child's anxiety and the ways you could better handle it. Here are some of the main points we made:

- Protecting or taking over for your child may make them feel better in the short run but will maintain their anxiety over time. It is more useful to encourage your child to face their fears.

- If your child asks for help, it is best to give guidance in how to solve the problem and then encourage your child to solve it for themself.

- If your child regularly asks for reassurance, you should assist your child to do detective thinking. Then let your child know that you have confidence that they can solve the problem and that you will ignore further requests for help.

- Remember to reward your child for behaviors that you are happy with.

- If you find it difficult to let your child make their own mistakes, you need to do detective thinking yourself to convince yourself that your child will not suffer in the long run if things do not always go well.

Some Sample Programs

It is not always necessary to use every one of these techniques and components with each child. Some types of problems need certain techniques more than others, and some children will find that some techniques make more sense to them than others do. Therefore, even though it is important for you and your child to understand all of the core skills (detective thinking, stepladders, problem solving, and parenting), you may find that the program you and your child complete will make use of some skills more than others.

We will now revisit the five children we've mentioned throughout this book and describe the final program each of them selected. You will notice that the most essential technique—stepladders—was included in each child's program. *Your child will not learn to master their fears if they do not do lots of stepladder practice.*

Talia

You may remember that Talia had a fear of water. Overall, she was a confident, outgoing nine-year-old, but Talia was afraid of swimming, and this was starting to affect her confidence with friends.

In this type of case, where the problem is very restricted and the child is not generally shy or sensitive, the program can be a very quick and straightforward one that involves only stepladders and detective thinking. Talia's program, therefore, began with Talia and her parents using detective thinking to find evidence about the risks of being in water and then brainstorming all the sorts of situations that made Talia afraid. They then organized these situations into a stepladder—from easiest to hardest. Because Talia's fear was a very specific one, it was quite easy to come up with a lot of steps that very gradually got harder and harder. Also, because Talia really wanted to get over her problem and go swimming with her friends, her parents only had to use a few small rewards from time to time to get her to do her practice. Most of the time, they just needed to remind her of her final goal—going to the beach with her friends. The whole program took Talia only about five weeks, and, before long, her fear of water was far behind her.

Ethan

Ethan had a much broader and more general problem than Talia. He was shy, sensitive, and had little self-confidence. Because of his fears, Ethan avoided many social interactions and had few friends. He also had times of feeling low.

Because Ethan's fears were very much a result of the way he thought about things and because he was an intelligent young man, Ethan's parents decided to focus heavily on the detective thinking component of the program. They spent a great deal of time working on getting Ethan to think more accurately about his abilities and, most importantly, about what other people thought of him. The most important lessons that Ethan needed to learn were these: you can do things well and even if you do something badly, other people will not necessarily think badly of you, and even if they do, it is not the end of the world. Ethan did well with his lessons, but it was hard for him to really believe in those concepts. He did begin to shift his beliefs, but they did not change completely.

To really reinforce these new beliefs, Ethan's parents included stepladders in his program. Because Ethan was so unconfident and also a little depressed, he really needed lots of encouragement and motivation to work on what were some pretty difficult tasks. So, Ethan's parents made sure that the stepladders had lots of very small steps, and they gave him lots of rewards and encouragement along the way. This meant that Ethan's program took quite a long time—in fact, it became a way of life that Ethan and his parents continued, to some extent, for more than a year. By making sure that the steps were small enough that he managed to do them on most occasions, Ethan was able to have plenty of successes and lots of rewards and encouragement from his parents, which, slowly but surely, began to boost his confidence.

Finally, while doing his stepladders, it became clear to Ethan's parents that he really did lack a few basic skills and the ability to really get along with other kids. This was very understandable given that Ethan had had hardly any friends over the years. In his first year of middle school, Ethan was also starting to be teased by a few of the kids. So, Ethan's parents made sure that they also included some work on his social skills in his program. Ethan and his parents practiced different ways of meeting new kids and of talking to them. Ethan then made sure that he practiced these new skills during his stepladders and in daily life.

Because the teasing was not too severe, he didn't want his parents to talk to the schoolteachers about it. Instead, he practiced ways of dealing with the teasing, especially trying to let the other kids know that he was okay with their comments and that they didn't bother him. Luckily, this seemed to be enough, and the teasing stopped after a short while. This success was a huge boost for Ethan's confidence.

Ethan is still working on his anxiety, and it will be a long-term task for him. But over the course of several months, he was already a different boy than the one who began the program. As Ethan's confidence began to build, his depression also became less of an issue. Ethan and his parents were happy with the changes and didn't feel that he needed to do any special work on his earlier low moods.

Hayley

Hayley had two quite separate problems—constant worry and a fear of choking. At the beginning of the program, the focus was on controlling worry and helping Hayley's parents deal with Hayley's challenging behavior. Once Hayley began working with stepladders, she was able to begin addressing her fear of choking.

To deal with her worries, Hayley focused on learning and then practicing detective thinking. This was very important for her as she constantly expected the worst in all situations. Without having the detective thoughts in place, Hayley would never have agreed to try and face her fears. Hayley and her parents got into the habit of looking for evidence for all of the worried thoughts that any of them had as a way of practicing detective thinking as often as possible. As Hayley's skill increased, her parents took less of a role in guiding her through the process until they were able to just say, "What would a detective say about that?"

Hayley did two main stepladders that addressed her worries. The first was for increasing her contact with other children, and the second was for getting her work done within a time limit and without trying to make her answers perfect. Hayley proceeded slowly with these stepladders. She had a setback on the first stepladder when one of her good friends got annoyed because Hayley didn't invite her to her house one weekend. Hayley wanted to stop the stepladder there, but after doing a lot of detective thinking work and also looking back at what Hayley thought life would be like if she didn't worry so much, she was able to keep working. To increase her confidence, she went back two steps, repeated them, and then kept going.

Hayley's fear of choking was addressed with a very long stepladder that involved making a list of all the foods she was scared of eating and then slowly working through the list. For the tough foods, like lamb chops, the steps also involved how small she was able to cut the pieces up and how long she could chew each mouthful. The early steps were quite difficult, but once Hayley reached the step of eating a steak sandwich, all the rest of the foods on the lists were easy, and her eating went back to normal very quickly.

Hayley had had a long time to practice being fearful and worried, so it took a few months for any noticeable progress to be made. This was frustrating for her parents, but they persisted with implementing the skills, expecting Hayley to be able to manage her anxiety. Over time there were breakthroughs, some of which came quickly while others were hard fought. The important thing was that Hayley started to gain weight, she could now complete tests at school, and she could get to sleep without needing to worry about things that might happen the next day.

Kurt

Kurt had two main problems—repetitive washing, because of a fear of germs, and a more generalized anxiety that affected all sorts of different areas. Because of the complexity of these problems, Kurt's first step was to be very clear about all of the behaviors and features that went with each type of difficulty. Kurt labeled his anxieties his "washing problem" and his "worry problem" so that he could keep them straight in his head.

There were a lot of similarities between the two problems, but there were also some differences that Kurt needed to be clear on.

Kurt's father was supportive, but didn't have a great deal of time to work with him, so Kurt's mother took the lead in working on the program with Kurt. They began by working on detective thinking. For his washing problem, Kurt needed to learn that he was not picking up lots of germs and that even if he was, they would not hurt him. For his worry problem, Kurt needed to learn the general rule that the world was not a particularly dangerous place and that he was not especially likely to get hurt. Because there were so many things that Kurt worried about, it was quite easy to think of lots of evidence to prove to himself that he was not thinking accurately. Kurt was able to begin to use his detective, James Bond, to help him through some tough situations.

As with all the other programs, Kurt's included stepladders. Kurt's stepladders were a little harder to think up because his worries were so much less concrete than the other children's. But by thinking hard, Kurt and his mother were able to come up with several stepladders and lots of steps. In chapter 6, we gave you some examples of creative stepladders for Kurt and other children who had these less concrete fears. The especially hard part for Kurt came when he had to go through several days without washing. But his determination and the rewards his mother used helped him get through it. After many weeks, it began to get easier.

Lashi

Lashi was a young girl whose parents had separated. She worried that her mother might be injured or killed and that she would never see her again. As a result, she became upset whenever she had to separate from her mother. Because Lashi was only seven, her mother decided to use calm thoughts on cue cards instead of full detective thinking, and she also taught Lashi relaxation skills. The relaxation fit with her mother's general philosophy in life since she herself had done several relaxation courses over the years.

Lashi really enjoyed the relaxation, especially because it gave her some special time alone with her mother. She never really learned to completely relax, but she was able to do it enough that it gave her the start that she needed before moving on to stepladders.

The stepladders were the main part of Lashi's program. Lashi and her mother worked out a number of stepladders for different portions of her problem—going to school, staying overnight at other people's houses, being left with a sitter, and so on. Each stepladder was broken down into small steps, and Lashi picked some fun rewards for doing each one. Many of the rewards involved special time with her mother. Part of the program also involved Lashi's mother not allowing Lashi to ask for too much reassurance.

Lashi's mother also realized that the separation had affected her in many ways too. Most importantly, she realized that following the breakup of the relationship, she became more scared of losing Lashi. As a result, she had started to be a little too protective of Lashi and was perhaps a bit too forgiving of her fears. Lashi's mother had to admit that sometimes when she let Lashi stay home from school, she really didn't mind too much. So Lashi's mother decided to work on being a little less protective herself and to be tougher in encouraging Lashi to face her fears. As part of this change, Lashi's mother began to do some detective thinking about her own worries—what would really happen if Lashi became a little scared, would Lashi really hate her if she made her go to school, and so on.

Finally, when Lashi was doing pretty well in separating from her mother, she and her mother worked out another stepladder for Lashi's other fears of injections and hospitals. Because both of Lashi's areas of fear—separating from her mother and injections—were quite concrete, the program for Lashi was fairly straightforward, and it was not long before she started to show some great improvements. The whole program was done in around twelve weeks.

Ang

You may remember Ang as a young boy who was still in preschool. His main fear was about being separated from his mother and going into his room to sleep with the lights out. But he was also a shy and quiet young boy who was quite reluctant to speak to others. Because of his very young age, Ang's parents did not try and teach him the full detective thinking technique but simply taught him to verbalize his worried thought and then verbalize a calm thought in its place.

Ang's quite concrete fears and avoidance meant that his program focused almost entirely on stepladders. Because he was so young, his parents developed most of the stepladders for him based on their knowledge of Ang's fears and by a little trial and error. In the end, Ang and his parents worked hard on three main ladders: (1) gradual steps to separate from his mother without tantrums; (2) gradual steps to sleep in the dark; (3) gradual steps to increase his talking with people outside the family. Ang soon became very excited by the rewards he received after each step, most of which focused around fun activities with his parents.

Quite early in the program, Ang's mother realized that she had been finding it extremely difficult to separate from Ang herself and that when Ang threw tantrums or showed other forms of distress, it broke her heart. As a result, she learned that she had subtly been allowing Ang to avoid his fears—she had often not dropped him places where she needed to; she had often stayed at home with him rather than take him to preschool or leave him with his father; and even on preschool mornings, she had hesitated to leave. Once she began to change these habits (even though it wasn't easy for her), Ang's tantrums initially increased. However, it took only a couple of weeks for the gradual stepladders and the rewards to begin to build his confidence and his extreme distress began to reduce.

After a few months, Ang was happily waving good-bye to his mother when he went off to preschool and he was sleeping in his room with only a small light in the hall. He was also getting much better at saying hello to people he didn't know and was starting to talk more with others, although this was still an area on which his parents were continuing to work.

Maintaining Gains

Probably the main questions on your mind now are these: Where do we go from here? How long do we keep practicing, and when can we put all this behind us and forget all about it? Unfortunately, these questions don't have clear-cut answers. Every child is different, and every situation varies. Some children we have treated make huge gains in a few short weeks and never look back. Others change slowly and to only a small degree and may really need to keep their practice going for months or even years.

The typical child is probably somewhere in between. They may practice hard for ten to fifteen weeks and make positive changes. At this point, these children can stop doing the set, formal practices, but they and their parents need to keep in mind all that they have learned, and continue to do so for the rest of their lives. They need to keep reminding themselves of the principles of detective thinking and stepladders, and whenever they get a chance, they should do the occasional practice. This doesn't mean having to do formal practice, but simply that they should practice whenever life throws something a little tough their way. For example, when your child has exams or a big sporting event or perhaps has to give a speech at an awards night, it's a chance for your child to remind themself of the techniques learned here. If your child finds that their anxiety is high, it is a chance to practice the techniques properly again for a week or so, just to get back on top of things. The practice your child has to do should not be too painful over time because many of the techniques should become a natural and normal part of their life. As your child builds confidence, makes new friends, and has successes, the techniques, such as detective thinking and problem solving and even stepladders, will be something that they do anyway as part of living.

Relapse

There is the possibility of what professionals call *relapse*—that is, that at some point, your child will once again begin to experience problems with fears and anxiety. This is not necessarily going to happen, and for many children, it never does. But as described in chapter 1, for a variety of reasons, including their genes, your child is likely to be a sensitive child, and so there is always the possibility that anxiety will once again rear its head. This may happen for a number of reasons. First, once life starts to feel good again, it is understandable that children and their parents often stop practicing their techniques. Sometimes, in these cases, anxiety just has a habit of very gradually creeping back. Second, bad things do happen in life. Your child may lose someone close to them, or they could fail an important exam, move to a new house, or be in a car accident. And when something bad happens in life, it makes many of us think for a while that other dangers are very likely. For sensitive children, this might be enough to bring back the negative thoughts and feelings of anxiety. And finally, anxiety and fears can return, in some cases, during times of general stress. For example, if you or your partner becomes unemployed or if you have a burglary or you separate, these general stresses that enter family life and affect all of you may cause your child to lose confidence and begin to have fears again.

If relapse does happen, don't panic. Simply going back to basics and practicing the techniques that worked the first time should get things under control quickly. When your child's return of fear has been triggered by another problem, such as stress within the family or a major calamity, it is important to allow all of you time to deal with that stress first. For example, let's imagine that your partner lands in the hospital after a serious work accident and the whole family is distressed. Your child might lose some confidence, and you may find that some of the fears that they had before, or even some new ones, might develop. It is important not to immediately start to do detective thinking, stepladders, and so on, in a frantic fashion. Rather, allow everyone time to adjust to the changes in your life and to deal with the practical problems and the emotions of the situation first. Once you get a little control over the stress in your life, then you can begin to practice the anxiety control techniques again if they are needed.

An important point to remember is that if your child does show some signs of anxiety again, it will take much less time to get on top of that anxiety the second time around. Your child should now know the techniques well and will be able to put them straight into practice. In addition, the anxiety will not have had long to take hold.

We certainly hope that nothing terrible happens in your child's life and that they manage to live a life free of interference from anxiety. But even if there are difficulties along the road, it is good to know that your child has now learned some techniques and skills that will be of benefit throughout their life.

Taking Time to Chill: Positive and Negative Coping Strategies for Stress

In the future, it will be very important to encourage your child to take positive steps to manage general everyday stress. Because your child is probably a sensitive person, learning these skills will help them to develop ways of looking after themself in life. Taking a proactive approach to stress will reduce the likelihood of more serious problems, such as continuing anxiety, depression, and substance use. To help your child manage everyday stress, you might, for example, encourage them to take up yoga or to practice relaxation, if these are things that they would personally find helpful. Ensure that your child devotes time to regular exercise and proper nutrition. It is also especially important for most people to spend time socializing with friends and family. Anxious children have a tendency to focus excessively on tasks such as studying or work. The problem with spending all of their time on any one activity is that they are likely to burn out and they will find it more difficult to achieve their goals. As a parent, you need to recognize that a balanced life between work (or school), self-care (like exercising), and a social life is crucial to emotional and physical health.

As your child enters adolescence, it will also be important to acknowledge the temptations of negative coping strategies as a way of dealing with stress. It's important to acknowledge that some people cope with stress by using drugs and alcohol, withdrawing from friends and family, and neglecting activities such as diet, sleep, and exercise. If you discuss these approaches, their disadvantages, and alternative options in an open way with your child, they will be more likely to make positive choices in the future.

Planning for Future Challenges

Before finishing the program, it is important to plan for the future. Managing anxiety will take continuing work, as we discussed above. By looking at future events that may cause anxiety and planning for them using the anxiety management skills, you can prevent major setbacks. That is not to say that there will be no times of high anxiety for your child, but with work, the level of anxiety will be no different than what most children experience during their lifetimes. For some children, immediate future plans will include finishing their current stepladders. You and your child will need to review how far you've gotten and how you intend to finish off the steps or goals that are left. For those children who have reached their original goals, it is useful to ask what the next big life challenge will be and set this as a goal that will be tackled with the help of anxiety management skills. For example, if your child is currently in second grade and you know that camp and other group activities you'll want your child to participate in will start in the next few years, you might like to make a long-term goal of preparing for this event by breaking the potential fear down into manageable steps that can be completed well before the event even occurs. Keeping an eye on your child's future skill needs, as well as on current ones, helps you to be proactive in ensuring your child's successes.

PARENT ACTIVITY: Preparing to Set Goals for the Future

Take some time to think of your child's future.

What skills will your child need in the next few years (e.g., for sleep-overs, camp, staying home alone after school)?

_____

_____

_____

What challenges will your child have to face (e.g., starting high school, moving to a new house, having new siblings)?

_____

_____

_____

Use these ideas to plan long-term goals with your child.

ACTIVITIES TO DO WITH YOUR CHILD ...

CHILDREN'S PRACTICE TASK 7: Reaching My Goals

The final practice task asks children to put in extra effort in reaching the goals on their stepladders. They should plan when they will face steps and what coping skills they can use to help them manage their anxiety. You will need to keep repeating this practice task for several weeks or possibly several months, depending on the complexity, number, and length of your child's stepladders. Each week, help your child to make appropriate plans and help them implement chosen steps. Once you get to the end of your child's stepladders and you are ready to stop having anxiety management sessions together, complete the final children's activities (#24–27) that focus on reviewing progress and the future. (Visit http://

www.newharbinger.com/49913 to download this practice task and the final children's activities, which you will find in the Activity Book.)

CHILDREN'S ACTIVITY 24: How Could I Help Others?

As a way of consolidating your child's anxiety management skills, it can help to have your child "help" other children who have similar problems. By helping others, children consolidate their own skills and also preempt fears and worries that they may one day face. This is a useful preventative task and also boosts self-confidence as children realize that they have useful knowledge.

Make up several stories of other children who have anxiety and ask your child to come up with ideas for how those children could learn to cope better. Discuss each "case" with your child and have them suggest what each child might do to overcome anxiety. Cases might include the following:

- Jack has a fear of bugs; he feels sick when he sees them and has to leave any situation where he sees a bug, even if it is only on TV.

- Annie has her first summer camp coming up; she has never stayed away from home and is worried about what might go wrong.

- Melissa started a new school last year; she hasn't made very many friends and has become really shy.

- Tim worries all the time about his mom getting sick or hurt. He tries his best to always be with her so that he can take care of her.

- Sam starts high school next year and is really nervous. He worries about getting lost in the large school, finding the work difficult, making friends, and what the teachers will be like. His worries make it difficult to get to sleep.

CHILDREN'S ACTIVITY 25: What Have You Achieved?

Talk with your child about how far they have come over the past few months, and don't allow a discounting of these achievements. Your child has learned new skills that have enabled them to face the things they used to worry about, and that is a very big accomplishment. Tell your child what you are proud of about these recent achievements—and give special praise for the effort put in as well as for the fears that they have conquered.

Also have your child acknowledge any goals that they are still working toward, and then you can both talk about when and how to tackle these. It can help to write down new goals that your child can keep working on over the next few months or even a year.

CHILDREN'S ACTIVITY 26: Stopping Fears and Worries from Coming Back

Explain to your child that the only way to keep fears and worries under control is to keep practicing their skills (like detective thinking and problem solving) and to every so often remind themself that they are strong enough to fight the bad feelings. Your child can do this by facing the once-feared event every now and then as a reminder of how brave they now are.

Talk with your child about the possibility that one day they might once again feel very scared or worried. Make an agreement that if that's the case in the future, your child will come to you and talk about what is happening, and, in turn, you will give them your attention and try your best to understand and give the help they need to face the new challenge. Explain that although your child may feel very anxious at the time, facing fears the second time is usually much quicker and a lot easier than what they have been doing over the last few months.

CHILDREN'S ACTIVITY 27: Facing a Really Big Challenge

In this final activity, you should ask your child to set a challenge by doing something enjoyable that they previously would have avoided, or by identifying a big challenge to be faced in the near future (such as going away to camp, starting high school, or joining a sports team). Once an activity is chosen, write an action plan that will help your child to be successful. This might include what needs to be done to start the activity, ways of reducing any anxiety felt, and where your child might be able to get help to achieve the goal. We hope that by aiming to do something challenging that is also enjoyable, your child will also increase social contact, allowing them to experience and overcome more anxiety—and ultimately helping your child to perfect their anxiety management skills.

CHAPTER HIGHLIGHTS

In this chapter you and your child reviewed…

→ all the skills taught in this program;

→ a summary of how the children featured in this book completed their individual programs;

→ the progress you have made toward the goals set in the first weeks of the program;

→ how keeping up the practice of your new anxiety management skills will maintain the gains and progress your child and you have made;

→ what to do when a relapse occurs—particularly in times of stress—and how working through the program skills and steps again can quickly overcome the problem; and

→ why it is important to actively manage everyday stress by taking good care of yourself; getting plenty of rest; balancing work, school, and social activities at all times; and avoiding negative coping strategies such as neglecting yourself or your friendships, or using drugs or alcohol.

You and your child will need to do the following:

* Continue to work on stepladders and to practice other anxiety management skills such as detective thinking, problem solving, social skills and relaxation. When the final steps on the stepladders are done, the final children's activities will be completed.

* Review goals and make plans to keep facing fears that may arise in the future.

Congratulations!!!

You have come to the end of the program. You have taught your child valuable skills that will assist them in the future when they struggle with other issues. If you and your child have worked through the chapters and exercises in this book carefully, it has probably been a long, hard road.

Hopefully, it has also been a worthwhile one. Your child should be quite different from the one who started the program. Of course, change can range from large to small—everyone is different, and how much your child has changed will depend on so many things.

To finish the program, give your child a certificate to recognize their effort and achievement. (Use can use the certificate below or, if you prefer, download it at http://newharbinger.com/49913.) During the goal setting activity at the beginning of the program, you planned a special family activity. You should plan to do this in the next week or two. It might also be nice to have a family dinner party with all your child's favorite foods as a surprise reward for these achievements. Don't forget to reward yourself as well for your commitment in helping your anxious child learn new skills and face their fears.

CONGRATULATIONS!!

You are now certified in

Brave Behavior

Detective Thinking

Facing Fears

You should be very proud of all the things you have achieved.

Take a look back at the beginning of the workbook where you set your goals.
Remember you agreed that if you all worked very hard you do something special together.
So go and enjoy yourself, you deserve it.

CHAPTER 11

Looking Forward: The Teen Years

The teenage years, a time of major transition between childhood and adulthood, are full of challenges. These years bring anticipation and excitement, and also many worries about the changes young people are experiencing.

During these years, teens start high school, work out how they fit in with friends, seek acceptance within the wider peer group, deal with their own and others' expectations about academic performance, negotiate conflicting needs and expectations about autonomy and independence from family, experience body changes, and deal with sexuality and gender identity as they explore relationships. It can also be a time of family changes as parents experience transitions and challenges in their own lives, relationships, and careers.

Coping with all of these transformations can be a major stressor for young people who have experienced difficulties with anxiety as children. Anxiety disorders are the most common problem experienced by adolescents. Up to 30 percent of thirteen- to eighteen-year-olds have some anxiety symptoms and around 8 percent have severe anxiety (Lawrence et al. 2015; Merikangas et al. 2010). Depression and eating disorders also become far more common from middle adolescence (Rapee et al. 2019). Having completed this program, your child will have learned skills to manage anxiety and will have developed independence and confidence that will provide significant protection against developing severe anxiety. However, some children will continue to experience anxiety into their teen years, or anxiety that was once well managed may be exacerbated by all of the stressors listed above.

Parents and caregivers can be at a loss about how to help their teen, as many challenges are ones that they have not faced themselves or they may have struggled with themselves in earlier years. Often the young people they care for do not believe their parents have relevant experience and advice to offer.

The following information highlights how to recognize anxiety in teens, when you should seek professional help, and how to adapt and use the skills you have already learned in this program to work on fears or worries that arise once you are parenting a teen.

Recognizing Anxiety

Parents will notice many changes in their child across the adolescent years. Many of these transformations are normal and an adjustment to developmental changes. Stress, anxious feelings, and mood changes are experienced by most young people and are a normal part of adolescent adjustment. Let your teen know that feeling stressed or anxious is normal and that there are ways to manage it.

Some changes can be symptoms of a recurrence of anxiety problems or the development of further issues such as depression or eating problems. Young people who have previously had problems with anxiety can be more susceptible to a recurrence of anxiety as well as other mental health issues in adolescence. Concerning changes that parents and caregivers may notice in young people include:

Changes in emotions and mood

- feeling on edge or keyed up
- more irritable and volatile than usual
- restlessness and finding it hard to concentrate
- feeling overwhelmed

Social changes

- increasing isolation and spending a lot of time alone

- avoiding interactions with friends

- avoiding outside activities and sports previously enjoyed

- avoiding school

Physical changes

- increasing minor illnesses

- headaches

- stomachaches

- persistent changes in eating—either more or less

- intense panic feelings, including racing heart, dizziness, difficulty breathing, sweating or shaking, feeling numb or not really there

Sleep changes

- difficulty getting to sleep and restless sleep

- a shifting sleep cycle (This is typical for growing teens but staying in bed for long periods can also be a sign of avoidance or low mood.)

- nightmares

- overall tiredness

Changes in school and other performance

- concerning changes in achievement and involvement

- not coping, overwhelmed

- difficulty concentrating and finishing work

Anxiety in the teenage years can present itself as a return of their earlier problems or may emerge as quite new issues. Anxiety can be acute and tied to a specific stressful situation, or it can be more long lasting and pervasive, affecting different areas of a young person's life. A return of anxiety problems experienced before or the development of new issues is more likely to occur after a traumatic event or a series of adverse events or changes such as a rejection in social relationships, a significant loss, family changes, or moving.

The types of anxiety that occur in teen years include those that are also common in childhood. As a teen, separation anxiety may present itself as reluctance to attend school or to socialize or as a persistent worry and a sense of responsibility in ensuring that a parent is safe and well. It may seem like a loss of confidence and increased anxiety in situations outside their home. School avoidance can be complicated by being a victim of or observing bullying.

Generalized worries in teens often broaden to include worry about their future and finances, and they may start to worry about how much they worry. These teens can struggle with decision making, overprepare for events, procrastinate about assignments, go blank during exams, and set often unattainably high standards for themselves.

Young people who have been shy or socially anxious as young children may develop more persistent and pervasive problems with fears of evaluation in performance or social situations. In fact, self-consciousness and social anxiety can increase quite a bit from around ten to thirteen years of age. This may be seen in their reluctance to participate in class discussions, avoidance of interacting with peers both in-person and online, and avoidance of family events. A fear of asking questions in class as a younger child may reemerge and broaden to other social or performance situations if the young person experiences rejection or negative feedback.

Some anxiety disorders—such as panic disorder, generalized anxiety disorder, and social anxiety disorder—most commonly emerge in the teenage years and can persist into adulthood. The onset of puberty, with body changes and development, can exacerbate self-consciousness and intensify concerns about fitting in and being accepted socially. Similarly concerns about performance and being evaluated negatively can intensify in teenage years as academic demands grow and pressure and expectations about exams, future study, and work increase. Teens can be overcome by concerns about study and performance, leading some to become overly perfectionistic about achievements and making mistakes.

Young people with previous experience of anxiety in childhood have an increased risk of developing mood disorders such as depression. This is particularly the case for young people with generalized fears and social anxiety who may avoid many social situations because of fears of negative evaluation. This can lead to being excluded and rejected by their peers and social group, confirming their fears of negative outcomes.

Some teens can also find relief from anxiety in using alcohol and other drugs to reduce physiological arousal, particularly when they are in social situations or under stress. Talk openly with your teen about the risks of using alcohol and drugs as negative coping strategies and aim to work with them to find other ways of coping with stressful situations or social pressures.

Rosanne's story

Rosanne was fifteen when she experienced her first panic attack. She was at a friend's party when she began to feel dizzy and sick. Her vision became blurry, and everything seemed to be happening from a long way off. Rosanne was convinced she was going to faint and yelled at her friends to call an ambulance. Many medical tests failed to find any physical problems, but from that time on, Rosanne began to be very afraid of any situations—such as flickering lights, fairground rides, or even exercise—that caused strange feelings in her body. Rosanne continues to have panicky feelings from time to time and is now limits her life and avoids going anywhere that she fears might set off another attack.

Mason's story

Mason, age fourteen, had always been shy and lacking confidence. However, he had worked with his parents on increasing his social skills and tackling his fears about speaking up in class and giving presentations. When he was thirteen, his family had to move to another city, and Mason found adjusting to the new, larger school difficult. Mason developed intense fears about attending school, worrying that he would make mistakes in class and that people would laugh at him. He was invited for a visit by his neighbors, invited to a party, and invited to join the local basketball team, but he refused to go to any of these activities. His parents were concerned about how unhappy and withdrawn Mason seemed. He was calling himself a loser, not enjoying anything he had liked before or trying anything new. They talked with their family doctor who organized a referral for assessment and treatment with the local adolescent service.

When to Get Professional Help

There may be times when you need to seek additional professional help. This may be when you first become aware that your teen is feeling anxious or after you have tried for a while to assist them. Consider seeking additional help in the following situations:

- Anxiety or other issues are significantly interfering with everyday learning, socializing, and life in general.

- The problems are intense, persistent, interfering, and distressing.

- You are concerned about the young person's depressed mood.

- You have concerns about the young person's safety.

Sources of help may vary in your community. However, your teen's medical practitioner, pediatrician, or school counselor can be a starting point for accessing psychological help through local adolescent mental health services and private mental health professionals.

There may also be many resources, including treatment programs, available online for young people who cannot attend in person. Talk through these options with your teen and aim to work collaboratively with them in seeking further help.

Seeking professional help may make your teen feel they are failing or disappointing you or that they are different and not normal. Let them know that you understand but that you need some extra help: "I'm not quite sure if I know how to how to help you myself. I want to help you get on top of this, and we will find help together."

How to Utilize Skills With Teens

The core skills of understanding how thoughts, feelings, and behaviors are linked, and using detective thinking, problem solving, and facing fears by using stepladders are still the main pathway to managing anxiety in adolescents and indeed for adults.

When anxiety arises again, approach it as you have done before. Consider the anxiety as a problem to be solved using the skills and techniques you and your teen have used before. This can be done by working through the core skills using the same worksheets or adjusting them with a new look if this suits your young person. This approach is aimed at reducing distress and preventing complications by minimizing the effect on your teen's school life, social life, and developmental progress.

While the key skills of identifying thoughts and feelings, detective thinking, and stepladders are the same, adolescents may respond to a change of wording so these skills to appear less child focused—for example, switching detective thinking to "realistic thinking" or "helpful and unhelpful thoughts." Some teens may prefer to rename stepladders as "facing fears" or "fear challenges." The principles, strategies, and troubleshooting approaches remain the same.

The optional chapters on assertiveness and social skills (chapter 8), including dealing with bullying, and on relaxation skills (chapter 9), including meditation, are highly relevant to young people. These chapters are well worth reviewing or practicing from the start if you did not need to use these skills when your child was younger.

Reassurance doesn't make anxiety go away, and paradoxically it can make the anxiety worse. Having a young person experience anxiety, mood disturbances, or distress is in turn very distressing for parents and caregivers. Parents have a natural tendency to want to take away the painful feelings by reassurance. This is not helpful in the long term, though it may make you feel better in the present moment. Parents can get caught in a trap of reducing their own anxiety by offering reassurance to their child.

Detective Thinking

Read back over the chapter 3 on detective thinking to remind yourself of the key ideas about helping your teen think more realistically about a situation that has led to worry and distress. The detective thinking process involves identifying the worried thoughts, using questions to help find evidence that the worried thought might not be absolutely true, and then finding a calm and realistic thought. Compared with children, teens can be encouraged to find more detailed evidence and to consider what the consequences of the situation will be and whether they would be able to cope even if their anxious prediction comes true.

Detective thinking can be done in a planned way using the forms in the Activity Book (available for download at http://www.newharbinger. com/49913) when they know they will be entering a situation that is anxiety provoking, when they are facing a fear or when planning to do a step on their stepladder. Read through the questions to challenge the worried thought and find evidence that the thought is not absolutely true. Help your teen link fears to specific events and feared outcomes rather than becoming caught up in your teen's overwhelming fears and catastrophizing.

Detective thinking can also be done on the run when there is an immediate situation that causes distress. With your teen, practice quickly identifying a worried thought, asking a key evidence-finding question—such as "What else might happen?" or "If it happens, can you cope?"—and then thinking of another more calm and helpful thought.

Some teens may respond to developing a humorous approach to detective thinking such as speaking the worried thought in the voice of a cartoon character. Let this come from them without crossing the line of humiliating or belittling them or minimizing their concerns. Other teens may prefer to move on from calling the process detective thinking. As mentioned above, teens and adults most commonly describe the process as realistic thinking as it is designed to encourage thinking about the likelihood, costs, and consequences in real-life situations. This is very different than "positive thinking." The realistic focus is important because "bad" things do sometimes happen, and it is important to acknowledge that while they may feel upset or uncomfortable at the time, your teen will be able to cope.

Remember that anxious thoughts may relate to an immediate situation that is causing distress and also to a more general anxious prediction about your teen's future. Sometimes parents can be surprised at the depth of distress their child feels in a situation. This may be a clue to explore with your teen their broader and deeper concerns.

Stepladders

By using the worksheets in the Activity Book (available for download at http://www.newharbinger.com/49913), which you have used before, you and your teen can develop a list of steps to gradually tackle any new fear or the recurrence of an old fear. Review chapter 5 ("Facing Fear to Fight Fear") to refresh your ideas on developing stepladders and chapter 7 ("Troubleshooting Stepladders") to review the troubleshooting skills, if needed.

Again, the concept of facing fears to provide opportunities to challenge anxious predictions and the process of building stepladders is the same across age groups. Remember that the four Rs—realistic, responsive, repetitive actions, and rewards—are the keys to success for an effective stepladder program:

- being *realistic* about the goals

- being *responsive* by adjusting the program if needed

- utilizing *repetitive actions*—that is, using lots of steps to strengthen learning that the really bad thing will not happen

- using *rewards* to acknowledge your teen's diligent efforts to face their fears

Your teen may want to use a reward program to acknowledge their progress or provide motivation when the steps seem difficult. For other young people, completing the steps and checking them off is sufficient reward. You and your teen will need to work out what works best in your situation. Whether you use a reward system or not, your social recognition of the effort they are making and your matter-of-fact acknowledgment of how hard they are trying to overcome their fears is very important.

As a parent, you can support the new learning your teen has gained with every step they try. When you check in with them about how a step went, you can ask some questions in a low-key way to strengthen and consolidate what they have learned. These questions build on their developing capacities to analyze and verbalize their experiences:

- What did you think would happen?

- What did happen?

- How much did that surprise you?

- What did you learn?

Make sure your questions are put in an interested, supportive, and curious way rather than belaboring the point or lecturing your teen. The most effective and long-lasting learning is achieved through the young person coming to the conclusions about the outcomes themselves. You are there as a cheerleader—to support and encourage.

For some teens, a "scientific" approach to stepladders can be a useful and different way to gradually facing their fears. Encourage them to approach the steps as mini-experiments.

Before trying a step or a challenging situation, ask these questions:

- What's the hypothesis? What do you expect will happen?

- What is the likelihood of the bad thing happening as a percentage?

- After the step has been attempted, discuss these questions:

  - What are your observations? What actually happened?

  - What are your conclusions for the experiment?

These steps and experiments are useful to challenge beliefs and assumptions. When young people learn that there is mismatch between their expectations of a bad thing occurring, how likely it is to occur, and what actually happens, they are establishing new learning. They are learning that that there is a different way to look at these anxiety-provoking situations, that there may be a different likelihood of bad things occurring, and that they may be able to manage the situation very differently than how they expected.

There will be times when not everything goes as planned. This can occur especially for social anxiety when your teen tries a step or an experiment for a fear involving a social interaction or a performance of some type. The outcome of trying a step may be not as positive as they, or you, may have hoped. For example, when giving a speech or presentation, they may hesitate or forget their place in the talk. However, the important learning is that the really bad outcome, the total disaster or humiliation they feared, didn't occur.

When checking in with your teen after a step doesn't go according to the original plan, you can ask if it was as bad as expected or if it was manageable: How did they manage? What were the real consequences, and how long did they last? Acknowledging their emotions and helping your teen to evaluate the outcome fairly (rather than catastrophizing) are ways that you can help them in the aftermath. This is really important and useful learning for teens. Parents and caregivers can provide important support by acknowledging in an age-appropriate way their bravery in trying to face their fears.

As young people are involved in wider life experiences and situations, they will have opportunities to face spontaneous challenges to fears.

Encourage your teen to take on these challenges when opportunities arise. This may be as simple as catching public transportation independently to catch up with friends at a shopping center or learning about a new school club in an area of interest. If needed, you can create small stepladders to assist them in succeeding if the challenge provokes more than a small amount of fear or worry. For example, your teen might be worried that they won't know what to say if they go to the new club. A stepladder providing opportunities for the teen to have conversations with unfamiliar people might assist in their confidence. Give praise and acknowledgment for these spontaneous steps and include credit for them if you have started a new reward program.

How Parents Can Help

Remember, reassurance and permitting avoidance do not make anxiety go away. Paradoxically, they can make the anxiety worse. As we mentioned above, having a young person experience anxiety, mood disturbances, or distress is in turn very distressing for parents and caregivers. Parents have a natural tendency to want to take away the painful feelings by reassurance or stepping in to help. This is not helpful in the long term, though it may make you and your child feel better in the present moment. Parents can also get caught in a trap of reducing their own anxiety by offering reassurance to their child. Remind yourself of the principles and strategies in chapter 4, "Parenting an Anxious Child."

LISTENING AND COMMUNICATION

Aim to be calm, to listen respectfully, and to show you understand what your teen is experiencing. It is most helpful if teens feel heard, rather than have you explain what they did wrong or how to solve the problem. As you talk with your teen, keep these things in mind:

- The aim is to keep communication open and to stay in touch with how they are feeling.

- Help your teen name how they are feeling. Ask, "What's your strongest feeling right now?"

- Use open-ended questions—such as "What are you worried will happen?"—to help your teen identify their anxious expectation. Ensure you don't minimize or dismiss the current situation. Sometimes young people can communicate anxiety and distress in tentative, oblique, or dysregulated ways. If you are worried that you didn't realize or pick up on something at the time, go back and check it out with your teen when life is calmer. If needed, apologize to them that you missed something important they were trying to tell you.

- Get some separate help or mediation if there is disagreement between parents about how to help your teen with their anxiety or other issues. Teens need parents and caregivers with a united front rather than be stressed by disagreements that can undermine their confidence.

Unhelpful Parent Comments	Helpful Parent Comments
It's nothing, don't worry about it.	You're worried about... (reflect what they are telling you is the problem)
Don't sweat the small stuff.	This reminds me a bit of when you...
That's babyish.	You've handled this before.
Toughen up; you're too old for this now.	What worked before when you felt like this?
Calm down. Don't panic!	I can see that this is really stressing you out. Would you like to [suggest an activity they enjoy such as exercise, walk, or cook together]?

Unhelpful Parent Comments	Helpful Parent Comments
Just do it.	I can see you're finding this tough. What part of the job can you start with?
It's going to be okay. Everything will be fine.	You're worried about getting a bad grade and what that will mean for next year. Worrying about the future can feel overwhelming.
I'll fix it for you. You should do this...	What are your options? Who might be able to help out? What usually gets you through problems like this? There are a lot of potential problems here, but let's work out which ones can be fixed and which ones we can't change.
Yes, it's a real disaster.	You were expecting to get a better mark on this assignment, and now you're worried you might not get into the advanced class.

STAY HOPEFUL AND SUPPORT THEIR AUTONOMY

- Remain confident in your teen's ability to deal with recurrence of anxiety and new problems.

- Don't jump in with a solution or take over. There is a fine line between being supportive and taking over. Offer to help implement solutions that your teen has created—for example, reading over an email where they are asking for an extension on a school assignment rather than writing the email for them.

- Encourage but don't force them to tackle their worries.

- Strengthen their perception that you think they are capable and you are hopeful for their ability to overcome their fears.

HELP WITH REMINDERS OF THEIR SKILLS IN ANXIETY MANAGEMENT

- Try to be a supportive cheerleader. Remind your teen of what they have learned in similar situations in the past. Help them think about how these skills can apply or be adapted to their current worries.

- Help them set small, achievable goals.

- Encourage your teen to complete practice and steps alone as well as with you, and in as wide a variety of situations as they can manage to consolidate their skills.

ENCOURAGE HEALTHY BEHAVIORS AND SELF-CARE FOR YOUNG PEOPLE AND FOR YOURSELF

- Support their developing expertise to take care of themselves, develop healthy behaviors, and regulate their worries and moods.

- Encourage and model an adequate sleep routine, healthy nutrition, and regular eating.

- Promote genuine and positive connections with family and peers.

- Support and promote recreation, exercise and sports, creative hobbies, and time in nature.

- Learn and practice relaxation or consider other self-care activities such as mindfulness, meditation, and yoga.

- Talk openly with your teen about using alcohol and drugs as a negative coping strategy and aim to work with them to find other ways of coping with stressful situations or social pressures.

Social Skills and Assertiveness

Relationships with peers and others, the desire to feel accepted, and the need for assertiveness and social skills have a whole new degree of difficulty in the teenage years. As a parent, you will not have all the answers to advise your teen in middle and high school. It is important that you step back and allow them to lead in how to handle situations, unless there are serious or safety issues involved. While your teen's choices may not always be what you hope for, allowing them to learn independence and cope with consequences, and your being there to comfort and support them when things go wrong is your priority when parenting a teen.

The social skills needed in the teen years are more complex and subtle than those needed as a child. As they grow, teens will need to communicate effectively with school staff and potential employers as well as to navigate more complex peer relationships, including dating. Review your teen's developing social skills with these new social situations in mind. If you identify that a lack of confidence or assertiveness is having a negative impact, role-play situations and create social situation stepladders where skills can be practiced using the techniques and suggestions in chapter 8, "Social Skills and Assertiveness."

Relaxation

Learning to relax the mind and body is important for people of all ages, and it is just as important for older children and teenagers as for younger children. With older children, you may wish to discuss with them how much help they need; they may, for example, prefer to write their own meditations for practice. Relaxation and meditation skills are increasingly being taught in schools. If your teen has had this experience, use this as an opportunity for them to teach you and/or other family members what they have learned and to talk together about how to use these skills.

If not, or if the approach was not a good fit for your teen, look together at the scripts in chapter 9, "Relaxation," and practice a few together.

Alternatively, there are many good relaxation apps available for download these days that can provide a good framework. It is useful for both teens and adults to have a number of relaxation strategies to be used in different situations—for example, having a longer relaxation script for winding down at night before sleep as well as a quick mindfulness or breathing exercise to be used in the moment. Practice these relaxation skills in a variety of situations such as sitting in the car, at a desk, in the library, or even in a toilet cubicle so that the relaxation skills are ready to go when—and where—needed.

CHAPTER HIGHLIGHTS

→ It is common for anxious children to experience fears and worries as they move through the challenges of teenage years. These can seem like fears they have had before or different fears may develop.

→ Some anxious teens may develop low moods or depression, may misuse alcohol and drugs to help manage their feelings and fears, or may develop difficulties with eating.

→ Parents should seek help if they are concerned about how they or their teen is managing or if they are concerned about their teen's safety. Support your teen by making sure parents and caregivers are as consistent as possible in their approach to helping their teen manage anxiety.

→ The key skills of identifying thoughts and feelings, using detective thinking, and facing fears gradually using stepladders are useful for teens and for adults.

→ Refreshing and relearning relaxation skills is useful for everyone involved. Take the opportunity to refresh your own skills by getting your teen to teach you.

References

Caspi, A., G. H. Elder Jr., and D. J. Bem. (1988). "Moving Away from the World: Life-Course Patterns of Shy Children." *Developmental Psychology* 24: 824–31. https://doi.org/10.1037/0012-1649.24.6.824.

Cobham, V. E., M. R. Dadds, S. H. Spence, and B. McDermott. (2010). "Parental Anxiety in the Treatment of Childhood Anxiety: A Different Story Three Years Later." *Journal of Clinical Child & Adolescent Psychology* 39 (3): 410–20. https://doi.org/10.1080/15374411003691719.

Eley, T. C. (1997). "General Genes: A New Theme in Developmental Psychopathology." *Current Directions in Psychological Science* 6 (4): 90–95.

Lawrence, D., S. Johnson, J. Hafekost, K. Boterhoven De Haan, M. G. Sawyer, J. Ainley, and S. Zubrick. (2015). "The Mental Health of Children and Adolescents: Report on the second Australian Child and Adolescent Survey of Mental Health and Wellbeing." Department of Health [Australia]. Available at https://www.health.gov.au/resources/publications/the-mental-health-of-children-and-adolescents.

Lee, S., A. Tsang, J. Breslau, S. Aguilar-Gaxiola, M. Angermeyer, G. Borges et al. (2009). "Mental Disorders and Termination of Education in High-Income and Low- and Middle-Income Countries: Epidemiological Study." *British Journal of Psychiatry* 194 (5): 411–17. https://doi.org/10.1192/bjp.bp.108.054841.

Lyneham, H. J., and R. M. Rapee, R. M. (2006). "Evaluation of Therapist-Supported Parent-Implemented CBT for Anxiety Disorders in Rural Children." *Behaviour Research and Therapy* 44: 1287–1300. https://doi.org/10.1016/j.brat.2005.09.009.

Merikangas, K. R., J.-p. He, M. Burstein, S. A. Swanson, S. Avenevoli, L. Cui, C. Benjet, K. Georgiades, and J. Swendsen. (2010). "Lifetime Prevalence of Mental Disorders in U.S. Adolescents: Results from the National Comorbidity Survey Replication-Adolescent Supplement (NCS-A)." *Journal of the American Academy of Child & Adolescent Psychiatry* 49 (October): 980–89. https://doi.org/10.1016/j.jaac.2010 .05.017.

Rapee, R. M., M. J. Abbott, and H. J. Lyneham (2006). "Bibliotherapy for Children with Anxiety Disorders Using Written Materials for Parents: A Randomized Controlled Trial." *Journal of Consulting and Clinical Psychology* 74 (3): 436–44. https://doi.org/10.1037/0022 -006X.74.3.436.

Rapee, R. M., J. Fardouly, M. K. Forbes, C. Johnco, N. R. Magson, E. L. Oar, and C. Richardson. (2019). "Adolescent Development and Risk for the Onset of Social-Emotional Disorders: A Review and Conceptual Model." *Behaviour Research & Therapy* 123: 103501. https://doi.org/10.1016/j.brat.2019.103501.

Rapee, R. M., H. J. Lyneham, V. Wuthrich, M.-L. Chatterton, J. L. Hudson, M. Kangas, and C. Mihalopoulos. (2021). "Low Intensity Treatment for Clinically Anxious Youth: A Randomised Controlled Comparison Against Face-to-Face Intervention." *European Child & Adolescent Psychiatry* 30: 1071–79. https://doi .org/10.1007/s00787-020-01596-3.

Ronald M. Rapee, PhD, is distinguished professor in the school of psychological sciences at Macquarie University in Sydney, Australia; and director of the Centre for Emotional Health. He has been involved in an advisory capacity with the DSM-IV and DSM-5, and has sat on both public and scientific advisory committees for national and international organizations. He is developer of Cool Kids, a scientifically proven treatment program for anxious young people that is used by health departments, therapists, and organizations in over thirty countries.

Ann Wignall, DPsych, was principal clinical psychologist at Northern Sydney Health, and service manager for child and youth mental health. She established the Child & Adolescent Anxiety Clinic at Royal North Shore Hospital in 1995, and ran national training programs for treatment and early intervention in anxiety and depression.

Susan H. Spence, PhD, is a clinical psychologist and researcher specializing in the assessment, treatment, and prevention of child and adolescent anxiety and depression. She is an emeritus professor at Griffith University, Queensland, Australia; and has a strong international reputation, having received several significant awards for her contribution to youth mental health.

Vanessa Cobham, PhD, is a clinical psychologist specializing in the treatment of anxiety and post-traumatic stress in children and adolescents. She is a professor at The University of Queensland, and an advanced clinical psychologist within Children's Health Queensland's Child and Youth Mental Health Service. She is from Brisbane, Australia.

Heidi Lyneham, PhD, is a clinical psychologist and researcher who focuses on assessment and treatment of emotional difficulties in children and families, particularly in improving access to services. She is clinic director at the Centre for Emotional Health at Macquarie University, Sydney, Australia.

MORE BOOKS from
NEW HARBINGER PUBLICATIONS

**RAISING GOOD
HUMANS**

A Mindful Guide to
Breaking the Cycle of
Reactive Parenting and
Raising Kind, Confident Kids

978-1684033881 / US $16.95

**END THE MEALTIME
MELTDOWN**

Using the Table Talk Method to
Free Your Family from
Daily Struggles over Food
and Picky Eating

978-1684039463 / US $18.95

**ANXIETY RELIEF
FOR KIDS**

On-the-Spot Strategies to Help
Your Child Overcome Worry,
Panic, and Avoidance

978-1626259539 / US $17.95

**THE RESILIENCE
WORKBOOK FOR KIDS**

Fun CBT Activities to Help You
Bounce Back from Stress and
Grow from Challenges

978-1684039166 / US $18.95

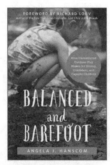

**BALANCED AND
BAREFOOT**

How Unrestricted Outdoor Play
Makes for Strong, Confident,
and Capable Children

978-1626253735 / US $18.95

**PARENTING A
TEEN GIRL**

A Crash Course on Conflict,
Communication and Connection
with Your Teenage Daughter

978-1608822133 / US $22.95

newharbingerpublications
1-800-748-6273 / newharbinger.com

(VISA, MC, AMEX / prices subject to change without notice)
Follow Us 🅞 f 🇾 ▶ 🅿 in

Don't miss out on new books from New Harbinger.
Subscribe to our email list at **newharbinger.com/subscribe**

Did you know there are **free tools** you can download for this book?

Free tools are things like **worksheets, guided meditation exercises**, and **more** that will help you get the most out of your book.

You can download free tools for this book— whether you bought or borrowed it, in any format, from any source—from the New Harbinger website. All you need is a NewHarbinger.com account. Just use the URL provided in this book to view the free tools that are available for it. Then, click on the "download" button for the free tool you want, and follow the prompts that appear to log in to your NewHarbinger.com account and download the material.

You can also save the free tools for this book to your **Free Tools Library** so you can access them again anytime, just by logging in to your account! Just look for this button on the book's free tools page. ➤ **+ Save this to my free tools library**

If you need help accessing or downloading free tools, visit **newharbinger.com/faq** or contact us at **customerservice@newharbinger.com**.